A Game of Thrones:

The Jacobites, Louis XIV, and the Intelligence Battle for the British Isles

Neil Kent

Clément Chevalier

A Game of Thrones:
The Jacobites, Louis XIV, and the Intelligence Battle for the British Isles

Neil Kent

Clément Chevalier

Academica Press
Washington

Library of Congress Cataloging-in-Publication Data
Names: Kent, Neil, Chevalier, Clément (authors)
Title: A game of thrones : the jacobites, louis XIV, and the intelligence battle for the british isles | Kent,
Neil | Chevalier, Clément.
Description: Washington : Academica Press, 2025. | Includes references.
Identifiers: LCCN 2025938602 | ISBN 9781680537673 (hardcover) | 9781680537697 (paperback) | 9781680537680 (e-book)
Copyright 2025 Neil Kent

Special thanks to Natalie Chevalier for her copious editorial assistance in producing this book

TABLE OF CONTENTS

FOREWORD xi

INTRODUCTION 1

CHAPTER 1
THE KING'S SECRET CHAMBER 5

CHAPTER 2
DYNASTICS ISSUES 41

CHAPTER 3
THE ORIGINS OF THE FALL OF THE STUARTS (1649 – 1688) 53

CHAPTER 4
IMMEDIAT CONSEQUENCES OF
THE GLORIOUS REVOLUTION (1688-1689) 71

CHAPTER 5
SCOTLAND'S ROLE AFTER
THE GLORIOUS REVOLUTION (1688-1715) 83

CHAPTER 6
THE COURT OF JAMES II AT
SAINT-GERMAIN-EN-LAYE (1688-1689) 97

CHAPTER 7
ENGLAND AND HOLLAND AGAINST
LOUIS XIV AND THE JACOBITES (1688-1690) 105

CHAPTER 8
SECRET NEGOCIATIONS AND
THE WAR OF THE GRAND ALLIANCE (1692-1697) 123

CHAPTER 9
THE WAR OF SPANISH SUCCESSION (1699-1702) 135

CHAPTER 10
INTERNATIONAL INTRIGUES (1702) 141

CHAPTER 11
NATHANIEL HOOKE (1664-1738)
AND THE SCOTTISH EXPEDITION (1703-1708) 153

CHAPTER 12
A GEOPOLITICAL CRISIS IN FRANCE AND
RENEWED PLANS FOR ACTION IN SCOTLAND (1709-1710) 183

CHAPTER 13
NEGOCIATIONS AT THE TREATY OF UTRECHT (1710-1712) .. 193

CHAPTER 14
JACOBITES HIBRYD USE OF INFLUENCE
AND INTELLIGENCE IN ENGLAND (1712-1713) 223

CHAPTER 15
THE FAILURE OF THE JACOBITE'S CAUSE (1715-1745) 235

CONCLUSION 253

BIBLIOGRAPHY 263

INDEX 269

LIST OF ILLUSTRATIONS

1. James II (1633-1701), by Nicolas de Largillière, 1686;

2. Louis XIV, King of France, by Hyacinthe Rigaud;

3. 'Antoine Rossignol, maître des comptes,' in Charles Perrault's book, Les Hommes illustres qui ont paru en France pendant ce siècle, Paris, 1696. Anonymous engraving;

4. King William III and his wife Queen Mary, Engraving from R. White, Private Collection of S. Whitehead, 1703;

5. John Wallis, by Sir Godfrey Kneller, Bt (died 1723);

6. The Château Neuf de Saint-Germain-en-Laye and its gardens, seen from the right bank of the Seine (1664 - 1665), by Adam Frans van der Meulen;

7. The White Rose of York, symbol of the Jacobites;

8. James Drummond, 2nd Duke of Perth (1674-1720) - National Galleries;

9. The Battle of the Boyne, 1 July 1690, by Jan Wyck;

10. Portrait of Queen Anne of England, in a tinted engraving from an atlas commissioned by Augustus the Strong, King of Poland and Elector of Saxony, 1707;

11. Marlborough first duke, by Godfrey Kneller, 1705;

12. James Francis Edward Stuart c.1703, attributed to Alexis Simon Belle;

13. Antoine de Guiscard (1658-1711), Private Collection ;

14. Destruction of the Soleil Royal at the Battle of La Hougue 1692, Adriaen van Diest, 1700;

15. The Abbé François Gaultier (d.1723), by Alexis-Simon Belle (1674-1734), National Trust ;

16. Jean Albert d'Archambaud, Count of Bucquoy, known as Abbé Bucquoy, Dutch engraving;

17. Nicolas Mesnager (1658-1714), by Hyacinthe Rigaud;

18. John Campbell, 2nd Duke of Argyll (1680-1743);

19. Depiction of the Battle of Sheriffmuir in November 1715, by John Wootton (1686- 1764);

20. 'Bonnie Prince Charlie,' by John Pettie, 1893.

FOREWORD

One of the advantages enjoyed by French kings in the Game of Thrones with their British rivals for much of the seventeenth century was superior intelligence. Neil Kent and Clément Chevalier highlight the role of the great codebreaker, Antoine Rossignol, whom Cardinal Richelieu made head of the royal Cabinet Noir founded in 1628. According to Charles Perrault of the Académie Française (founded by Richelieu), though the usually inscrutable Richelieu rarely displayed visible enthusiasm, at their first meeting Rossignol "gave such astonishing proof of his [codebreaking] ability that this great Cardinal ... was unable to conceal his astonishment."

Appropriately, as well as meaning "nightingale," Rossignol was also argot for a skeleton key to unlock locked doors and cupboards. Some of the main ciphers he unlocked were British.

However, Louis XIII and his ministers did not require the assistance of Rossignol and the Cabinet Noir to read the coded letters sent by Charles I to his French-born Queen, Henrietta Maria in the Civil War during her exile in France. Their decrypted correspondence was published by Parliament under the title "The King's Cabinet Opened" with a hostile commentary which claimed that "The Queen appears to have been as harsh and imperious towards the King as she is implacable to our Religion, Nation and Government."

In the secret Game of Thrones, Louis XIII comprehensively defeated Charles I. Richelieu rewarded Rossignol by making it possible for him to purchase aelegant château at Juvisy, twelve miles south of Paris. Louis XIII demonstrated his personal interest in codebreaking and high esteem for Rossignol by paying several visits to his château. So did Louis XIV early in his reign. A painting by Pierre-Denis Martin shows him arriving at Juvisy on horseback. By contrast, no English codebreaker received any sign of appreciation from the Stuart kings.

The Cabinet Noir founded by Richelieu also provided Louis XIII, Louis XIV and their senior ministers with gossip and signs of subversion discovered in intercepted domestic correspondence. The celebrated letter-writer Madame de Sévigné occasionally included complaints at the delays to her correspondence caused by Louis XIV's letter-openers: "Messieurs, at least take the trouble to put [my letters] back in their envelopes so that, sooner or later, they reach their destination."

Louis XIV also took a personal interest in the use of seduction for intelligence gathering. The most successful seductress was Louise Renée de Penancoët de Kérouaille. The French ambassador in London, Colbert de Croissy, passed on Louis's personal congratulations to de Kérouaille after her seduction of Charles II in 1671. The ambassador informed Louis: "I have made the young lady joyful by assuring her of the pleasure with which His Majesty [Louis XIV] learned of her brilliant conquest. There is every prospect that she will long hold on to what she has conquered." In 1673 Charles made de Kérouaille Duchess of Portsmouth. She accompanied Charles II to the theatre far more frequently that the Queen and became a regular informant of the French embassy.

By the 1690s, however, Louis's interest in intelligence gathering had waned. William of Orange, who became King William III shortly after the Glorious Revolution of 1688, had a more sophisticated grasp of intelligence than any previous British (or French) monarch. By the end of 1689, the veteran British codebreaker, John Wallis, had succeeded in breaking ciphers used by both Louis XIV and Colbert de Croissy (now French foreign minister). French intelligence (codebreaking included) continued to be outclassed by Britain's during the reign of Queen Anne (thanks to her ministers, however, rather than the Queen).

Perhaps the most bizarre moment in the Anglo-French Game of the Thrones was the appearance of the maverick French spy, the marquis de Guiscard, at a British cabinet meeting on 8 March 1711. When his offer to spy for Britain was exposed as fraudulent, Guiscard drew a penknife from his pocket and stabbed Robert Harley (later Earl of Oxford), head of the Tory government elected in the previous year. Harley recovered but Guiscard died in Newgate Prison from wounds inflicted on him by ministers who came to Harley's rescue. Public interest in the assasination attempt was so great that the Newgate jailer pickled Guiscard's corpse in a barrel, put it on display and charged a penny each to the many who came to view it.

As Neil Kent and Clément Chevalier show, the French fell behind even in the use of "honey-traps" for intelligence gathering. During the Congress of Utrecht in the Netherlands, which negotiated peace treaties to end the War of the Spanish Succession, luxurious brothels were set up to ensnare the negotiators. The French historian Casimir Freschot, then resident in Utrecht, describes one of the brothels as an "enchanted palace" set amid beautiful gardens. He adds that the French delegation were its chief customers.

Britain won the Game of Thrones. Neil Kent and Clément Chevalier are indispensable guides to understanding its victory and the roles of players in secret diplomacy. Under Richelieu, France had been the world leader in intelligence. It has never been so since.

Christopher Andrew

My ill-fated star has made its malign influence felt on the armies of Your Majesty, armies always victorious until the day they fought for me. I therefore beg you to no longer take any interest in my troubles, but to allow me to withdraw with my family to some corner of the world, where I can no longer be an obstacle to the normal course of your prosperities and conquests.[1]

These were the words of the deposed King of England, James II Stuart, to King Louis XIV in 1702, during a period of economic and military crisis in France. This quote perfectly symbolises James II's state of mind between 1688 and 1701.

---

[1] James II writing to Louis XIV after the naval defeat at La Hougue (1692). Quoted in Dulon, Jacques, Jacques II Stuart, Sa Famille et les Jacobites à Saint-Germain-en-Laye, 1897, 158 pages.

INTRODUCTION

The historical backdrop to this era includes the pivotal year of 1688, which witnessed the Glorious Revolution in England. This revolution, driven by domestic political strife, resulted in the ousting of King James II Stuart (James VII of Scotland) and his exile. The resolution to this turmoil came externally, with the arrival of William III of Orange, the Protestant Stadtholder of the Netherlands. France, under Louis XIV, offered support to the exiled English king, motivated by a blend of Catholic solidarity and strategic isolation in continental Europe. Louis XIV sought to forge an alliance of Catholic monarchies as a counterbalance to the encroaching Protestant powers. Meanwhile, the Netherlands, divided in its policy, capitalised on the shifting landscape. Thus, the international landscape in 1688 was fraught with tension, propelling Europe towards the War of the League of Augsburg, soon to be known as the War of the English Succession, signalling another chapter in the continent's relentless march towards conflict.

Until the close of the 17th century, European kingdoms were engaged in a delicate balancing act, striving to maintain their geopolitical positions while ensuring internal political stability. France, under the autocratic rule of Louis XIV, exemplified a more straightforward case. The Sun King's absolute authority allowed for a stable political landscape and facilitated a ready recourse to war, underpinned by a standing army. In contrast, England's situation was markedly more complex. Domestically, the nation grappled with a frayed social fabric and a political arena deeply divided. Loyalists to the exiled king coexisted uneasily with Protestant factions, including Whigs, Tories, Jacobites, Catholics, and Protestants. The country was far from the united entity we recognise today, with its territory and society fragmented. During this era, states wielded varied political influences, and monarchies employed comprehensive diplomatic machinery to navigate foreign affairs. This world of diplomacy was inhabited by prominent figures, some publicly recognised due to their titles and governmental roles. However, a more covert group operated in the shadows—agents and spies, employed by political factions, particularly in England amid its domestic upheavals. The activities of these agents, though ostensibly straightforward, often involved duplicitous undertakings. Information gleaned from adversaries became a potent tool in this clandestine warfare. Thus, European relations, far from being random or incidental, were the outcome of intricate influence games and internal confrontations, including those within the enigmatic realm of espionage. This interplay of power dynamics and intrigue underpins the central theme of this book: a war of thrones, shaped as much by shadowy machinations as by overt political actions.

This book sets out to demystify the complex international landscape from 1688 to 1715, focusing on France under Louis XIV, England alongside the Jacobites, and Holland, all through the lens of espionage and the intelligence war.

In the first chapter, we will delve into the secretive world within governments, and unveil the integral role of espionage in statecraft, revealing how even young monarchs were inducted early into these practices. This training encompassed various political realms, including diplomacy, military strategy, and covert plots. The idea that effective governance also involves the art of concealment is a key theme.

The second chapter is foundational, offering readers insights into the European context from 1630 to 1688. We will look at the geopolitical situation, when Louis XIII of France and his minister Richelieu, then at the head of the most powerful country in Europe, were able to rely on a highly effective network of spies, under the leadership of the king's cryptographer, Antoine Rossignol (1600-1682). Taking advantage of this exceptional network, French intelligence served a strong state, and Louis XIII's minister, the Duc de Richelieu, fought against attempts by Charles I's England to establish his family in Brandenburg and Hanover.

In the third chapter, devoted to the fall of James II Stuart, we will see that Louis XIV was at the head of a kingdom that was still the most powerful in Europe, but the perpetual wars that were being waged in Europe in his name or against him made the spy network more difficult and less effective. He began to be countered by foreign cryptographers.

Little by little, he paid less attention to espionage, and by the end of his reign, it could be said that English and allied spies and their cryptographers were taking precedence over those of France.

From chapter 4 to chapter 14, we enter the heart of our subject, and study the geopolitical situation that followed the fall of James II, and which gave rise to the Jacobite party, trying by all means to restore James II and then his son James Francis Stuart to the throne of England. We shall see that the flight of James II Stuart was supported by a network of spies that was still very effective, but counterbalanced by the allies. We will see that the Jacobites were gradually abandoned by Louis XIV, not only because the King was weary of turning his back on their cause, but also because he could no longer rely on his network of spies, which was being countered just about everywhere. We will be looking at these cryptographers and spies in the service of the English monarchs between 1688 and 1715.

The final chapter deals with the definitive fall of the Jacobite party, when King Louis XV could no longer stand up to the inexorable unification of Great Britain, which was now a major European power, if not the major power. James Francis Stuart, son of James II Stuart, was to pay the price for this geopolitical situation, and all the Jacobites with him. The cause would be heard when it became clear that Louis XV's support would be no more than lip service, no longer relayed by a spy network that was being beaten everywhere, particularly by English cryptographers. However, we shall see that before the Seven Years' War, Louis XV still had the opportunity to fight the English on the continent, by playing on European diplomatic relations. Certain key figures, including spies, were able to distort relations between England and Russia, for example, when the former used German pressure to keep Russia in its fold. We will sometimes quote Professor Christopher Andrew, the Former British Security (MI5) official historian and co-convenor of Cambridge University Intelligence Seminar. This comprehensive approach ensures that the reader is not left adrift but is guided through the ongoing complexities and intrigues of this pivotal period in European history.

CHAPTER 1

THE KING'S SECRET CHAMBER

This first chapter will take us entering squarely into the subject of our book, which is aptly titled to reflect the clandestine battle for supremacy over the British Isles, a contest that entangled France, England, the Jacobites, and Holland. Yet, our narrative endeavours to explore far beyond the mere machinations of political power struggles. We embark on an examination of the expansive and enigmatic realm of espionage and intelligence, operated by a network of spies under the auspices of the aforementioned sovereign states.

To fully grasp the essence of this clandestine world, it is imperative to consider the context within which these spies operated, often pledging their services to multiple states concurrently. Statecraft, thus, was enveloped in layers of secrecy for reasons we shall unveil: it encompassed both domestic and foreign policies, the latter of which, referred to herein as international affairs, demanded thorough comprehension by monarchs. Achieving such understanding necessitated the guidance of seasoned specialists, tasked with navigating the intricacies of global diplomacy to fulfil the monarch's strategic objectives. These specialists, alongside a vast network of spies that infiltrated European courts, acted as the operational arms of centralised intelligence bureaus, orchestrating the covert agendas set forth by their rulers.

Intriguingly, the King's Council, originally not devised for clandestine operations, required the backing of an unseen entity dedicated to managing not just the deployment of agents throughout Europe but also overseeing all correspondence linked to royal affairs, known as the Cabinet Noir. The communications of such critical nature were of course encrypted, necessitating the expertise of cryptography specialists or adept individuals. This crucial correspondence invariably made its way through the postal system, which was frequently commandeered for the king's purposes. To maintain the confidentiality of these operations from the monarch, it was imperative for the crown to appoint trustworthy individuals, starting with the ministers themselves. The Minister of Foreign Affairs, for instance, held a title and role explicitly indicative of the sensitive nature of their duties.

This clandestine network relied on the formal structures of official services, possessing branches and operational capabilities shrouded in secrecy. These operatives, frequenting the halls and antechambers of international courts, often engaged in alliances with diplomats to acquire and relay information, notwithstanding their simultaneous obligations to multiple states. The scope of their endeavours spanned a broad spectrum, influenced by the ebb and flow of international politics and extending to more concentrated domains such as military intelligence. Their activities encompassed surveillance within regions, fortifications, and even the battlefield, with propaganda also playing a major role. Even in this era, what we currently recognise as the media served as a significant instrument of influence, with certain pamphleteers and publishers of newspapers and gazettes crafting content for various domestic or international factions. Of course, discovering these clandestine operations, or more perilously, the agents themselves, amounted to an act of state treason, leading to imprisonment or, for the fortunate few, repurposing to serve another sovereign.

Risk was the limit of espionage. By informing a sovereign, an individual was breaking into the world of international relations, escaping his social or political status - initially as a mere subject - and this break-in had a price - which he was paid or had to pay. In a society where everyone's place was well-defined, first and foremost by their birth in a particular place or milieu, the informant distinguished himself and made a name for himself. But more often than not, such distinction was shrouded in secrecy, or at least discretion. When the secret was revealed, the social order was disrupted and a dazzling reparation was required - death being the most absolute form of reparation. In return, the greater the service, the more valuable it was. As the medium of information was writing, it was around writing that the paradox of espionage was played out: the letter was the surest tool and the most compromising evidence. Between the methods of the information that was the basic data - situation on the one hand, initiatives on the other - and the motivations that justified the act, the writing of the information - both material support and definitive compromise - was the final commitment that made a subject an "agent," and the privileged place of risk.[2]

I. The Collection of Secret Informations.

"If you can't hide, you can't rule."[3]

Scholars have frequently remarked on Louis XIV's penchant for secrecy from an early age. This trait, while not unique to any single state of the 17th century, was particularly pronounced in the French monarchy. The absolute nature of French kingship, underscored by the sovereign's image and prerogatives—wherein the king was beyond accountability for his actions—necessitated a culture of state secrecy. This inclination towards the clandestine can be traced back to Louis XIV's formative years as monarch, suggesting that his affinity for secrecy was not only innate but also honed through his royal upbringing.

Furthermore, beyond these observations, it's evident that secrecy served as both a shield for the sovereign and a strategic veil for the operations of the royal state. In the complex tapestry of international relations described earlier, secrecy emerges not merely as a preference but as an imperative for political manoeuvrings. Thus, the mysteries and secrecy enveloping the monarchy naturally integrate into the fabric of international diplomacy, embodying a critical aspect of the conduct and preservation of state power.

1. Methodes Used:

The concept of secrecy was inherently woven into the fabric of absolute monarchies, where the sovereign's word was law, immune to public scrutiny or debate. Louis XIV, shaped by the tumultuous

---

[2] Bély, Lucien, *Espions et ambassadeurs au temps de Louis XIV*, Ed. Fayard, 1990, p. 208
[3] Sentence attributed to Louis XI of France (1423-1483)

experiences of the Fronde and aware of the historical conflicts that marked his predecessors' reigns during the Wars of Religion, was determined to consolidate his rule, enforce internal harmony, and secure the French state's supremacy over both domestic and foreign adversaries. The warfare engaged in by Louis XIII and Richelieu against the Habsburg dynasty was overtly justified by the defence of the kingdom's religious interests, despite Louis XIII's precarious hold on authority—a situation Louis XIV was keen to rectify. From an early age, Louis XIV was instructed in the importance of vigilance and espionage as tools for maintaining and extending his power. The shadows of the royal court were thus inhabited by covert agents, whose efforts in espionage played pivotal roles in the orchestration of conflicts, negotiations, and treaties. The king's challenges were not limited to external foes; internally, he encountered resistance from the parliament and sovereign courts, entities theoretically under his dominion yet practically independent. These bodies' reluctance or outright opposition to royal directives could compel the king to adopt measures that invited controversy. This fraught relationship between the monarchy and the aristocratic classes that constituted the parliament fuelled the civil unrest and revolutions which episodically rocked England throughout the latter half of the 17th century. Here, secrecy takes on its full meaning, since aren't the factionalists plotting in secret against the authority and the very person of the king?

Louis XIV mastered the art of omnipresence through a network of informants, encompassing not only the nobility but also individuals engaged in espionage as their profession.

His tutelage as monarch emphasised political ethics, drawing from the teachings of Aristotle, Alexander the Great, mediaeval literature, and Erasmus. Starting in 1649, the young Louis XIV was granted access to the council chambers, enabling him to witness firsthand the machinations of governance. He was as much an observer as he was the subject of observation, occasionally concealing himself to overhear discussions, with his responses meticulously documented. Despite not positioning himself as a scholarly figure, Louis XIV's engagement in secretive practices stemmed from a deliberate intellectual strategy.

If there is one thinker who could have influenced Louis XIV's education in this area, it is Machiavelli, unsurprisingly. His comments are admittedly blunt, but he argues that when it comes to virtues, "what is needed is for him (the king) to appear to have them,"[4] because the prince's only ambition is "the conquest and preservation of his State."[5] And finally he adds: "What the prince really is, what his moral nature is, reserved in the secret of his conscience, is of no concern to his subjects, for the reality of his power, like their obedience, is entirely invested in appearances."[6]

It is also not impossible that Louis XIV was introduced to the writings of Girolamo Cardano (1501-1576). In his work *Proxeneta seu de Prudentia Civili Liber* (1627), Cardano wrote that "this beautiful art of feigning, dissimulating and persuading, which gives so many advantages and is so necessary to civil life" or "These feints are justified by the innocence and justice of the design that puts them into practice, and their necessity favours and suffers them in the Court of kings, princes and their ministers, where "feinting and dissimulation are the advantages of men of spirit"[7] Indeed, the readership of Cardano's and similar texts extended beyond Louis XIV to other European monarchs, and we shall see that these texts provided a framework for the way politics was conducted in Europe.

As we have seen, Louis XIV's penchant for secrecy became apparent early in his life, notably during his adolescence when he and his mother encountered various diplomatic envoys. He quickly discerned that diplomacy was a realm of strategic display, where every gesture was weighted with significance and could potentially spark severe diplomatic conflicts.

By the mid-17th century, it was uncommon for monarchs and princes to engage in direct meetings. However, in 1644, a notable exception occurred when Louis XIV hosted of France, Charles I's wife, who was escaping the turmoil of the English Civil War. Despite criticisms of his educational regimen as being overly lenient, Louis XIV displayed an early

---

[4] Machiavelli, *The Prince*, chapter XVIII.
[5] *Ibid.*
[6] *Ibid.*
[7] Girolamo Cardano, *Proxeneta seu de Prudentia Civili Liber*, 2nd ed. Paris, 1652, p.238.

inclination towards martial endeavours, actively participating in military campaigns rather than confining his learning to the classroom.

The intricate web of European monarchy, marked by a blend of alliances and rivalries, was unified by a common goal: the preservation of their realms. This particularly applied to the monarchies of France and England. In this shadowy game of power, what one ruler did clandestinely, another mirrored. This dynamic was especially pertinent to Louis XIV and James II Stuart, contemporaries facing similar geopolitical challenges. James II's extensive knowledge of France, among other nations like Spain, due to his experiences living in these kingdoms, placed him in a unique position to navigate the complexities of international diplomacy. But what cannot be overstated is that young princes were sometimes taught in the same places as their co-religionists. This was the case for James II Stuart, who, belonging to the same family as Louis XIV, often travelled to France to partake in educational endeavours, including those in military tactics, for example.

Thus, it is plausible to infer that the protagonists of our study either collaborated directly or, at minimum, possessed a mutual understanding throughout their tenures. Initially, as young princes, they might have found themselves at odds over various political dilemmas. However, towards the twilight of James II's reign, they seemingly united in their opposition against William III of Orange and his adherents. Despite this apparent partnership, James II maintained a distinct approach to secrecy, overseeing his court with vigilance and the support of an extensive espionage network spanning both France and England. It goes without saying that Louis XIV did the same.

Having explored the theoretical underpinnings of secrecy and concealment within the realm of statecraft, we now shift our focus to the practical applications of these concepts.

2. Intelligence Specialists:

"Louis XIV reigns over a paper kingdom"[8]

These are the "missive letters," documents of a highly personal nature not meant for public circulation. Crafted either by the state secretaries or within the king's private cabinet, these letters underscored the intimate role of a personal secretary, whose title itself stems from the word "secret." The 16th and 17th centuries witnessed the development of a comprehensive doctrine on the education and duties of these secretaries. The doctrine outlined that a secretary should collaborate closely with the king, especially in the dispatch of correspondence to foreign dignitaries, demanding exceptional tact and sensitivity. Armed with an extensive knowledge of history and languages, a secretary was expected to employ a language that was not only pure, perfect, and elegant but also capable of subtly conveying the monarch's intentions, including any desires for deception. Furthermore, these treatises on secretaryship posited that a secretary must possess an intimate understanding of the monarch he serves, transcending mere linguistic proficiency.

The system saw the appointment of four secretaries, each serving on a quarterly rotation. Notably, some had prior experience in diplomatic roles, including figures such as Bartet, Verjus de Crécy, Hennequin, Callières, and Guilleragues. The crafting of the king's personal correspondence took place within the sanctum of his cabinet, facilitated by the "secrétaire de la main" or "à la plume," who had the unique skill of replicating the king's handwriting:

> To have the pen is to be a public forger and to do for a fee what would cost the life of anyone else. This practice consists in imitating the King's handwriting so exactly that it cannot be distinguished from the handwriting that the pen forges, and in writing in this way all the letters that the King must or wants to write in his own handwriting, and yet not taking the trouble.[9]

---

[8] Sarmant Thierry, Stoll Mathieu, *Régner et gouverner*, coll. Tempus, Ed. Perrin, 2019, 896 p., p. 245.
[9] Saint-Simon, *Mémoires*, Paris, Gallimard, collection de la Pléiade, under the dir. of Y. Coirault, p.24.

From 1657 to 1701, President Toussaint Rose held the esteemed role of secretary with the pen. He had been a fixture in the king's life from a young age, and had closely followed all of his decisions since Mazarin's death. He attended council meetings and took notes, which were then reported to the king. An important man in the shadows, the courtiers feared him because he was in the king's "secret" and knew all the ins and outs of the internal struggles at court. Saint-Simon gives us a portrait of him:

> It is not possible to make a great king speak with more dignity than Rose did, nor more appropriately to everyone, nor on every subject, than the letters he wrote in this way, and which the king all signed with his hand. [He was extremely faithful and secretive, and the king relied on him completely.[10]

However, he would publish a selection of missives intended for the general public, and even a Formulary of the King's Cabinet in 1663: "Cabinet letters are either in the King's hand, genuine or imitated, or in the secretary's hand, according to what pleases His Majesty." Further on he specifies that "Letters are folded in four and closed with silk, namely: with white silk, when it is for the Pope; with blue silk for all princes, both sovereign and otherwise, and with red silk for all others." The Seal of France was affixed to communications intended for French and English subjects, while letters to other nations bore the Seal of France and Navarre, typically stamped in red wax, except during periods of mourning when black or violet wax, matching the mourning silk, was used. Mourning correspondence featured paper with blackened edges, in contrast to the gilded edges of regular missives. A very standard practice was used for private letters to other monarchs. To show his attachment to his family in France and England (James II Stuart was Louis XIV's cousin), the king ended his letter with the phrase "I pray God to have you in his holy and worthy keeping." In return, he wrote "Je suis, Monsieur mon frère." These letters, devoid of envelopes, were simply folded and addressed, showcasing the king's personal touch.

Toussaint Rose's death was enveloped in as much mystery as his life, marked by his silent guardianship of royal secrets until the very end. In his final moments, he refused the rites of confession and medical intervention,

---

[10] *Ibid.*

choosing to depart as enigmatically as he lived. His dedication to secrecy was commemorated in verse, highlighting his refusal to divulge even personal transgressions:

> Here lies old President Rose
> Cabinet Secretary
> Who in dying was so secret
> That he kept his mouth shut about his own sins.[11]

Historical records identify three categories of royal correspondence: autograph letters directly penned by the monarch, letters drafted by the secretary with the pen in the king's script, and missives composed by the secretary or his cabinet counterparts. The act of signing these documents was a prerogative reserved for the Secretaries of State, a distinction not afforded to Cabinet Secretaries. Thus, while personal letters to the royal family bore the king's own signature, those emanating from central administration bore the signature of a clerk on the king's behalf, reflecting the structured hierarchy of royal communication. The voluminous nature of diplomatic correspondence often precluded genuine personal expression, suggesting that Louis XIV's private viewpoints are unlikely to be gleaned from these formal communications.

Conversely, lettres de cachet served as confidential instruments for issuing specific royal commands, often involving the imprisonment of individuals in the Bastille, or otherwise their exile. These orders were directly signed and sealed by the king himself. It was in this context that Louis XIV, having been angered by the conduct of one of his greatest spies, Louise de Kéroualle, Duchess of Portsmouth (she had become the mistress of King Charles II of England, which we will discuss later), was not far from personally sending her a lettre de cachet ordering her exile, which a diplomat, Honoré Courtin, advised the King against, in view of the great services Louise had rendered.

---

[11] *Ibid.*

3. The Black Chamber:

Within the French monarchy, the intricate web of state secrets was closely guarded by key figures such as Jean-Baptiste Colbert, François Michel le Tellier de Louvois—both senior ministers to the King—and Jean-Baptiste Colbert, Marquis de Torcy, the Minister of Foreign Affairs. Central to the orchestration of Louis XIV's espionage network, however, was Antoine Rossignol. Rossignol's expertise in cryptography enabled the establishment of the king's clandestine communication network, known as the "Black Cabinet."

The "Black Cabinet" operated as a highly efficient service, a legacy of previous monarchs, where the Grand Esquire issued commands to horsemen and couriers. These messengers, dispatched to foreign lands with official passports or safe-conducts, were formally recognized by other states and afforded diplomatic protections, signalling the dispatch of significant communications. The reliability and adaptability of these agents were crucial, given their role in the delicate balance of diplomatic interactions, where they might be intentionally delayed or intercepted based on the shifting sands of political alliances. This network extended to encompass correspondence between the King's ministers and agents, both domestically and internationally, ensuring the king remained informed. Despite the era's limitations in terms of infrastructure, Louis XIV's reign saw significant advancements in the postal system, enhancing the capacity for secure message exchange. The management of the Cabinet Noir's communications fell to the Ferme des Postes, which in turn delegated responsibilities to local post offices or courier services. These operations, overseen by postmasters who were royal officers, relied on horseback transportation to carry out their sensitive tasks.

To ensure the secure and timely delivery of crucial correspondence, particularly in the realm of diplomacy, international protocols and agreements between sovereigns were established. The overarching principle was straightforward: a letter should be delivered swiftly without any compromise to its contents. Yet, under Louis XIV, the "Black Cabinet" wielded exclusive authority to oversee state correspondence, allowing for surveillance interventions that contradicted the aforementioned principle.

During periods of conflict, when intelligence held paramount value, the royal administration covertly orchestrated delays, negligence, and even instances of petty theft. A notable instance occurred in 1668 when Condé requested Louvois to postpone decisions in Paris, aiming to conceal Louis XIV's plans to annex Franche-Comté from the Burgundians. Similarly, in 1685, Louvois employed impostor thieves—soldiers in disguise—to intercept and plunder a dispatch from the Emperor.

Following such interceptions, a meticulous system was activated: the purloined letters were conveyed to a trustworthy individual for examination, ensuring minimal exposure. Louis XIV instituted a specialised foreign post office tasked with the retrieval of these specific letters. After Louvois's demise, Louis-Léon Pajot, the head of the general farm of posts and relays in France, was inducted into the king's circle of confidence.

During times of war, managing correspondence evolved into a critical aspect of counter-espionage, granting authorities the power to inspect and decipher any letters or dispatches deemed suspicious. This strategy was particularly evident in the period surrounding James II Stuart's ousting and throughout the War of the League of Augsburg. The Black Cabinet executed numerous interceptions, notably capturing letters from Holland and those associated with a certain Caillaud, a merchant from Rotterdam identified as the leader of a spy network. This scenario underscored the utilisation of experts skilled in code-breaking. The entire postal network fell under the vigilant surveillance of the royal administration, with particular scrutiny directed at the clerks it employed. Instances were noted where clerks divulged sensitive information, enabling its dissemination through gazettes for public consumption. Despite stringent oversight, the inherent nature of postal operations, especially at the kingdom's borders, facilitated inevitable interactions with counterparts from adjacent nations. It is therefore easy to see that all these agents, clerks, couriers and postmasters were both corruptible and sometimes corrupt. The services of one are bought in order to betray another, a foreign agent is turned against his country, and so on.

4. Encrypted Correspondence:

The imperative for governments to safeguard their confidential communications has led to the advancement of cryptology, particularly through the development of the "mixed" or "nomenclator" method. This approach combines letter-by-letter substitution with an encryption alphabet and code substitution ("codic"), where words, syllables, and proper nouns are represented by numbers. While the practice of encrypting messages dates back to antiquity, it was during the Renaissance that the art of letter coding gained prominence, also finding utility among renowned travellers like Descartes for secure communication.

Antoine Rossignol (1600-1682) emerged as a leading figure in encryption since the era of Cardinal Richelieu and continued his service under Louis XIV, earning widespread acclaim across Europe for his expertise. Rossignol developed encryption tables for the king's use, sometimes working directly beside Louis XIV in a room adjacent to his study. Together with his son Charles-Bonaventure, Rossignol created the "Grand Chiffre," a sophisticated encryption system, and played a foundational role in establishing Louis XIV's Cabinet Noir. His contributions also popularised the term "Darkroom," setting a standard for services dedicated to the encryption and decryption of texts internationally. Rossignol's innovations significantly enhanced the complexity of encryption techniques.

At the time, he was in rivalry with the English codebreakers, such as John Wallis (1616-1703), professor of mathematics at Oxford, and his grandson William Blencowe (1683-1712), and finally John Keill (1671-1721). John Wallis was instrumental in developing cryptanalysis during the English Civil War, by deciphering royalist messages. William Blencowe, his grandson and pupil, was the unofficial cryptographer to William III of England, then the first official Royal Encipherer to Queen Anne of England, enabling these monarchs to foil many attempted negotiations. He was succeeded at the court of Queen Anne by John Keill, a Scottish mathematician.

During peace treaties, European plenipotentiaries carried cipher tables to facilitate secure communication, ensuring swift and confidential dispatches to their home courts. Louis XIV, in response, engaged in similar cryptographic practices. The use of various ciphers extended beyond peace treaty negotiations to include negotiation memoranda and agent communications. Each envoy received a unique cipher from the minister. At a time when Louis XIV was facing numerous coalitions, royal secrecy was perfectly well protected throughout Europe, and very difficult to decipher.

Informers often included private citizens compensated for their intelligence contributions. A notable instance in 1712 involved a parish priest, or the abbot François-Louis Gaultier, based in London, who utilised a range of pseudonyms for key British figures in his communications. Queen Anne was coded as Prothose, her half-brother James Francis Stuart, the Pretender to the English throne, as Montgoulin, diplomat Henry St. John, the 1st Viscount Bolingbroke, as M. de Montplaisir, the Tories as M. Bonhomme, and the Whigs as M. de Ruzé. These correspondences employed "sympathetic" or invisible inks, such as lemon juice, to clandestinely communicate information such as military movements (which we will discuss later in the context of the war). Agents were assigned specific addresses for mailing, ensuring that messages reached precisely intended destinations. Queen Mary, James II's daughter, enlisted individuals like Fuller, Lady Melfort's valet, and a young man named Crone, for secret communications with London. While some messages were verbal, others utilised invisible ink and were worn concealed within the large breeches fashionable at the time. On one mission, after being ferried to the Kent coast from Calais by order of the local governor, Fuller and Crone split paths to London; Fuller reported directly to the King at Kensington, whereas Crone ended up divulging everything after being apprehended and intoxicated in a London tavern.[12]

Finally, it should be remembered that each secret agent often represented the interests of a specific minister, leading to rivalries among ministries and offices, which were seen as significant power bases. A notable rivalry occurred between the Secretary of State for War, Chamillart, and the Secretary of State for Foreign Affairs, Colbert de Torcy, igniting a covert conflict between their respective agents. The

---

[12] Du Boscq, G. and M. Bernos, *La Cour des Stuarts à Saint-Germain-en-Laye 1689-1718*, Paris 1912, VIII., Paris - Emile Paul -1912, p.206

discord arose from possessing contradictory intelligence, culminating in Chamillart, whose purview was not foreign affairs, being compelled to concede.

The Case of the Celle Post Office:

Despite meticulous efforts, espionage networks were adept at intercepting mail from France, especially during the War of the League of Augsburg. Celle, located near Hanover in the domain of the Duke of Brunswick—an ally of William III of Orange and an adversary of Louis XIV—became a crucial interception point. The town's post office specialised in the interception, decryption, and examination of French communications headed to Sweden, Saxony, and Denmark, significantly informing William III of French strategies. The new ciphers poured in and were requested again and again, so much so that the Celle post office had to admit that it could not decipher so many dispatches so quickly. Nevertheless, the post office remained active throughout the war. On the other hand, the letters exchanged between the French negotiators show us that the Amsterdam route was the safest, as it was swamped with an array of dispatches and letters that overwhelmed large postal hubs, preventing effective filtering.

After conflicts disrupt standard communication channels, as seen when trade halts post-war, reinstating regular correspondence becomes crucial for maintaining dialogue between political figures and operatives. Following the Treaty of Utrecht, which concluded the War of the League of Augsburg in 1712, Torcy, the French Foreign Minister, reached out to his English counterpart, St. John, 1st Viscount Bolingbroke: "It would, I think, be very necessary in such a situation to facilitate the passage of letters in order to communicate more frequently the things that it is essential to know on both sides. To this end, the *packet-boats* from Dover to Calais could be re-established as they were before the ban on trade."[13] In the end, the reopening of this communication route made it possible to bypass the indirect route via the Netherlands.

---

[13] Archives des affaires étrangères, courriers particuliers, England 239, fol.61, letter from Torcy to St. John, 19 July 1712.

5. Officials Privy to Secrets:

In theoretical terms, governance in France was an exercise in absolute decision-making by the monarch. Contrastingly, in England, James II's efforts to solidify absolutism—marked notably by his endeavour to re-establish Catholicism and curtail the powers of Parliament—faced inherent limitations. Despite his intentions, the necessity for parliamentary cooperation remained a barrier he could not surmount, with Parliament firmly opposed to relinquishing its influence. France, too, boasted a formidable parliamentary structure, albeit one under the sway of the influential aristocratic families known as the Robe. Louis XIV embarked on a successful campaign to diminish the power of the nobility, and despite occasional resistance, the French parliament largely conformed to the king's directives. James II's attempts to emulate this dynamic in England faltered, precipitating his fall amidst enduring religious and political strife—a theme that resonated through more than a century of debate. This dichotomy underscored a fundamental difference: in France, the monarch and his office prevailed within the framework of absolute monarchy, whereas in England, political figures navigated the complexities of a parliamentary monarchy ensnared by party politics.

Yet, in both realms, the monarchs relied on a coterie of trusted advisors, including secretaries and confidential counsellors, to navigate both domestic and international challenges. Louis XIV convened the Grand Council (or Conseil d'en haut, named for its location within the royal residences), where he presided over discussions, reserving the final say after all opinions were presented. The Council's agenda spanned the gamut of state affairs, with a pronounced focus on diplomacy and military strategy. Over Louis XIV's reign, 17 ministers served, their primary duty being to support the king on critical issues while upholding the utmost secrecy regarding state matters. Below is a non-exhaustive list of the ministries relevant to the subject of our book:

The Government of the Kingdom of France between 1688 and 1715:[14]

Secretaries of State of the King's Household (the office of Principal Minister was abolished in 1661 on the death of Mazarin): Jean-Baptiste Colbert de Seignelay (1672-1690), Louis Phélypéaux de Pontchartrain (1690-1699), Jérôme Phélypeaux de Pontchartrain (1693-1715).

Secretaries of State for Foreign Affairs: Charles Colbert de Croissy (1680-1696), Jean-Baptiste Colbert de Torcy (1696-1715).

Secretaries of State for War: François Michel Le Tellier de Louvois (1677-1691), Louis François Marie Le Tellier, Marquis de Barbezieux (1691-1701), Michel Chamillart (1701-1709), Daniel Voysin de la Noiraye (1709-1715).

The Government of the Kingdom of England between 1688 and 1701-1715:[15]

Monarchs of England: James II (1685-1688), Mary II (1689-1694), William III (1689-1702), Anne (1702-1707).

Sovereigns of Great Britain and Ireland: Anne 1707-1714), George I (1714-1727).

Ministers of the Crown: John Churchill, 1st Duke of Marlborough and Lord Godolphin (called Godolphin-Marlborough ministry, 1702-1710), Robert Harley, 1st Earl of Oxford and Henry St. John, 1st Viscount Bolingbroke (called Oxford-Bolingbroke ministry, 1711-1714), Charles Townshend, 2nd Viscount Townshend (called Townshend ministry, 1714-1716).

---

[14] The dates in brackets indicate the start and end of the ministries.
[15] Lucien Bély, in his book Espions et ambassadeurs au temps de Louis XIV, ed. Fayard, 905 pages, provides an overview of historical works on English diplomatic personnel: Thomson, M.A. *The Secretaries of State, 1681-1782*, Oxford, 1932 / Sainty, J.C., *Officials of the Secretaries of State (1660-1782)*, London, 1973 / Horn, D.B., *The British Diplomatic Service*, Oxford, 1961 / Lachs, P.S., *The Diplomatic Corps under Charles II and James II*, New Brunswick, 1966 / Lane, M., *The Diplomatic Service under William III*, Transactions of the Royal Historical Society, X (1927), 87-109 / Snyder, H.L., *The British Diplomatic Service during the Godolphin Minister*, in Studies in Diplomatic History, Hatton and Anderson eds, 1970.

Lord High Treasurer (heads a commission of leading figures. He is not yet Prime Minister, and will not be until the reign of George I in 1721): Charles Montagu, 1st Earl of Halifax (1714-1715), Charles Howard, 3rd Earl of Carlisle (1715).

High Chancellor (dependent on the Ministers of the Crown): Lord Jeffreys (1685-1688), John Somers (1693-1700), Nathan Wright (1700-1705), William Cowper, 1st Baron Cowper (1705-1710), Simon d'Harcourt, 1st Baron d'Harcourt (1710-1714), William Cowper, 1st Baron Cowper (again, 1714-1718).

High Chancellor Commission (governs in the absence of the High Chancellor): John Maynard, Anthony Keck, William Rawlinson (1689-1690), John Trevor, William Rawlinson, George Hutchins (1690-1693), John Holt, George Treby, Edward Ward (1700), Thomas Trevor, Robert Tracy, John Scrope (1710).

However, the hierarchy of governance extended beyond those appointed to the crown's highest echelons. Alongside ministers, the machinery of government included secretaries of various ministerial departments and, crucially, the unseen architects of policy and strategy: the secret advisers.

One notable figure was a Picardy gentleman, Truffier d'Augicourt, who began his tenure as a secret adviser to Louvois in 1670. Louis XIV, too, counted among his covert council the Duc de Chevreuse, a figure who, while not a formal member of the king's councils, engaged in discussions and collaborated directly with the monarch during quieter moments. The Duc was known to consult with and receive counsel from Fénelon, among others, who provided advice and support in navigating the complexities of state affairs. The Duc de Chevreuse was known for his forthrightness, offering candid assessments of courtly figures upon the king's request. In an international context, Louis XIV's placed a Frenchwoman, Marie-Anne de La Trémoïlle, Princesse des Ursins, alongside the Queen of Spain following his grandson's ascension to the Spanish throne She maintained regular correspondence with various important figures at the French court. We shall see later that the choice of women in these most crucial affairs was no accident.

France:

The social origins of negotiators and diplomats typically aligned closely with the elite sectors of society: the court and sword nobility, high clergy, or the distinguished robe nobility. In England, while there were instances of the king employing individuals from more modest backgrounds, such as Abbé Gaultier, a simple priest, and Mesnager, a former merchant, the first ambassador appointed was the Duc d'Aumont, a figure of notable high birth. The Duc notably criticised the monarch's strategy of appointing individuals from lower social strata to confront princes, highlighting an instance where one, described pejoratively as a bourgeois, found himself ill at ease in dealings with Queen Anne.

In France, the diplomatic corps consisted of 100 members, among whom 36 bore noble titles, with court nobility frequently spearheading major official embassies. Missions to less prominent principalities were often assigned to the lesser nobility, who were designated as "envoys" rather than ambassadors. According to the historian Lucien Bély, 21% of diplomats hailed from the military nobility, with negotiations occasionally unfolding directly on the battlefield (notables like Huxelles, Harcourt, Berwick, and Villars served both as marshals and negotiators). Political engagement, at times of a temporary nature, could serve as a catalyst for advancement within military ranks. The clergy comprised 11% of those serving abroad, including both high-ranking figures such as cardinals and abbots, and individuals from the robe nobility or the bourgeoisie.

Beyond these prominent figures, clerks and servants also played roles in negotiation processes, ascending through administrative ranks to become key negotiators. While some emerged from the legal profession, few diplomats originated from the bourgeoisie or the realms of arts and letters, indicating a predominantly aristocratic composition of the diplomatic and negotiating bodies. There were also many foreigners serving the French crown: loyal followers and family of the Stuarts (Hooke, Bourk and Berwick), Germans including La Marck and the Count of Rottenbourg, Italians including Rossi and Marcin, a private soldier, and Swiss and Dutch merchants. The negotiators were sent in order to Madrid for the most part, the United Provinces, Rome and finally England.

England and Holland:

In England, the diplomatic landscape featured 38 diplomats from count or ducal families, the nobility, and the provincial gentry. Political figures like Marlborough, Horatio Walpole, and James Vernon mingled with those from mercantile backgrounds, including Molesworth and John Methuen, alongside a few from humble origins, such as Matthew Prior, a carpenter's son. A significant portion of these diplomats held seats in either the House of Lords or the House of Commons, underscoring a trend where most emerged from government ranks rather than the king's inner circle, contrasting with the French model.

The Revolution of 1688 marked a decisive moment, demanding allegiances be declared. Figures like Charles Mordaunt, Earl of Peterborough, and the Molesworth family aligned with William of Orange, receiving rewards for their loyalty: the Molesworth family, for example, who had been involved with Cromwell and later took part in the Irish Puritan revolution, but who had taken part in William's victory at the Boyne, were restored to their titles and lands and were called to the Privy Council. Others, like Lord Stair, returned from exile to embrace the Protestant cause, while some, such as the Duke of Hamilton (formerly Early of Arran), navigated more tumultuous paths, transitioning in his case from imprisonment in the Tower of London until 1712, to a diplomatic position when the Tory government released him and sent him to France as ambassador.[16]

In the Dutch Republic, the transformation from a monarchical to a republican system did not diminish the nobility's role in diplomacy; 43.5% of diplomats hailed from noble backgrounds, particularly those who held sway in urban governance as burgomasters and councillor-pensioners. The representation of military figures among these diplomats was minimal. Instead, the republic's diplomatic engagements were predominantly managed by its administrators, with merchants serving as intermediaries and lawyers also playing significant roles. Dutch diplomats primarily

---

[16] James Hamilton was killed in a duel in London on 15 November 1712. Charles, Lord Mohun, had a disagreement with Hamilton over land and inheritance. The dispute lasted several years, and Charles Mohun finally challenged Hamilton to a duel in Hyde Park. Both were seriously injured, but it was Hamilton who died.

operated in key regions, with assignments prioritised to England, France, the Spanish Netherlands, and the Baltic countries, in that order. A hallmark of the Dutch diplomatic approach was the notable stability and specialisation of its negotiators

6. Confidence of the King:

Secret advisers played a crucial role in assisting the King to navigate various pressures, ensuring he remained uninfluenced by external factors. A pivotal moment occurred in 1701, highlighting the influential role of women in shaping political decisions: As James II Stuart lay dying in exile at Saint-Germain en Laye, Louis XIV contemplated bestowing the title of king upon Stuart's son, Jacques François Stuart. Jean-Baptiste Colbert de Torcy, the Minister of Foreign Affairs, opposed this move, a sentiment echoed by other ministers who feared it would incite English animosity. However, James II's wife, Marie de Modène, and Madame de Maintenon, Louis XIV's secret spouse, successfully swayed the King's decision, securing recognition for Jacques François Stuart—a decision Torcy lamented as influenced unduly by two women. This episode sparked widespread commentary, with pamphlets praising Madame de Maintenon for her wisdom over the collective counsel. Ultimately, Louis XIV, anticipating inevitable conflict with England, resolved that he had nothing further to lose by this decision. But as the king chooses his advisers, and sometimes refers to other opinions, he surrounds himself with those he considers the best. His government, even in the shadows, is therefore personal and absolute.

Ambassadors working together:

The situation we are describing seems to have only one outcome, that of war and conflict resolution. However, despite the backdrop of hostilities, ambassadors—men of significant stature, hailing from the aristocracy or even princely lineages—entrusted their spies and agents with the machinations of deception and subterfuge. In contrast, these dignitaries themselves often maintained relationships that, on the surface, appeared to be cordial friendships. While one might speculate these interactions to be mere facades, there's reason to believe they were, at times, infused with genuine, unbiased empathy.

Some embassies were well-known, and travelled throughout continental Europe by land and/or sea. These journeys lasted several weeks or months, and we know of accounts of them that were printed and published for the general public to read. Along with the writings of adventurers who travelled the world (and these adventurers often worked for a specific employer or state), the texts presenting the great embassy journeys introduced readers to the world and its peoples.

The Duc d'Aumont, for example (to whom we will return later), was sent to England in 1712, marking the rekindling of Franco-British diplomatic ties. The extent to which people were sensitive to the end of violence and war can be gauged from a number of factors, not least the resumption of trade: in the north of France, the Duc d'Aumont was acclaimed and received the blessing of the people. In his correspondence with the French Foreign Minister, the Duc d'Aumont articulated a dual purpose: to signal France's commitment to peace and to subtly deride Holland, anticipating its isolation should the anticipated peace with England materialise. Interestingly, the paths of the Duc d'Aumont and the English envoy, Matthew Prior, converged, leading to an encounter. Aumont greeted him warmly: "I have arranged people of good will and the most honourable on the road to do him the honours of both this province and Picardy."[17] The meeting took place a few days later, on the road, but it apparently did not live up to diplomatic expectations, even if the demonstrations of friendship were sincere. A notable incident underscored the diplomatic decorum of the time: upon learning of his English counterpart's impending journey along the same route, the Duc d'Aumont, aware of the logistical challenges posed by the narrowness of the road and the impossibility of their entourages passing each other, opted to allow Prior precedence while waiting where he was.[18]

---

[17] Archives des affaires étrangères, Angleterre 240, fol. 279, letter from the Duc d'Aumont, de Boulogne, 21 December 1712.
[18] To get an idea of the importance of such a trip, here's what a negotiator's crew contained: 5 carriages, 129 leaded cases, 8 cases containing playing cards and sweets, 20 cases of wine, prints representing the king (for royal propaganda). For a

However, these journeys involved considerable expense, and the king soon resolved to move his embassies only at less cost.[19] As the 18th century progressed, the grand displays of aristocratic camaraderie that characterised the previous century became less common, with discretion and incognito modes of travel gaining preference.

II. **Diplomats in Action.**

1. Diplomatic secrecy:

The realm of international relations, or foreign affairs, inherently demands a culture of confidentiality. During the reign of Louis XIV, discussions on such sensitive topics were strictly limited to those expressly invited, underscoring the paramount importance of secrecy amidst escalating conflicts. The era tolerated no breaches in the discretion surrounding royal deliberations.

In this environment, where politics was deeply enshrouded in secrecy, each minister served as a custodian of this confidentiality, playing a vital role in a complex diplomatic chess game. Responsibilities often overlapped, with ministers holding various areas of expertise converging to counsel the king on unified matters. This scenario fostered a competitive landscape among their agents, where possession of crucial information could significantly sway the king's favour and, consequently, his decisions.

You will correspond constantly with our ministers in other foreign courts, for our best service and your mutual information and assistance in your respective negotiations; and you will also maintain good correspondence and good relations with all the ambassadors, envoys and ministers of the princes and states in friendship with us, and as far as you can penetrate into the designs of their respective superiors, and of what

---

Frenchman, the main concern was wine and silverware. The wine was loaded onto carts of 4 to 6 horses. But even then, customs sometimes caused problems.

[19] For example, ambassadors refused to leave if they were not provided with enough money: 20,000 ecus, pages and servants, and a coach costing 20,000 livres.

you discover of this nature, you will report it constantly to one of our principal secretaries of state.[20]

Weekly, Louis XIV held audiences with ambassadors at his court, from Paris to Versailles, adhering to a meticulous protocol that distinguished between ambassadors and mere envoys.[21] Louis XIV's reception of James II of Stuart was a secret that was brought out into the open, and certainly even the conclusion of old private agreements that were hidden from the general public. In 1670, had Charles II of England not asked his sister Henriette (Louis XIV's sister-in-law) to negotiate a rapprochement between France and England?

Diplomatic missions often extended into hostile territories for discussions between ministers and their co-religionists (as we have said, kings do not meet). Instances include Torcy's 1709 mission to Holland to negotiate with Grand Pensionary Heinsius, which concluded unsuccessfully, and the 1712 mission of English Secretary of State Henry St. John, Viscount Bolingbroke, to France, which was met with enthusiasm in Paris. These high-level engagements were supported by a vast bureaucratic network (clerks, secretaries, interpreters, etc.), who were not of high lineage, and therefore could not aspire to prestigious missions throughout the courts of Europe, but who were often recognised for their talents and confidence. These "no-names" operated discreetly in the shadows, behind the scenes of the monarchy. Colbert de Croissy and Colbert de Torcy meticulously preserved and filed all documents concerning foreign relations to create a comprehensive memory of state affairs.

In the 17th century, the concept of maintaining permanent representatives at foreign courts was nascent yet gradually taking shape. These envoys were stationed abroad to closely monitor the host country's

---

[20] Instruction given to Sir William Trumbull, 1685.
[21] The reception of the Sultan's envoy at the French Court in 1669 is a case in point. Following the announcement of the arrival of a minister from the Sublime Porte, Louis XIV decided to conduct a ceremonial event himself, designed to impress his interlocutor. But there was a mistake, because the person who was coming was just an embassy envoy. The king realised this but continued the reception, only to be mocked later. To make up for such a fine spectacle given in honour of a private individual, he asked Molière and Jean-Baptiste Lully to compose the opera-ballet Le Bourgeois-Gentilhomme (1673).

policies. Despite their covert operations, these agents possessed considerable authority to negotiate and conclude treaties. For instance, in 1711, Abbé Gaultier journeyed from England to France, engaging with Torcy to discuss peace propositions. Following this, the English poet Matthew Prior[22] was dispatched to France with a modest letter from Queen Anne Stuart, aiming to secure a significant pact.

Post-1659, as Spanish dominance waned, France's diplomatic influence surged, taking proactive steps on the international stage. The strategic manoeuvres of French diplomatic networks during this period are noteworthy. The 1668 Peace of Aix-la-Chapelle served as a strategic manoeuvre for Louis XIV in anticipation of the Dutch War. French diplomats were tasked with the covert mission of isolating the United Provinces, a preliminary move that required the negotiation of a clandestine treaty with Spain to divide its territories and ensure its neutrality. The Chevalier de Grémonville was instrumental in finalising these agreements in 1668 and 1671. Moreover, disrupting the Triple Alliance was critical. Colbert de Croissy in London executed this task with finesse, while efforts in the east, including an alliance with the Elector of Bavaria secured by Robert de Gravel in 1670, fortified French positions for the forthcoming conflicts. The diplomatic effort extended to Portugal, where Saint-Romain was dispatched to consolidate support across the Iberian Peninsula. In Germany, Verjus de Crécy sought to align with princes, fostering peace and mutual protection agreements. By 1672, with the declaration of the Dutch War, swift military action was imperative. Arnaud de Pomponne and Courtin ensured Swedish support through a treaty signed that same year. Prince William of Fürstenberg (a friend of Lionne's) was tasked with sowing discord and plotting in anticipation of the French offensive. However, by 1674, as the war intensified, Fürstenberg, leading a French delegation, was perceived as a hostile entity in Germany, resulting in his capture by soldiers given his lack of official diplomatic status and perceived role as an enemy agent. Nevertheless, no charges could be pressed against Fürstenberg due to his clerical status and protection by the Vatican. Post-war, he was named Bishop of Strasbourg

---

[22] Matthew Prior was renowned for his free speech with kings and princes. Louis XIV liked him and once shared a glass of wine with him at Marly.

and was poised to become Prince-Elector of Cologne, a prospect that ultimately did not materialise. Louis XIV later appointed him to the prestigious Abbey of Saint-Germain-des-Prés in Paris.

Thus, it becomes evident that every negotiator dispatched by the king must embody the essence of discretion to avoid becoming a potential hostage. Beyond their representational duties, these diplomats were tasked with gathering intelligence and conducting negotiations on the sovereign's behalf. Consequently, every diplomat transformed into an agent with clandestine missions, privy exclusively to the objectives at hand. Yet, the art of negotiation is fraught with challenges; any sign of concession could inadvertently signal a kingdom's vulnerability—an untenable position. In times of conflict, negotiators risk being branded as traitors or defeatists, necessitating a veil of anonymity both in presence and purpose. This clandestine nature of diplomacy paved the way for some artists, who later rose to prominence, to initially serve their country as covert operatives. Discovery of such agents by enemy forces often led to the unearthing of extensive conspiracies. A notable instance occurred in 1712 when the capture of a French gentleman exposed a secretive communication channel linking Vienna, Hanover, and St. Petersburg. The ensuing investigation sparked discussions of execution, prompting the Court to say that he would be "a victim of his monarch's orders." Ultimately, he was released.

This is a small digression, which not only holds interest but also, under a veil of caricature, reveals how certain behaviours became both a challenge and a source of intelligence. Specifically, the misconduct of the King's official agents led to unique intelligence-gathering methods.

Specifically, the misconduct of the King's official agents led to unique intelligence-gathering methods. In Utrecht, 1712, during the congress, establishments of debauchery were deliberately created to entice the less disciplined and to extract information from them. The French historian, chronicler, and translator Casimir Freschot, who resided in Utrecht at this time, documented such anecdotes in a chronicle.[23] He states that one of the places of debauchery was characterised by beautiful gardens, and

---

[23] Freschot, Casimir, *Histoire amoureuse et badine du congrès et de la ville d' Utrecht, en plusieurs lettres écrites par le domestique d'un des plénipotentiaires à un de ses amis*, Liège, Jacob Le Doux, S.D. (1714), in-12, front.

presented an "enchanted palace," where the nights had no end, "all in a freedom that made one forget all the considerations capable of interrupting or chagrining debauchery."[24] The French were the most loyal customers: "The gentlemen and members of the retinue of the French ambassadors were the ones who seemed to take more interest in it than the others, because they had pushed things further...."[25] In these settings, some women were employed specifically to glean secrets from their incautious visitors, making the leakage of sensitive information somewhat commonplace.

In an attempt to mitigate the sometimes undesirable consequences of such libertine activities, what may be considered the earliest forms of condoms were devised:

> certain very fine caps or bladders, which are applied to the instrument of pleasure, and which, more effective than if they were made of iron, put him in a position to brave the peril in the very fort where he is hiding. [This bladder or cap] is tied with a ribbon in the place where this shirt is missing; and it is necessary to wait until the brave man is animated with all his bravery, and puffed up with all his courage. [a merchant with a monopoly on] this mysterious veil which she herself applies to those who are rude enough not to understand the method.[26]

The diverse composition of the delegations, including officers, often led to overindulgence owing to the protracted nature of their assignments. One officer, enamoured with a village girl, engaged in a duel and suffered an assault. Similarly, churchmen, distant from their spiritual duties, succumbed to sensual pleasures; one young abbot even promised marriage and amassed debts, compelling his convoy's lenders to demand repayment from the ambassador.

2. Military Secrecy and Espionage:

Amidst advancements in warfare, the realm of intelligence was simultaneously evolving, becoming more sophisticated and technologically adept. The military campaigns under Louis XIV were

---

[24] *Ibid*, pp. 142-143.
[25] *Ibid*.
[26] *Ibid*.

characterised by a series of sieges and, less frequently, open-field battles. The organisation and efficiency of the French army were significantly enhanced by Louis XIV's regulatory reforms, and the science of fortification reached new architectural zeniths.

Conducting war thus necessitated a veil of secrecy, even as armies manoeuvred under the watchful eyes of foreign observers. Key figures, including the ministers of war and foreign affairs along with military generals, were integral to this covert approach, imbuing the military domain with a distinctive mystique. The centralised decision-making process under Louis XIV, an absolute monarch, renders historical accounts somewhat scant, complicating efforts to fully grasp the strategic motivations behind these operations.

The meticulous planning for the invasion of Franche-Comté in 1668 exemplifies this clandestine approach. Remarkably, Louis XIV remained at the court, ostensibly engaged in leisure, as military preparations were quietly advanced in eastern France. With troops, horses, and supplies strategically amassed in border towns, the mobilisation was poised for action. The king's sudden appearance, leading a grand parade alongside Condé, underscored the strategic secrecy that also extended to the court's internal power struggles. The minister Louvois sought to limit Turenne's importance while at the same time wishing to restore Condé to the King's good graces, after his actions against him during the Fronde des Princes. Similarly, the preparations for war against Holland were shrouded in such secrecy that the procurement of powder and ammunition across Europe was conducted completely undetected.

3. Cabinet Strategy:

The work prior to the declaration of war was therefore primarily orchestrated within the King's Council, encompassing ministers, secretaries of state, marshalls, and various military commanders. Each member brought to the table a wealth of expertise in their specific fields, contributing significantly to the strategic discussions. This was particularly true for military personnel who, having operated across diverse battlefronts, offered detailed insights into the geography of relevant territories. Vauban, for example, was celebrated not just for his engineering prowess but also for his geographical knowledge, and played a crucial role in these deliberations. Armed with maps and informed by these comprehensive briefings, decisions were made to deploy forces strategically across the complex European landscape. This process birthed the concept of cabinet strategy, which saw a particular application in the standoff with William III of Orange in 1693. Embracing what was termed the "learned" strategy, Louis XIV was cautious of engaging William III in open battle, acknowledging his limitations. Instead of a direct assault through Belgium, where the Stadthouder's fortifications presented formidable defences, Louis XIV directed Marshal de Luxembourg to strike at Neerwinden. The engagement, though narrowly won, was marked by heavy losses. The campaign unfolded across multiple fronts, with a constant stream of information making its way back to the King's office. This data was predominantly geographical in nature, aimed at informing the strategic deployment and development of military forces. Guided by insights from his envoys and military leaders, Louis XIV initiated a decisive engagement against the Savoyard troops at the Battle of La Marsaille on October 4, 1693.

Collection of Information:

The ministerial departments enabled the secretaries of state to gather information pertinent to their areas of responsibility. The networks of informers bolstered the state's key figures, with tensions arising frequently due to the competitive nature of politics, which unfolded both within the nation's borders and on the international stage. Military campaigns and diplomatic negotiations were arenas ripe for contention, and Louis XIV exhibited masterful skill in navigating the intricacies of his ministry, exploiting rivalries to the state's advantage. Notable were the disputes between Colbert and Louvois, and Chamillart and Torcy. Generals, too, maintained their own networks of informers to secure intelligence on enemy movements and strategies. However, personal alliances played a significant role in maintaining positions of power and securing the favour of influential individuals. Marshal de Villars, for instance, adeptly navigated these networks, though his reputation for underpaying informants resulted in a delay in receiving crucial information: "In the field, the ability of an army commander is measured by the spies he knows how to use to find out about the opposing forces and their situation."[27]

One example was the planned French landing on the British Isles in 1690, when a planned French incursion into the British Isles in 1690 required the full activation of all available intelligence networks and communication channels. Since the tumultuous events of 1688, Louis XIV had harboured aspirations to restore James II to the British throne, employing observers to monitor and relay developments back to the French administration: "Most of these regiments were raised by gentlemen who had never been in the army... it was tailors, butchers and shoemakers who formed the companies, who maintained them at their own expense, and who were their captains."[28] It was also reported that James II was indecisive and that this created unnecessary political tension. Amidst these strategic considerations, Louis XIV's reluctance to overtly align with anti-Protestant sentiments stemmed from a desire to uphold an image of autonomy from the Vatican, keen to avoid being perceived as beholden to Catholic doctrines. What's more, if James II Stuart returned to the throne, he would be king of both Catholics and Protestants. D'Avaux continued: "The Irish are irreconcilable enemies of the English, so that, if we let go of their hands, they would slit the throats of those who are here in a short time."[29] Furthermore, James II harboured a certain jealousy against France and did not want his return to the throne to be completely attributed to Louis XIV.

Military Campaigns:

In the realm of military surveillance, the focus here is on intelligence collected along a specific war front, particularly under the watch of one Claude Leblanc, the intendant of Maritime Flanders. His jurisdiction lay on a critical frontier, historically the entry point for enemy forces in each conflict against France, including during the War of Spanish Succession. To anticipate the movements of the opposing army, Leblanc needed to

---

[27] Bély, Lucien, *Les secrets de Louis XIV*, Le grand livre du mois, p. 305
[28] Based on the memoirs of the Comte d'Avaux, ambassador extraordinary to Louis XIV.
[29] *Ibid.*

ascertain the location of its baggage trains and troops. Remarkably, the local populace, bearing the brunt of occupation and thus directly affected, proved more reliable than spies and informers in observing the activities of foreign soldiers within their territory. Leblanc discovered plans to besiege Lille, prompting him to notify Versailles with urgency. However, Chamillart, the Secretary of State for War, dispatched his directives too late, as the enemy forces had already embarked towards the city. Nevertheless, Leblanc's network continued to provide valuable insights, allowing Chamillart to issue timely orders to fortify Lille's defences on a subsequent occasion. Claude Leblanc thus solidified the reputation of his informant network, which had expanded its reach even to London. The actionable intelligence he gathered enabled enemy convoys to be intercepted. Local inhabitants were also mobilised, and villages were visited to ask for the enemy's exact positions.

The Battlefield:

Local intelligence plays a crucial role in military strategy, not just for predicting enemy movements but also in understanding the battlefield's dynamics: terrain, force strength, bridge locations, and resource availability. Scouts are often dispatched into enemy territory, blending with the local populace to gather essential insights. For instance, a river traversing a plain could spell disaster for an unprepared army. This strategic gathering of information was instrumental in Marshal de Villars's success in capturing the enemy's baggage and supplies in 1712, which facilitated a straightforward victory in Denain. At the time, Eugène de Savoie was besieging Landrecies with the allied forces, stretching his supply lines thin to Marchiennes and Denain. The initiative to strike at Denain originated from Jean-Lefebvre d'Orval, a parliamentarian from Douai, who suggested the manoeuvre to Minister Voysin. Armed with this insight, Villars feigned an assault on Landrecies to divert attention, while Marshal-Count Pierre de Montesquiou executed the decisive attack on Denain. The subsequent capture of Marchiennes, the repository of the allied army's provisions, compelled the adversaries to abandon their positions in the region.

Partisans played a crucial role as scouts, closely monitoring enemy movements on land, while naval operations demanded meticulous espionage within harbours and merchant networks. Ships were dispatched with operatives to gather and convey critical intelligence prior to engagement. A notable instance occurred in 1692 when Tourville effectively blockaded the English Channel, facilitating the passage of French vessels. Despite this strategic advantage, Louis XIV harboured reservations about his admiral's capabilities, compelling him to confront the English fleet, which had yet to unite with its Dutch counterparts. However, the timely relay of information faltered, leading to the unexpected merger of the two enemy fleets. Tourville, hindered by delayed intelligence, was confronted by the combined naval forces. Despite the evident disparity in strength and his officers' counsel to evade battle, Tourville adhered to the king's unequivocal command. The resultant encounter at the Battle of La Hougue on May 29, 1692, despite Tourville's valiant efforts, ended in a decisive defeat for the French. This event underscores the challenges faced by military commanders when direct orders clash with the realities of the battlefield. The reluctance or reinterpretation of orders by several marshals, driven by their assessment of situational dynamics, underscores the potential for strategic miscalculations and their catastrophic consequences.

4. International Networks:

For the power brokers of the era, information was not merely useful; it was the lifeblood of their influence, allowing them to monitor developments within the court and foreign lands, thereby securing, consolidating, and enhancing their standing. This dynamic was not limited to the realms of commerce and finance, where merchants and bankers utilised networks to gather intelligence; intellectuals too leveraged their circles of influence for similar purposes. Within this intricate web, every individual could potentially act as a spy or informant, weighed by the balance of risk against reward, with financial compensation often serving as a key motivator. It was, therefore, also financial payments that made it possible to track and trace informers. During the War of the Spanish Succession, for example, the actions of Louis XIV's Cabinet Noir could be tracked. It was the diplomat Jean-Baptiste de Poussin,[30] Louis XIV's emissary to London in particular, who set up this network. His notable achievements included persuading the renowned economist Charles Davenant, leading to the censorship of passages unfavourable to France in *The True Picture of a Mern Whig* (1701). However, shortly afterwards, Louis XIV officially acknowledged James III as the successor to James II, resulting in Poussin's expulsion from London by William III. He joined the Tory MPs, and Davenant did not escape unscathed as he was henceforth referred to as a *Poussineer*.

Certain networks are unravelled, laying bare the duplicity of certain spies and informers, who are as much henchmen as important figures. Financial transactions traced back to these actors served dual purposes: silencing potential threats or incentivising revelations.

5. Propaganda:

However, the war on information also extended into the realm of public opinion and propaganda. Guided by the monarchy, its aim was to control public opinion, not only at home, but also abroad, by mobilising foreign opinion from France. The battleground for this endeavour was primarily the written press, recognised for its enduring impact contrasted with the ephemeral nature of what could be termed "fake news," which may only influence the short-term discourse.

Intellectuals and men of letters were enlisted to endorse the king's policies, with both pro-French and pro-English narratives proliferating in press publications. Individuals like Obrecht from Strasbourg played key roles in distributing news across the empire and dispatching pamphlets to Germany within diplomatic parcels. Counter narratives, such as those by Davenant against England and La Chapelle against Switzerland (through "Lettres d'un Suisse à un Français"), sought to undermine French positions, with the latter contending against the pro-Habsburg *Gazette de Berne*. Remarkably, an English translation was even sent to Queen Anne of England and all the members of Parliament. Historian Joseph Klaits

---

[30] He had a real career in diplomacy, first with Cardinal de Bouillon in Rome in 1691, then with Tallard in London. He was expelled from England after the controversies surrounding Charles Devenant.

underscored the significant reach of these efforts, estimating that each copy of such publications could attract up to twenty readers, amounting to a potential audience of seventy thousand. Moreover, some texts were crafted under the guise of high-profile identities, with alterations made to the paper's appearance to suggest origins from Paris or other significant locations.

The power of propaganda was significantly amplified through newspapers and gazettes that circulated across Europe, reaching especially those nations most involved in current affairs. Louis XIV, for instance, was particularly aggrieved by the disparaging and crude caricatures of his persona that proliferated in the United Provinces amidst his conflict with William of Orange. He regarded such defamation as a potential casus belli, a stance that, predictably, did little to curb the enthusiasm of libelers in Holland, England, and even France. In this context, it's noteworthy that in 1695, the London Commons chose not to renew the Licensing Act, paving the way for a new legislation aimed at more effectively regulating the publication of newspapers and the operation of printing presses. The House of Lords initially advocated for the reinstatement of the old legislation, but their efforts were ultimately unsuccessful. The failure to pass the Licensing Act resulted in an era of newfound freedom for publishers, who were then at liberty to disseminate their content without censorship. This legislative shift marked the emergence of the first independent newspapers.

6. Geographical Scope:

In the late 17th and early 18th centuries, the pervasive presence of spies throughout the capitals and courts of Europe meant that any rumour potentially advantageous to their causes was swiftly appropriated. Information dissemination was not solely the domain of the national or independent press; it thrived in the public sphere, particularly within the communal spaces of cafés, where the pulse of public sentiment could be keenly felt. Peter Wenworth, for example, who canvassed London's cafés, wrote to his brother the Earl of Strafford (plenipotentiary in Utrecht): "At the Café Saint-James, they hope that the Dutch will stand firm with the

Emperor and be able to conquer France for themselves."[31] Similarly, John Drummond amplified the rumours circulating in the wake of newspaper headlines, especially in France, concerning Queen Anne and the political fates of Lord Oxford and Lord Bolingbroke.

By 1707, London boasted around three thousand cafés, with Queen Anne being aware of nearly five hundred frequented by the bourgeoisie, who avidly discussed the latest developments. The *London Gazette* stood as a significant source of news, and some cafés took it upon themselves to produce and distribute their own newsletters to patrons. Lloyd's café distinguished itself in this regard, often serving as a venue where news was read aloud. Considering the vast number of periodicals, each reaching thousands of readers, the importance of information warfare during this period becomes evident. Spies, deeply embedded in this network of communication, played crucial roles in gathering and disseminating intelligence, thereby bolstering the strategic operations of government departments.

7. Threats:

In France and England alike, the Bastille and the Tower of London served as emblematic strongholds for detaining individuals implicated in affairs of state secrecy, embodying the very essence of governmental clandestineness. In both realms, the shadow of suspicion could precipitate imprisonment, while proven culpability often warranted the death penalty. Sovereigns calibrated their punitive measures based on the gravity of the offence and the stature of the implicated parties, employing incarceration as a means to mute potential dissent without inviting public scrutiny or political fallout. In France, however, Louis XIV was able to demonstrate versatility in his choice of detention sites beyond the Bastille, including Mont Saint-Michel, the Lyon prison, the Château d'If facing Marseille, and Pignerol in the Alps

By the turn of the 18th century, the Bastille was processing approximately a hundred cases annually, with thirty-seven individuals

---

[31] Coombs, Douglas, *The Conduct of the Dutch. British Opinion and the Dutch Alliance during the war of the Spanish Succession*, The Hague-Ashimota, 1958, p.338.

receiving decade-long sentences and eleven facing even lengthier confinements. The existential reality of a spy, intrinsically linked to wartime activities, necessitated their imprisonment until the cessation of hostilities. During these tumultuous periods, a collective paranoia permeated society, fostering an environment ripe for the proliferation of surveillance practices that extended to the monarch himself. This era was characterised by a strict adherence to dress codes that mirrored one's social station; deviations from this norm were often construed as attempts at concealment, thereby arousing suspicion. Disguises adopted by individuals—be they feigned monks, soldiers, or nobility—served as red flags. Moreover, the very act of travelling, particularly with unusual frequency, was seen as indicative of espionage, marking the individual as a potential foreign agent and subject to the scrutinising gaze of state security apparatuses.

The case of René-Auguste Constantin de Renneville, incarcerated in the Bastille from 1702 to 1713, stands as a particularly illuminating example to underscore our discussion. De Renneville aspired to expose the inner workings and secrets of this notorious fortress to the wider public. Claiming residence in Holland and asserting his arrival in France was at the behest of Louis XIV's Cabinet Noir, de Renneville intriguingly lacked any formal documentation or passport to substantiate his mission. His account provides a vivid portrayal of life within the Bastille's walls, suggesting that incarceration was often the result of knowing too much, with many prisoners opting to keep their secrets. Intriguingly, the prison's officers sometimes designated inmates to serve as informants. De Renneville recounts encounters with a diverse array of fellow prisoners, including prelates, abbots, pastors, valets, soldiers, prosecutors' clerks, colonels, and magistrates, indicating the political significance and varied backgrounds of those detained. Archival research corroborates that the Bastille's inmates were typically of notable status and held for reasons deeply political. Some imprisoned spies were desperate to communicate with the outside world, not necessarily to divulge secrets but to assert their existence to those beyond the prison walls. Ingenious methods were employed to relay messages, including one instance where an inmate used a crossbow to launch messages wrapped in drug packets, inscribed with blood. Despite their isolation, prisoners were not entirely forsaken, remaining under the vigilant watch of their captors who were as keen on extracting secrets as they were on overseeing their confinement.

The art of secrecy aligned seamlessly with Louis XIV's temperament, as he adeptly navigated the realms of deception and concealment from a young age to advance his agendas. Upon ascending the throne, he strategically limited his circle of advisors, a testament to his cautious approach towards counsel. His military engagements across Europe stemmed not merely from ambitions of power but from a palpable need for self-defence. To adeptly govern France and safeguard the state, Louis XIV undertook the establishment of an elaborate intelligence network, dubbed the "Cabinet Noir."

This clandestine network spanned Europe and beyond, comprising a cadre of adventurers, spies, and occasionally, civilians, who frequented the royal courts of the world. These agents acted as the government's sensory organs, privy to the king's confidential endeavours. Their reports, borne of keen observation and crafty intelligence gathering, contributed significantly to the crown's strategic planning. The complexity of these covert communications was further enhanced by advancements in cryptology, resulting in codes that sometimes remained forever undeciphered.

Versailles itself was a hotbed of espionage, with spies blending into the grandeur of the royal court. The palace's corridors were rife with surveillance, underscoring the notion that even the walls had ears. Louis XV, continuing the legacy of his predecessor, engaged in practices such as intercepting and scrutinising letters and orchestrating operations to detain or abduct foreign dignitaries. The battlefields, too, were arenas of hidden intrigue, with agents navigating the perilous spaces between opposing forces to relay critical information.

> In a word, my son, it means having your eyes open to the whole world; learning at all hours the news of all the provinces and all the nations, the secrets of all the courts, the moods and weaknesses of all the princes and all the foreign ministers; being informed of an infinite number of things that we are thought to be ignorant of; penetrating among our subjects what they hide with the greatest care.[32]

---

[32] Louis XIV, *Memoirs*.

CHAPTER 2

DYNASTICS ISSUES

The tumultuous struggle for supremacy in the British Isles was a conflict deeply rooted in the international policies of the late 17th to mid-18th centuries. This era was characterised by intense diplomatic and military contests between three major powers: the Kingdom of France, the Kingdom of England, and the Republic of the Seven United Provinces of the Netherlands. These complex and often volatile relations were a key aspect of the international system of the time, unfolding amidst the dynastic wars that embroiled these nations. France, then the most formidable kingdom in Europe, found itself contending with two burgeoning maritime powers that challenged its supremacy both on land and at sea. England, a kingdom that had been embroiled in internal conflict for over half a century, struggled to solidify its political identity and secure a position befitting its potential. Despite internal turmoil, England had already set its sights on maritime dominance, positioning itself in direct competition with the Netherlands, another major regional power. This tripartite struggle had multifaceted origins, which will be explored in detail in this first part of the book. We aim to elucidate the intricate web of political, military, and diplomatic manoeuvres that shaped the trajectory of these three states and their quest for dominance in this pivotal period of European history.

Firstly, it is essential to contextualise the dynastic elements at play, particularly concerning England and Scotland, which are central to our discourse. We will embark on a detailed historical journey, tracing back in time to unravel the intricate political, religious, and social complexities of the era. A key focus will be understanding the roots of Jacobitism in the British Isles: how and why did this movement gain traction? We will also delve into the evolving relationship between the Kingdom of England and

France, tracing back to the reigns of Louis XIII of France and Charles I of England. It's crucial to recognise that the geopolitical dynamics between these two nations were not always marked by conflict. Notably, Charles I was the first to attempt forging closer ties with France, aiming to counteract Dutch maritime power. This effort, as we will explore, did not unfold as planned. Drawing nearer to the core theme of our book, we will illuminate the pivotal year of 1670 by dissecting the secret Treaty of Dover. This examination will pave the way for a deeper understanding of our central thesis: the power dynamics between states are inextricably linked to clandestine relations and secret treaties. Such undercurrents of hidden diplomacy and covert agreements played a significant role in shaping the historical landscape we aim to explore. For the moment, French intelligence almost single-handedly dominates the geopolitical debate, and it can be said that it dictates its will to other countries, which will no longer be the case since the reign of Louis XIV.

I. **The Stuarts**

1. **Origins and Dynastic Issues:**

During the 12th century, Scotland witnessed a transformative era known as the Great Century. King David I (1083-1153) was a reformative monarch dedicated to modernising the state. He established key roles within the royal government, each headed by Great Officers. These included the Chancellor (the King's intimate advisor), the Chamberlain (in charge of finance), the Constable (responsible for order in the palace), the Marischal (ensuring order within the palace), and the Stewart (Seneschal), tasked with organising the royal household. This Stewart role quickly became hereditary, and these senior officers were integrated into the royal family during the reign of Robert the Bruce (1274-1329), exemplified by the marriage of the 6th Great Stewart to the king's daughter.

2. **Family Matches:**

The lineage of the Stuarts began with Walter Fitzalan (or Fils-Alain), the great-grandson of Alain Dapifer, seneschal of Dol-de-Bretagne, who likely fought alongside William the Conqueror at the Battle of Hastings. Walter entered the service of David I of Scotland as the first royal grand seneschal, a position he passed down to his descendants. In 1371, Robert Fitzalan, the 7th Great Stewart and son of Walter Stuart, ascended to the Scottish throne due to his lineage and his role as co-regent of the Kingdom of Scotland.

Marie de Guise, wife of James V and great-granddaughter of Henry VII of England, was instrumental in the transition of the family name from Stewart to Stuart. Their son, James VI of Scotland, became King of England in 1603 as James I. His son, Charles I of England, was deposed and executed by Parliamentary forces led by Oliver Cromwell during the First English Civil War (1642-1651). Following Cromwell's death, a dynastic dispute paved the way for the Stuart restoration. After nine years in exile, Charles II was proclaimed King of England in 1660. Through his mother, Henrietta Maria of France, he was a first cousin of Louis XIV. On his death, his son James II Stuart became King of England. Succeeding Charles II, James II Stuart, a Catholic, pursued policies favouring France and displayed absolutist tendencies, leading to his unpopularity. After his ousting in the Glorious Revolution of 1688, he sought refuge in France, where Louis XIV recognised his son as the heir to the British throne under the name James III (also known as The Pretender). This period saw three Jacobite challenges between 1708 and 1719, with James III the Pretender attempting to reclaim his throne from France. In Great Britain, Queen Mary II, wife of William III of Orange, ascended the throne with her husband in 1689, followed upon their death in 1684 and 1702 by Queen Anne. Despite Anne's unstable health and relatively short reign, she was notable for restoring peace in 1713 and achieving political separation from Holland. However, her half-brother the Pretender, supported by a faction within Parliament, remained a Catholic and was bypassed in favour of George of Hanover, who ascended as George I. Interestingly, George was also related to the Stuarts through his mother, Sophia of Hanover, herself a descendant of James VI and I. Although Sophia was the designated heir to Queen Anne, she predeceased Anne, leading to George's succession to the throne.

II. King Charles I, Louis XIII, and Richelieu: espionage and alliances (1630-1641)

We have attempted to set out the problem of the succession to James II Stuart after his deposition, and we will take the liberty of saying that the King of England and Scotland was dispossessed of his crown by his daughter Mary (her father would understandably bear her an inexorable grudge, and would even go on to refuse to mourn her death in 1694, which shocked even his supporters[33]). Her marriage to William III of Orange had been desired by her uncle Charles II, despite the protests of Prince James, not yet King of England. In this, she was no exception to the rule, as her own aunt (sister of James II) had been married to William III of Orange's father, William II. The links with the Netherlands were therefore beginning to take on a serious dimension.

This Marian policy with the Netherlands was the result of a tactic imposed by the situation in Europe since 1630-1640, when Charles I's entire foreign policy had been to restore the lands of his nephew, Charles I Louis, in the Rhineland, while securing the French alliance. This alliance failed to materialise despite all the efforts made, forcing a shift in alliances towards France's enemies.

On the eve of the deposition of the Stuarts, the French and English intelligence services were in great demand, and the fight led by Louis XIV's cabinet to help James II regain his throne was rooted in the struggle that had already begun during the reign of Louis XIII in France and Charles I in England.

In 1630, Charles I's foreign policy saw his efforts to aid his nephew, Charles I Louis of the Palatinate (son of Frederick V of the Palatinate, King of Bohemia and Elector Palatine, and Elizabeth Stuart) to succeed his father, who had been deposed in 1620 in favour of his dynastic rival, Maximilian I, Duke of Wittelsbach of Bavaria. The English crown's aim was therefore to gain a permanent foothold on the continent, while dealing with the hostility of France, which wanted to retain its prerogatives over these territories. For many years, research revealed a certain inconsistency,

---

[33] After Princess Elisabeth-Charlotte, Princess Palatine (wife of Philippe de France, brother of Louis XIV), letter to her sister the Countess Louise, 5 March 1695.

even a weakness in the policy of Charles I, who distrusted France and therefore intended to move closer to Spain. However, English historians nuanced this view after the discovery of confidential documents relating to France, kept in the national archives in Kiev.

Between 1636 and 1639, the King of England's policy was characterised by a rather realistic approach: to obtain an alliance with France by concluding a treaty with Louis XIII. However, the King's Protestant subjects had worked to bring about this alliance, so that England would become involved in opposing the Counter-Reformation, which was gaining ground at the time. If it had gone ahead, England would eventually have taken part in the Thirty Years' War. Unfortunately, or fortunately, this rapprochement was not possible.

The government of Charles I was deeply divided, with the Earl of Leicester, Robert Sidney, and his allies (Algernon Percy, Earl of Northumberland, Philip Herbert, Earl of Pembroke, William Cecil, Earl of Salisbury[34] and Sir John Coke, Secretary of State) fervently defending the kingdom's participation in the Thirty Years' War. The motivation of the Northumberland-Leicesters was not only to counter the "political and spiritual tyranny" of the Papacy but also to combat the Counter-Reformation efforts spearheaded by the Habsburgs of Spain. By 1590, Protestantism dominated roughly half of the continent (France would also suffer from this state of affairs, with the famous "Amboise Conjuration"). After a hard-fought battle, Bohemia and the Palatinate fell under the influence of the Counter-Reformation, and even England took fright.

At the same time, it is important to understand that Spain was engaged in a battle against France, because the latter had closed the traditional route between Spain and Northern Italy towards Flanders (French occupation of Lorraine in 1633-1634). To do this, it intended to open up a maritime front in the English Channel, controlled by the English navy. England therefore had two options: to help France fight Spain, and thus keep the best part of the Palatinate for itself, or to help Spain keep its access to the continental road to Flanders.

---

[34] His two sons fought a duel in 1691, after an argument at a dinner party. The elder William was killed at the age of 19, and his brother converted to Catholicism and became a Trappist monk as a penance.

We can therefore say that the struggle that began between France and England was still latent, and, while not erupting into open conflict, manifested in a significant naval arms race that saw both nations deploying formidable warships, notably *the Sovereign of the Seas* by England and *the Crown* by France. It has to be said, however, that Charles I's preference leaned towards an alliance with France, as this could present a means to counterbalance Spanish power in the Netherlands and potentially dominate Europe. The financing of this ambitious naval buildup and the pursuit of an alliance with France led Charles I to levy the "Ship Money" tax. This tax, while intended to bolster the English navy, proved highly controversial and contributed to the growing discontent with Charles's rule, working against him when he had to be judged a few years later, and even leading to accusations of him having done it only for questions of personal prestige in European diplomatic circles.

In essence, Charles I's foreign policy was the result of desired but impossible alliances. In 1630, Spain had already turned its back on him, rightly believing that England's place was not very influential (this place was not definitively taken until a century later). This rebuff necessitated a pivot towards France, which was no easy task (and which therefore ended in another failure), and was a stopgap measure designed to regain control of the Palatinate as best as possible. In 1635, secret negotiations began with the aim of forming a league to recover the lands and dignity of Prince Elector Charles I Louis. In the spring of 1636, the Earl of Leicester was sent to France with the task of concluding an alliance. At the same time, and even more secretly, Thomas Howard, 14th Earl of Arundel was sent to Emperor Ferdinand II in Vienna. The balance of power thus established between France and the Austrian Habsburgs would have made it possible to obtain the best possible terms in future talks on the Palatinate.

In Paris, Leicester proposed an exchange between Lorraine (occupied by France) and the left bank of the Lower Palatinate, which had been held by the Spanish since 1620. Robert Sidney also proposed the services of the English navy to protect Picardy, and therefore Paris, from possible (and desired) Spanish incursions (control of the English Channel would also have made this possible). Furthermore, he was advised to consider this the best option, as the English ambassador suggested that his navy could also help the Spanish threaten north-eastern France. Charles wanted to strike a blow and encourage Louis XIII and his minister Richelieu to conclude this alliance. For his part, the Earl of Arundel in Vienna was powerless: Ferdinand II of Habsburg had no desire to confront Maximilian of Bavaria. Consequently, forging an alliance with France emerged as the final recourse available. The year 1636 was marked by France enduring setbacks at the hands of Spanish forces, notably the loss of Corbie and the consequential vulnerability of Paris, which led to Louis XIII's hesitancy in responding to English overtures. In this context, Charles decisively intervened.

In February 1637, Charles authorised Leicester to draw up a treaty of alliance with France. In fact, two treaties, one official and the other hidden, ratified an offensive and defensive alliance:

> His Majesty has now sent you... his ratification under the seal of the embroidery which, after a similar ratification under the seal of the French crown and signed by this king [Louis XIII], you may deliver to them... And the execution now rests on your hands: we expect it to be dispatched.[35]

The responsibility for advancing this alliance, thereby subtly shifting the onus to France, indicated the looming shadow of conflict with Spain. Despite the outward stance taken by the English monarchy, the internal desires of Charles remain shrouded in mystery, absent any definitive documentary evidence. In any case, the contemplation of war against Spain was fraught with risk due to the formidable Spanish military might, a fact Charles was acutely aware of. Thus, in February 1637, the King wrote to Thomas Wentworth, the Lord Deputy in Ireland: "What is the probability that I am wrong about Spain, you can now see as well as I do."

To bolster the stature of his nephew, Charles I Louis, Charles envisaged appointing him as the Lord Admiral of the Channel fleet. Successes under his command would not only elevate his nephew's prominence but also solidify the House of Stuart's influence in Europe, especially in the contest for control over the Palatinate. However, the strategic narrative took a different turn with the Earl of Warwick, Robert Rich, a staunch advocate for the "Blue Water" strategy, championing a

---

[35] Gregg, Pauline, *Charles 1er*, éd. Fayard, 1984, 522 p.

full-scale naval engagement against the Spanish armada in the English Channel—a vision reminiscent of Francis Drake's era under Elizabeth I. This naval dominance was seen as a precursor to any terrestrial confrontation on the continent, while provocations against Spanish colonies in the Americas were aimed at undermining Habsburg interests, setting the stage for a broader conflict in the English Channel.

In the spring of 1637, the geopolitical landscape of Europe seemed to indicate an unending conflict between Spain and England. In this climate of enduring hostilities, Louis XIII of France made a strategic move by drafting a version of the treaty in duplicate in the year 1637. Regrettably, only the latter of these documents has survived, a document believed to have contained additional significant elements. Nevertheless, the alliance, seemingly ratified, aimed at severing Flanders from Spanish control both by land and sea, was a development that Charles I greeted with a sense of relief, coupled with a renewed aspiration to reclaim the Palatinate for his nephew. However, initial actions to bring these ambitions to fruition were sluggish. Cardinal Richelieu, it appeared, was inclined towards decelerating the negotiation process. It was Charles himself who opted for a more assertive stance, initiating operations that ranged from intimidatory to outright aggressive. From July 1637 to September 1639, English strategy under Charles veered towards what could be termed Marian politics: Madame de la Vieuville, seeking refuge in London after her husband, the Duc de la Vieuville, was displaced by Richelieu in 1620, was prepared to return and challenge French domestic policies. Furthermore, Charles extended an offer of political sanctuary to all dissenters. This offer was extended to Marie de Rohan, Duchess of Chevreuse, a progeny of Henri de Rohan, a noted Protestant Huguenot leader. To her, he also proposed a matrimonial alliance with Prince Rupert, his nephew and the brother of Charles I Louis, who had distinguished himself in the Royalist cavalry. Finally, Charles I Louis was to take command of the Landgrave's army (formerly commanded by William V of Hesse-Cassel), albeit financed by France.

With these measures, Charles aimed to exert pressure on France, compelling it into substantive negotiations. This series of actions marked a dramatic transformation in Charles' persona. Initially inclined towards diplomacy and virtue, circumstances nudged him towards adopting a more confrontational posture. Moreover, Charles' reluctance to commit troops to the ongoing Thirty Years' War in Europe contributed to Cardinal Richelieu's growing wariness towards England. In 1639, amidst the escalating conflict with the supporters of the Scottish Covenant, Charles recalled Leicester from Paris, having previously negotiated a mutual non-aggression pact with France to safeguard England's southern coast. In a pivot towards continental politics, Charles participated in the 1640 Hamburg Conference, aligning England with France, Sweden, and the United Provinces in opposition to the Habsburgs. For this critical mission, he dispatched his foremost diplomat, Sir Thomas Roe, to Hamburg, while Leicester was instructed to return to Paris. This moment underscored the alliance with France as not merely strategic but verging on the essential for England's geopolitical stance. Simultaneously, the Battle of the Downs in 1639, pitting Spain against Holland, underscored the strategic importance of the English Channel as a vital maritime corridor for Spanish access to Flanders. In light of these developments, Charles' envoy in Vienna was ordered to maintain a stance of inactivity.

The position of Charles and England had devolved into one of humiliation, as foreign navies engaged in combat within British territorial waters, all while the English navy was preoccupied in Scottish waters due to the Bishops' War. This lack of military response from England coincided with a significant downturn in the fortunes of the once-dominant Spanish fleet, marking a pivotal shift in the maritime balance of power. This period also witnessed the gradual souring of relations between England and Holland, tracing its roots back to these maritime conflicts and strategic oversights.

Diplomatically, the situation was further complicated by the steadfast opposition of the Habsburgs by Maximilian of Bavaria, who held sway over the Palatinate. Maximilian's resistance posed a significant obstacle in the diplomatic exchanges between England and the Habsburgs, especially concerning the aspirations of Charles I Louis to ascend to the throne of the Palatinate. Complicating matters further, France began to extend overtures to Maximilian in an effort to forge a counter-alliance against the Habsburgs.

In this tangled web of alliances and enmities, Charles' strategy was unequivocal: he aimed to reclaim the Palatinate by aligning with France. However, with Charles engaged in Scotland and the Spanish preoccupied with issues in Flanders, all parties gravitated towards maintaining their established stances, relegating the issue of the Palatinate to a secondary concern. Faced with these circumstances, Charles found himself compelled to sever the alliance with France in favour of closer ties with Spain, presenting a solution that seemed to benefit all parties involved.

Negotiations with Spain commenced in London during the autumn of 1639, marked by the arrival of the Marquises of Velada and Virgilio Malvezzi, along with the diplomat Alonso de Cárdenas. To solidify the impending treaty, Charles offered the hand of his eldest daughter, Princess Mary, to Balthasar Carlos, the Spanish heir.

By autumn of 1640, the alliance with France had effectively dissolved. This development anticipated a rift within Charles' inner circle, particularly the Northumberland-Leicesters, who, as we can recall, had advocated for an unwavering alliance with France and participation in the Thirty Years' War. he Treaty of Berwick in 1639 concluded the first Episcopal war in Scotland, and in April 1640, Charles I convened the Short Parliament in an attempt to enforce the Anglican liturgy on the Scots. The subsequent military campaign failed, leading to the dissolution of Parliament, an action that found opposition among the Leicester-Northumberlands and others like Warwick and Francis Russell, Earl of Bedford. The divergence between Charles I and the Northumberland circle deepened with the support for Princess Mary's marriage to Balthasar Carlos. The convocation of the Long Parliament to secure funds for ongoing conflicts further destabilised the domestic front. The opposition from the circle heralded a political crisis in 1641, culminating in the eruption of the Civil War in the following year.

Against this backdrop, which did not seem to favour England, the intelligence services did their utmost to intercept mail from France, but Richelieu relied on a spy service that was far ahead of its enemies. He himself was a master of this art, and had chosen his men himself. This was the case with Antoine Rossignol (1600-1682), who had created an encryption table that was only solved at the end of the 19th century. His men were everywhere, and all over Europe it was very difficult to slip through the net. However, Charles I could already count on a number of key figures, who unfortunately only became active after his deposition and execution. John Wallis (1616-1703) officially served England between 1643 and 1703, but he also created a network of spies that would serve England's revival and European domination throughout the 18th century.

III. An Overview of the State of Affairs in 1688[36]

In 1996, French historian Bernard Cottret highlighted a resurgence in the academic study of Jacobitism: "in the last twenty-five to thirty years, the scientific study of Jacobitism has regained new vigour, thanks in particular to the courageous work of Eveline Cruickshanks, current President of the Royal Stuart Society."[37] This renewed scholarly attention sheds light on a pivotal moment in British history: the overthrow of James II, King of England,[38] Ireland, and Scotland, in 1686.

This momentous event, known as the Glorious Revolution or the Bloodless Revolution (though the latter term is a misnomer, as it was not entirely devoid of violence), saw James II dethroned by a coup d'état led by William III of Orange, Stathouder of the Netherlands. William's army, numbering over 25,000, including 7,000 French Huguenots, marked a significant Protestant intervention in British affairs. Following the deposition, England's Parliament, then under Whig leadership, assumed the monarch's powers.

Louis XIV of France, known as the "Most Christian" King and a first cousin to James II since the reign of Henry IV,[39] provided sanctuary to the deposed king and his followers in Saint-Germain-en-Laye. He openly

---

[36] Until 1700, France and England did not follow the same calendar. England used the Julian calendar, which was ten days behind the Gregorian calendar followed on the continent. From 1700 onwards, the difference was eleven days. In England, the year began on 25 March. For the purposes of this book, we will start the year on January 1.
[37] Cottret, Bernard, *History of England, 16th-17th centuries*, 1996.
[38] Before 1707, we speak of England, because the union of the crowns had not yet been established. After that date, we can talk about Great Britain.
[39] When James II arrived in France, people were surprised that he did not embrace Louis XIV, an omission that was put down to English manners, which differed from those of France.

protested the deposition, which had been fueled by Protestant forces. The term 'Jacobite,' derived from the Latin form of James's name, "Jacobus," soon came to denote the royalist supporters of James II. Among the approximately 40,000 Jacobite refugees, 60% were Irish, 34% English, and 6% Scottish. Overall, 40% were from aristocratic backgrounds, most of whom served as officers in the armies. They settled in Saint-Germain-en-Laye, forming a Jacobite Court. Concurrently, a significant Irish community formed in Nantes.

Understanding Great Britain's history involves recognising its distinctiveness, influenced significantly by its relations with other powers. Ever since the Auld Alliance of 1296, French kings have viewed this ally as a strategic counterbalance to English policy. The 1707 Act of Union, uniting England and Scotland, did not alter this dynamic. Louis XIV's aspiration to restore his cousin, James II, to the English throne, ultimately proved unsuccessful, illustrating the intricate interplay of dynastic, religious, and political factors in shaping Britain's unique historical trajectory.

CHAPTER 3

THE ORIGINS OF THE FALL OF THE STUARTS (1649 – 1688)

The dramatic situation in England had therefore culminated in the first revolution (1642-1651), with the death and execution of Charles I, but also some thirty years later when James II had to relinquish his crown to William III of Orange and flee to France, during the Glorious Revolution of 1688. At this stage, the balance of power saw Louis XIV's France still standing as the arbiter of Europe, a position that was being increasingly violently challenged, particularly by Holland. The French espionage network still relied on the work of Antoine Rossignol, who had created Louis XIV's famous Cabinet Noir with his son, Charles-Antoine Bonaventure (1649-1705). However, we set out in the first chapter the work that had already been done by the cryptographer John Wallis. His services were noticed by William III, who used them to counterbalance the network of French informers. From then on, Louis XIV's stranglehold on espionage affairs was undermined by the eminent work of the English informers and cryptographers, of whom Wallis was the leader.

I. A Difficult Political Situation in England (1649-1660).

1. The Trial and execution of King Charles I (1649):

With the King isolated and his cause seemingly lost, Charles I attempted to make a final stand by leveraging Scottish support. Cromwell and the Puritan "Independents," despite their initial alliance with the Scots during the Civil War, had never genuinely aimed to establish a Presbyterian church in England (in fact, at the start of the Civil War,

Cromwell had taken the lead of troops composed of the minor provincial nobility, often referred to as the "sword nobility," who had become revolutionary because they were impoverished and excluded from political and military life, and therefore had nothing left to lose. Their leaders were officers who called themselves Independents because they supported a Congregationalist religious policy.) After Naseby, they no longer needed the Scots and refused to pay the Covenanter armies. Charles sought to exploit Scottish discontent by aligning himself with their cause, signing a "Covenant" that acknowledged the Presbyterian Church in Scotland, and even pledged to experiment with Presbyterianism in England for three years. This move, however, came too late to change his fate. Scotland, already drained by its involvement in the English campaign and ironically weakened by Montrose's royalist campaign, found itself unable to mount a significant resistance against Cromwell's forces. The King's last-ditch effort faltered at the Battle of Preston, leading to his capture, trial, and eventual execution. Scotland was struck with horror. Six days later, the Scots faithfully proclaimed Charles II, aged 18, King of Great Britain and Ireland. The new king signed the Covenant almost without hesitation, as religious issues were of only relative importance to this cynical opportunist. He was crowned at Scone a year later, but it was the last breath of a doomed cause. Cromwell himself delivered the final blow at Dunbar (1650) and Worcester (1651). Charles II fled to the continent and Cromwell reigned supreme over Scotland.

The culmination of Cromwell's rule in Scotland was marked by General George Monck's rigorous enforcement of the Commonwealth's authority, effectively quashing any lingering resistance. The General Assembly was dissolved. The symbols of government were taken to London. Twenty-eight commissioners were installed to carry out the orders of the Commonwealth and, later, the Protectorate. The lands of those who had taken part in the last attempt at royalty were confiscated. A tax was imposed on all the inhabitants to pay the English armies garrisoned in a dozen castles. The country was left economically and spiritually drained.

However, despite the severity of his military campaigns, Cromwell proved to be a capable administrator. His tenure saw the restoration of order and the establishment of Puritan legal principles, leading to improvements in the judicial system, academia, commerce, and industry. Viewing this through perhaps a somewhat generous lens, the historian Burnet wrote: "the eight years of usurpation were a period of great peace and prosperity."

The failure of the Covenant to unify Scotland under a singular religious vision resulted in fragmentation within the Church, exemplified by the emergence of various factions, including the Caméronians. This group, named after Richard Cameron, a radical Covenanting leader, epitomised the extreme end of the Covenanters' spectrum. They revered the Covenant, placing it at the core of their faith, even above the Bible itself; it was considered eternal, since it was signed with God.

2. The Restoration of King Charles II (1660):

The restoration of Charles II to the throne in 1660 saw a tired Scotland's hopes for religious and political reconciliation quickly dashed. Upon his return, Charles, perhaps underestimating the complexity of the situation, reverted to the old Episcopal system, thereby reigniting religious tensions. The severe suppression of Presbyterian and Cameronian dissenters led to a resurgence of violence, with more than a third of the population defying the new religious edicts, preferring to hold their services in the open, away from the reach of soldiers. Upon the death of Charles II, James II, the "only stupid Stuart" (whose Catholic faith made his reign especially contentious in Scotland), ascended the throne. The first year of his reign became known in Scotland as the "black year" or "the season of slaughter." Before he had time to do too much harm, the English Revolution of 1688 drove him out of the country and placed William of Orange on the throne. Showing restraint, William, during the reading of his coronation sermon, refused to read the phrase: "... eliminate heretics and enemies of the true worship of God," declaring, "I refuse to place myself under the obligation of becoming a persecutor."

II. Louis XIV Established his Intelligence Services (1670).

1. The Treaty of Dover and his Secret Clauses (1670):

Prior to the alliance of the Stuart and Bourbon dynasties to reclaim sovereignty over the British Isles from William III, it is imperative to delve into the clandestine dealings that characterised the relationship between the two realms, particularly under the reigns of Charles II of England and Louis XIV of France. The backdrop of the 1670s provides a crucial context for understanding the subterfuge that defined this era.

Indeed, while the full-blown English Revolution was yet to occur, the adversities encountered by Charles II in this era were harbingers of the turmoil that was to come. This period was marked by a notable initiation of secretive diplomatic practices between England and France. Specifically, the covert Treaty of Dover, executed on 22 May 1670, epitomised the clandestine negotiations undertaken by the two monarchies, deliberately kept from the purview of their subjects. This pact can be regarded as the precursor to subsequent confidential dealings, particularly affecting Charles II's successor, James II, and Louis XIV.

By 1670, two decades had elapsed since the onset of the first English Revolution, a period characterised by the exile of Charles I's progeny and the rise of Oliver Cromwell's Puritan regime. Upon Charles II's restoration in 1660, the monarchy found itself in a transformed political landscape where the Parliament's authority, especially regarding taxation and military matters, had significantly expanded. Despite Charles II's covert allegiance to Catholicism, his position as the head of the Protestant Church served as a strategic facade to mitigate opposition from anti-Catholic and anti-monarchical factions. This delicate balance of power was persistently challenged, with the Parliament's reluctance to endorse the king's use of the standing army as a means to enforce his will, a stance influenced by the traumatic events of the 1640s. Nevertheless, in 1660, Charles II, during the Stuart Restoration, sought to promote domestic tranquillity. Yet, it was he who clandestinely negotiated with Louis XIV— a monarch he regarded both as kin and with suspicion—to secure financial support in exchange for his conversion to Catholicism

However, Charles II, distinct from his French counterpart Louis XIV, operated within the constraints of a constitutional framework that intertwined his monarchy with the legislative powers of the House of Lords and the House of Commons, thus reflecting the collective will of his subjects. This structural dynamic underscored that diplomacy was a tool to be wielded in favour of the parliamentary monarchy as a whole, rather than serving the singular interests of the monarch. Consequently, Charles II lacked the autonomy that characterised Louis XIV's reign, where the latter exercised absolute control over state affairs. This limitation spurred Charles II to seek avenues to consolidate power in a manner akin to the French model of governance.

The strategic matrimonial alliance with Catherine of Braganza, a Catholic, underscored this pursuit, yielding significant commercial advantages from Portuguese territories through a triangular agreement involving France. The Treaty of the Pyrenees in 1659, which aimed to resolve conflicts between Spain and France, included provisions that ostensibly restricted French support for Portugal. However, Charles II's marriage facilitated a loophole, enabling Louis XIV to indirectly support Portugal by channelling funds through England. This arrangement was further bolstered by the dispatch of General Schomberg, a Protestant, to lead the Portuguese military, coupled with a twenty thousand ecu financial package. At the same time, Charles II's sister, Henrietta of England, married Louis XIV's brother, Philippe d'Orléans, in 1661. Her mother knew France well, since Henrietta Maria, daughter of Henri IV, had married Charles I and fled to the castle of the Louvre (Paris) with her son. These close ties reveal one thing: Charles II preferred to ally himself with Catholic countries, whereas his brother opted for a Protestant alliance through his marriage to the daughter of Chancellor Hyde, from which two Protestant daughters, Anne and Mary, were born.

In 1662, the strategically significant port of Dunkirk was transferred from England back to France, a transaction reportedly facilitated by potentially dubious dealings, particularly involving Chancellor Hyde. This episode illustrates the enduring closeness between the Stuart monarchy and the French kingdom throughout its tenure over England. Amidst this backdrop, Charles II confronted the Franco-Dutch alliance, which, under the sway of merchant guilds in 1665, adopted an increasingly hostile posture. But despite this alliance, the Franco-English rapprochement seemed irresistible: the English monarchy had its agents within the members of its family. Henrietta Maria, Louis XIV's aunt, and Henrietta, known affectionately as "Madame" and Charles II's sister-in-law, emerged as key figures in this diplomatic dance. The latter maintained clandestine communication with Charles II, leveraging her covert moniker "Minette" to serve as an influential conduit for correspondence detailing mutual commitments between the monarchies. Initiatives for these exchanges were bolstered by figures such as Hugues de Lionne, the Secretary of State, Ruvigny, a Protestant officer, and Saint-Albans, the principal advisor to the Queen of England.

By 1667, amidst ongoing military skirmishes, England and the Netherlands endeavoured to forge a closer relationship, countering Louis XIV's aggressive stance towards the Dutch. Despite the Treaty of Breda, signed in July 1667, England and Holland signed a defensive treaty in 1668, replete with secret clauses that were not divulged to anyone, designed to force the King of France to abandon his conquests. Following this action, Charles II, in correspondence with Henrietta, expressed the constrained choices imposed by the European geopolitical landscape. In response, the Marquis de Croissy, brother to Colbert, was dispatched to London to finalise a treaty with England, skillfully navigating the colonial frictions with Holland to France's benefit.

However, the reins of the English government at the time were held by CABAL (Clifford, Arlington, Buckingham, Ashley, Lauderdale), most of whom were Puritans, with one notably staunchly anti-French. The shifting dynamics of alliances and conflicts in 1668 led to Portugal's estrangement from French influence. Consequently, the Peace of Aix-la-Chapelle in 1668 served merely as a temporary ceasefire, a strategic pause to secure formidable allies for ongoing hostilities. Louis XIV sought to enlist England's support to overcome the Dutch, an offer Charles II accepted, recognising France's preeminence in Europe. Nevertheless, the English Parliament, increasingly inclined towards William III of Orange—a nephew of Charles II and a Stuart on his mother's side—posed a challenge to the king's preferred diplomatic course. The financial aid promised by France through this alliance was, therefore, of paramount importance to him.

In the same year, Charles II's stance appeared to waver as he distanced himself from the proposals made by Louis XIV. The Duke of Buckingham persuaded Henrietta to undertake a covert mission to England aimed at advancing the Catholic cause. This manoeuvre prompted Louis XIV to seek a detente with Holland, facilitating a more conducive environment for Charles II's governance.

In February 1669, Charles II engaged in profound deliberations with his brother, the Duke of York, regarding the matter of converting to Catholicism. These discussions were notably attended by the Earl of Arlington, the Prime Minister, Sir Thomas Clifford, an adviser who was favourably inclined towards Catholics, and the Earl of Arundel, who was himself a Catholic. The accounts provided by the Duke of York, who would later ascend to the throne as James II, significantly highlight the importance of this event. It was during these conversations that the idea of seeking support from Louis XIV was first proposed. Despite the prevalent "natural hatred" of the English towards the French, as noted by Colbert, it was decided that any agreement forged would prioritise commercial interests over military ones.

In March 1669, Charles II dispatched a cryptic letter to Henrietta, wherein names were substituted with numbers to ensure that the communication remained intelligible solely to the intended parties. This act indicates Charles II's inclination towards securing financial support and an alliance from France in exchange for his conversion to Catholicism, which he perhaps viewed more as a strategic manoeuvre than a matter of personal conviction. Moreover, Charles II sought this support not only for religious reasons but also as a means to emancipate himself from the constraints imposed by the challenging Parliament. However, he postponed his decision, negotiating terms that included a financial contribution of two hundred thousand pounds and military support in exchange for the appointment of Catholics to pivotal government positions, the granting of religious freedom to co-religionists, and the public declaration of his own conversion to Catholicism.

2. Franco-British Secret Treaties:

Our exploration opens the door to one of the most enigmatic chapters in the history of the French monarchy towards the close of the 17th century, intertwining with the clandestine dialogues between France and England concerning Charles II's potential conversion to Catholicism. This discussion serves to illustrate that the veil of secrecy, far from being a novel phenomenon with the ousting of James II Stuart in 1688, has perennially constituted the backdrop against which international diplomacy unfolds. Hence, secrecy transcends its initial purpose, evolving into a realm of mystery in its own right.

In the year 1669, Charles II's cautious stance towards France was palpably influenced by the activities of Henry Jermyn, Earl of Saint-Albans. A devoted attendant to Queen Henrietta Maria of England, Jermyn's role as a mediator between England and France underscores the complexities of this period. The apprehension surrounding the potential public revelation of Charles II's conversion to Catholicism was well-founded; such an untimely disclosure, or worse, its discovery, risked igniting another armed insurrection in England, possibly leading to dire consequences reminiscent of past upheavals.

On 19 July 1669, a communique from the French minister Louvois disclosed the incarceration of a highly confidential detainee within the Alpine fortress of Pignerol. Yet, the formal arrest warrant was only dispatched on the 28th of July to a sergeant-major in Dunkirk, pertaining to one Eustache Danger apprehended in Calais. Instructions explicitly mandated the stringent surveillance of a valet associated with Danger, who was strictly prohibited from any form of communication or visibility. The convergence of evidence hints at a possible scenario wherein a double agent had intercepted covert communications relating to the perilously contemplated conversion of Charles II, an endeavour seemingly more audacious than that of his father, Charles I, who met his demise by execution. This narrative has led some scholars to speculate that "Valet Eustache Danger" could indeed be the enigmatic figure known as the Man in the Iron Mask.

Concurrently, escalating tensions between France and Holland underscored the imperative for an Anglo-French alliance. France proposed a joint military strategy: a terrestrial assault by French forces complemented by naval operations from England. The demise of Henrietta Maria in September 1669 necessitated her daughter, Henrietta, to assume her mother's role in the ongoing diplomatic negotiations. Charles II found himself enticed by Louis XIV's proposition to sever ties with Holland in favour of revitalising his sovereignty. Louis XIV envisioned for Charles a reign marked by territorial expansion, a subservient Parliament, and a stature befitting a monarch of considerable influence. Given the international political climate, there was a compelling case for an Anglo-French rapprochement, a strategy so adeptly orchestrated by Henrietta under Louis XIV's tutelage that even the English Parliament would find no grounds for objection.[40]

Thus, the document that has come to be recognised as the "Treaty of Dover" underwent a series of exchanges among the figures previously discussed.

It was the ambassador Croissy in London who initially received the draft of the treaty from Clifford. This draft was subsequently handed over to a certain Bellings for translation into French. The stipulations within the treaty were explicit, particularly concerning Charles II's conversion to Catholicism and the provision of a substantial financial sum to serve as a safeguard in the face of domestic unrest and as a buffer against potential conflicts with Holland. The English delegation, led by Arlington, was keen on expediting the negotiation process, cautious of Croissy's potential openness to alternatives proposed by Holland. The negotiations were conducted in French at the residence of Patrick Maginn, also known as "Priest Patrick," a cleric and double agent working for Charles II of England. The discussions were predominantly centred around the financial support from France, which was to amount to nearly a million pounds sterling, in addition to a significant provision of military equipment. Command of the joint naval force was to be entrusted to the Duke of York, the future James II. France agreed to maintain a stance of neutrality for one year while clandestinely supporting England. Ultimately, the agreement entailed the covert transfer of over three million pounds,

---

[40] One of the copies of the secret Treaty of Dover was found in Lord Clifford's travel office in Ugbrook Park.

facilitated through the smuggling of items like barrels and ropes. Despite these arrangements and subsequent efforts, as of 15 May 1670, France had yet to secure Charles II's public declaration of his conversion before Parliament. The acceptance of such a conversion by the armed forces in Scotland and Ireland, as well as by the colonel of the regiment of guards, was anticipated to be fraught with difficulties.

On the 1st of June, 1670, the Treaty of Dover culminated nearly two years of diplomatic negotiations and burgeoning ties between the monarchs of England and France. Aboard the vessel that transported Madame was Louise de Kéroualle, destined to become an influential figure in Charles II's court as his mistress and the Duchess of Portsmouth, fervently championing the French cause.[41]

The treaty's second article mandated Charles II to make a public declaration of his faith, yet, it also naively presupposed, reflecting a misjudgment of English political dynamics, that Charles could assure his subjects' loyalty despite a difference in religious affiliation. Should a rebellion occur, France committed to providing financial and military support. Furthermore, the agreement outlined a joint Anglo-French military campaign against Holland, with the stipulation that the treaty's contents remain undisclosed until the onset of hostilities.

We are thus in a position to understand more easily the situation of the House of Stuart on the English throne, with France backing what amounted to a veritable coup against the English Parliament. Despite enjoying the backing of both the Commons and the House of Lords, Charles's foray into religious policy was fraught with risk, largely aligning with Louis XIV's ambitions rather than his own interests. Charles accepted the French funds without publicising his conversion. The subsequent mysterious death of Madame[42] and the secret Treaty of London signing on December 31, 1670, underscored Louis XIV's realisation that Charles II had no genuine intention of publicly converting to Catholicism. It was only on March 28, 1672, that Charles II decided to declare war on Holland, leading to the naval defeat at Solebay on June 7, 1672, but also to French

---

[41] Louise de Kéroualle gave Charles II a son, and remained in contact with the French ambassador. She remained at the centre of political intrigues.
[42] Which will turn out to be natural after the autopsies.

victories on land. The English Parliament, believing the war was religiously motivated, failed to secure popular support. By 1674, the intended Anglo-French reconciliation envisaged by the secret Treaty of Dover had instead heightened animosity towards a France perceived as dangerously ambitious, both territorially and in its quest for dominance in overseas territories like the Americas.

3. The Special Role of Louise Renée de Penancoët de Kérouaille (1670-1688):

There are many precedents in the world of espionage, and the people who made it their speciality before the events we are studying were not all known or recognised as such. Espionage activities certainly did not begin in 1688, and we can affirm that the agents who provided information to the monarchs were not, as is generally thought, subject to morality. Agents who ventured into espionage from more humble beginnings often did so driven by financial necessity. The prospect of monetary reward, long-term honours, and sometimes the promise of elevated social status served as powerful incentives for these individuals to align with the interests of a monarchy. Conversely, agents hailing from more privileged strata, the so-called elite, already accustomed to the nuances of power and diplomacy, lent their services to the crown in exchange for honours and recognition. Moreover, an aristocrat was often well versed in the exercise of embassies and power, whereas private individuals who rose to the position of negotiator had to rely solely on their natural qualities to do so. All of the people we will be showing are examples of this. The character of Louise Renée de Kérouaille symbolises exactly what we are talking about: coming from the lower nobility of the provinces, nothing destined her to become an agent in the service of the monarchy, and all the more so because she was a woman. Even though she ended her "career" in 1688, she is an illustrious representative of the spies we are talking about. Her life as a double agent in the service of France shows us that in 1688, espionage activities were still going strong.

Louise Renée de Penancoët de Kérouaille was born in 1649 in a château near Brest. Her father and mother were noble but modest. Louise's striking beauty marked her for an unusual destiny far beyond the expectations set by her birth, and she was noticed by François de Bourbon, Duke of Beaufort, as soon as she left the convent in 1667. He offered to introduce her to the court, and she became maid of honour to Henrietta of England, known as Madame, Duchess of Orléans, in 1668. Her parents were aware of the effect she could have in front of the king, and they certainly hoped she would become his favourite. Louis XIV did notice her, but he was still too busy with the Duchesse de la Vallière and Madame de Montespan, his new favourite.

Louise accompanied Henrietta of England on her travels, given Henrietta's connection as the sister of King Charles II of England. Recognizing the potential diplomatic advantage, King Louis XIV of France deployed Louise in a strategic capacity. In 1670, amidst the Dunkirk affair—a matter imbued with both diplomatic significance and secrecy—Henrietta undertook a mission to England to meet her brother Charles II, whom she hadn't seen in nearly a decade. Despite Charles II's general antipathy towards France, his well-documented fondness for the company of women presented a unique diplomatic opportunity. During a reception in Dover, the Duke of Buckingham introduced Louise to Charles II.

Documentary evidence indicates that Louise was well aware of her mission, albeit accepting it with some reluctance due to the obligations of serving the King. Her influence on Charles II proved significant, playing a role in their eventual intimate relationship. On June 1, 1670, Henrietta successfully concluded her mission with the signing of the Treaty of Dover, wherein Charles II agreed to convert to Catholicism in exchange for an annual pension of 200,000 pounds. In a gesture of gratitude during the farewell ceremonies, Louise gifted Charles II a jewel, which led him to request her stay in England. Louise, initially hesitant to fulfil her espionage duties through intimate involvement with Charles II, sought refuge in a convent, a request that was denied. The sudden death of Henrietta on June 29, amid rumours of poisoning, prompted Charles II to consider severing ties with France. This development intensified the urgency of Louise's mission, compelling her swift return to England, now as a lady-in-waiting to Charles's wife, Catherine of Braganza, and stationed at Whitehall Palace under the guidance of the Marquis de

Croissy, the French ambassador. Based at Whitehall Palace and receiving her instructions from the Marquis de Croissy, the French ambassador. Louise received Charles II every evening, but it was during a reception hosted by the Countess of Arlington in October 1671 that Louise's position as mistress of the King of England was formalised. By early 1672, the Marquis de Croissy observed Louise's significant influence over Charles II, spawning rumours that "the silk ribbon around Mlle de Kérouaille's waist united France and England."

On 29 July 1672, Louise bore a son, Charles Lennox, who was later made Duke of Richmond in 1675. In recognition of her services, she was bestowed with the titles of Countess of Fareham, Baroness of Petersfield, and Duchess of Portsmouth in 1673. Sensing the need for further clandestine operations, Louis XIV, in 1675, introduced another player into the espionage game—Henriette Mauricette, Louise's sister, who was brought to England for a strategic marriage to Philippe Herbert, Earl of Pembroke. Thus began her journey as a spy, though her operations were more subdued compared to her sister's.

By the end of 1675, Charles II's attention had shifted to other women, including Hortense Mancini, Duchess of Mazarin. The following year, Louise faced personal turmoil with a miscarriage and contracted a venereal disease, which remained untreated.

As the 1680s dawned, the English Parliament grew increasingly wary of the king's leanings towards Catholicism, a movement they linked to Louise's influence. Her position at court became precarious as she was successively replaced by other women in the king's affections.

By 1682, Louise's time at the English court was drawing to a close. She returned to Louis XIV's court, where she was commended for her decade of service. However, her relationship with Charles II had made her a figure of suspicion in England. The English Parliament investigated her closely, accusing her of espionage and treason due to her covert activities for France.

In 1683, Louise's life took a new turn when she began a liaison with Philippe de Bourbon, Duc de Vendôme, the nephew of her initial benefactor. This new relationship incited jealousy in Charles II, leading him to request her departure from England, albeit with gratitude for her past services. Subsequently, Louis XIV summoned the Duc de Vendôme back to Paris, and Louise acquired the Duchy of Aubigny-sur-Nère in France.

On 14 February 1685, at a time when England was drawing closer to Holland, Charles died at the age of 54, after converting to Catholicism. James II Stuart, who did not think for a moment that he would have to flee to France a few years later, expressly asked Louise de Kéroual to leave England. Returning to France and living on her lands at Aubigny, she resumed a private life, and in 1688 took Henri de Lorraine, Duc d'Elbeuf, as her lover. Despite her dwindling fortunes, Louis XIV ensured her continued comfort.

In 1692, Charles Lennox was approached by English agents and returned to England, having renounced his Catholic faith and pledged his allegiance to William III. Louise de Kérouaille died in Paris at the age of 85, financially ruined.

The life of Louise de Kéroual, a spy for Louis XIV between 1670 and 1685, shows us that at the dawn of the English Revolution in 1688, espionage activities were already very prevalent, in various forms, illustrated by the actions of a woman from the small provincial nobility, who rose to become a member of the great nobility.[43]

III. The Glorious Revolution and the Jacobites (1688).

In 1688, James II, Charles II's brother, was deposed in what is known as "the Glorious Revolution" or "the Bloodless Revolution" (the latter term should obviously be qualified, as the war between James II's Catholic supporters and William III's Dutch army was a bloody one. In fact, it was only described as "peaceful" between 1688 and 1689). As we have said, James II had many difficulties, which we have traced back to the very origins of the Stuart dynasty. There are a number of factors that need to be highlighted in order to understand this:

---

[43] Louise de Kéroualle, through her son Charles Lennox, is the ancestor of Diana Spencer, Princess of Wales, as well as Camilla Parker-Bowles, Sarah Ferguson and Prince William.

The Duke of Monmouth, the illegitimate son of Charles II and Lucy Walter (from a family that had remained loyal to the King during the upheavals of the previous decades), was born in Holland in April 1649, where Charles had been exiled during the Civil War. James Scott, 1st Duke of Monmouth, was therefore Dutch... and Protestant! Married to a Scottish peeress, Anne Scott, he fought against the Netherlands under the orders of his uncle, the Duke of York (the future James II of England). As Charles II's brother had no children, parliamentarians hostile to James II tipped Monmouth to succeed his father, despite his illegitimacy. He went into exile in 1679 after plotting to regain the crown. His father's death prompted him to take up the fight, but he was defeated and executed on 15 July 1685.[44]

The new king decided to create a standing army. On this point, James II went against the English custom of assembling military forces only during times of war. Parliament was all the more concerned because the royal prerogatives allowed Catholics not to take the Test Act oath, which gave Catholics the same rights as other British and Anglican subjects. Since the seventeenth century, Catholics had been excluded from command of the King's armies.

In the same spirit, Catholics were allowed to take up senior positions in universities (think of the Duke of Monmouth, who was certainly a good soldier, but was given the title of Principal of Cambridge because he was Protestant).

Following the discovery of correspondence between James II and the Pope, we can now also see revealed the king's desire for closer ties with the Vatican, including plans to welcome an apostolic nuncio to London.[45] Of course, after all the political events closely or remotely linked to the religious reforms, this decision could have seemed almost violent for the country. It was against this backdrop that the King requested a declaration of indulgence, granting freedom of worship to Catholics and Dissenters. The Archbishop of Canterbury did not agree and was imprisoned.

---

[44] His execution was atrocious because it was totally botched by the executioner.
[45] According to Charles Gérin, in *Innocent XI et la révolution de 1688* - Revue des Questions Historiques, t.XX, p. 427-481, the Pope had chosen his side, but was receiving news of what was happening in Europe, including Leopold of Austria's support for the enemies of the Stuarts.

The dynastic aspect of James II's reign was indeed crucial, with the Protestant faith of his daughters from his first marriage—Mary and Anne—acting as a counterbalance to concerns about the potential for a Catholic monarch. Their Protestantism offered a semblance of continuity and stability in a predominantly Protestant England, aligning with the religious preferences of the majority and mitigating fears of a Catholic monarchy. However, the birth of a son to James and his second wife, Mary of Modena, a Catholic, in June 1688, dramatically altered the succession landscape, reigniting fears of a Catholic dynasty that could undo the religious and political gains made since the Reformation.

This domestic tension was compounded by the international context, particularly the actions of Louis XIV of France. His revocation of the Edict of Nantes in 1685, which had provided certain protections to French Protestants (Huguenots), signalled a stark turn towards religious intolerance, and fuelled fears of a similar religious crackdown in England under a Catholic monarch.

Given these circumstances, Parliament's invitation to the Prince of Orange to intervene (with the help of certain members of the English aristocracy, as we shall see later) seemed both a strategic and pragmatic decision. William, married to James II's Protestant daughter Mary, represented a viable alternative to James's Catholic line of succession. His reputation for opposing Louis XIV's expansionist policies in Europe further bolstered his appeal as a candidate who could safeguard England's Protestant faith and its liberties against both domestic and foreign Catholic influences. William's marriage to Mary was initially met with some reluctance by James, likely due to the political implications of aligning his daughter with a prominent Protestant leader. However, this union ultimately proved instrumental in facilitating the Glorious Revolution, as it provided a legitimate Protestant succession line that Parliament and the English people could rally behind.

Guaranteed major support on English soil, William triggered hostilities by landing with an army at Brixham in Torbay Bay on 15 November 1688. They had left Holland on 11 November, leading a formidable force of 14,000 mercenaries and 7,000 soldiers, including French Huguenots and Scottish rebels. Their fleet was huge and therefore difficult to repel. James II's flight from England in December 1688, ostensibly to protect his family, served as a de facto abdication, clearing the way for William and Mary's accession to the throne. Their arrival in London on 28 December 1688 was met with the support of Parliament, which quickly moved to formalise James's deposition. Wishing to reach complete agreement with the Church of England, William played the appeasement card, but added the Bill of Rights to the fundamental laws: Catholics could not accede to the throne, Parliament was renewed by free elections, and the standing army was suspended, becoming illegal again in times of peace. It could be argued that it was William III who gave birth to the parliamentary regiment in England.

What's more, a new discovery in British state documents shows that James II Stuart's daughter, Anne Stuart, played a more complex role than we thought. On 18 November 1688, Anne wrote a letter to her brother-in-law William III of Orange, wishing him well in his 'conquest' of England. What some believe to be a betrayal of her father, reveals that Princess Anne was in a difficult situation. Kept out of power, she was influenced by Lord and Lady Churchill. She was aware of William's plans and even corresponded with Mary of Modena. In her letter to William, certainly influenced by the Chruchills, she showed him her loyalty: 'I shall be ready to show you how very much I am your humble servant.'[46] But more than that, her gesture also enabled her to show off her husband, Prince George of Denmark (a supporter of James II Stuart). But when her husband defected to James II Stuart (along with a large number of other officers), and he took refuge in Whitehall, she fled and joined William's supporters in Nottingham.

From 2 January 1689, following James II's flight to France, a significant number of his followers, who refused allegiance to William and who were known as non-jurors or Jacobites (after the Latin name for James II), sought refuge in France, particularly in Saint-Germain, forming a government in exile under the auspices of Louis XIV. For several months, Louis XIV and his Council held war meetings with the help of a few of the English, Irish and Scottish Catholic military leaders who had taken refuge

---

[46] *Letter from Princess Anne*, november 18, 1688, SP 8/2/81, Part 2, Folios 152-153, The National Archives, Kew.

in France. There was talk of a landing in Kinsale, on the south coast of Ireland. 10,000 soldiers were to land on 12 March 1689. In July 1690, this army was soundly defeated at the Battle of the Boyne. In 1692, the Scottish clans joined the revolt, but were massacred at Glencoe in a very sad episode. That same year, Louvois, somewhat reluctantly (because he knew that the tide had turned and that William III was now to be reckoned with in matters concerning England) wanted to repeat the failed experiment of 1690 by setting out from La Hougue, but in vain.

Nantes, France, emerged as a crucial hub for Jacobite planning and operations, buoyed by an established Irish colony dating back to the Cromwellian period. James Sarsfield, 2nd Earl of Lucan, a major shipowner in the port, became a symbol of this diaspora's efforts, facilitating the emigration of the Irish to France, including, notably, 20,000 Irish soldiers, known as the 'Wild Geese'. The expeditions of 1706 and 1715 departed from the town.

The role of the Irish in the Glorious Revolution and its aftermath is particularly noteworthy, since it goes without saying that they took part in the war against William III of Orange. Under the leadership of James Sarsfield, they destroyed all of William's artillery, but had to retreat after their defeat at Aughrim. Under the Treaty of Limerick in 1691, Irish Catholics were granted a degree of religious freedom and their lands were returned to them. At the beginning of 1692, the majority of the Irish Catholic aristocracy fled to France.

Once the crown of England had been taken over by William III and Queen Mary II, the intelligence services were more active than ever. While Louis XIV was already counting on his position of strength in Europe to quickly restore James II to the throne, he had to contend with an entire network that had already emerged under the reign of Charles I, and which was beginning to make its mark under the new reign of William III under the leadership of the cryptographer John Wallis.

CHAPTER 4

IMMEDIAT CONSEQUENCES OF THE GLORIOUS REVOLUTION (1688-1689)

The deposition of James II of Stuart and the subsequent Glorious Revolution were indeed precipitated by a military invasion led by William III of Orange, but it should also be added that the international situation was one of heightened tension. Part of the English Protestant monarchy had actively collaborated to ensure that William III intervened. The historian Gérard Valin has produced an excellent and comprehensive analysis of the economical, financial and geopolitical elements that made up this situation.

In fact, this "invasion" brought religious and political stability, attracting large numbers of persecuted Protestants from the continent. But it was indeed a certain Dutch elite who emigrated with William, and became the custodians of the new English regime. In 1694, for example, the Bank of England was set up to lend the State the funds it needed to develop the river network and build a powerful and enduring fleet, the Royal Navy. On closer examination, the Glorious Revolution seems to have been a repeat of what had happened in Holland a few decades earlier, with strong urban, financial, intellectual and maritime growth. Stock exchanges emerged with the creation of the *Lloyd's of London*, stock exchange circles that met at *Jonathan's Coffee-House*. In 1698, the Royal Bank of Scotland created one of the first major stocks, the Darién Company. What's more, freedom of the press seemed assured, as the *Licensing Act was* abolished. These changes were sure to attract skilled labour, especially craftsmen and engineers from Europe, and breathe new life into the economy, laying the foundations for the Industrial Revolution along with a significant surge in innovation.

This era of ingenuity saw a large number of patents registered between 1690 and 1699, and these were soon rewarded by Parliament. Engineers and inventors were in the limelight. However, there was some debate within the scientific community. Two researchers, Douglas North and Barry Weingast, argue that it was the establishment of the parliamentary monarchy that led to the growth of public credit in the 18th century, but also to the protection of creditors' property rights against the arbitrary actions of the state. Bruce Carruthers and Stephan Epstein did not share this view, arguing that it was anachronistic because it focused too much on anti-state neo-institutionalism.

Finally, it was from the end of 1688 that the French intelligence services began to slow down their work. We have already mentioned John Wallis, who had been the leader of the revival of English cryptography, and therefore of the intelligence services. His second, William Blencowe (1683-1712), was to take up his work a little later and consolidate the world of espionage on behalf of England. But what made the difference was Louis XIV's growing lack of interest in espionage and cryptography. Turning away from it somewhat, he did not yet know that his support for the Jacobite cause was going to be undermined by this lack of expertise in the field. The Allies were going to take advantage of this.

I. The Jacobites Band Together.

1. Parlementary Strife and the Jacobites:

Talks began during the reigns of William and Anne. Despite the lack of enthusiasm among the English public for the union, two primary anxieties motivated the government's push for consolidation under the House of Hanover, which had a distant relation to James VI of Scotland: firstly, there was a longstanding apprehension regarding Scotland's potential to rise against England, especially while English forces were engaged in continental conflicts. This fear was compounded by the spectre of a Stuart restoration, which seemed increasingly plausible as Queen Anne, the last Stuart monarch, faced personal tragedy after personal tragedy with the death of all her seventeen children. So England had to "close the back door," as Bishop Burnet put it. We shall see that France will be counting on a return of the Stuarts and, later, an uprising in Scotland.

The opposition to the 1707 Acts of Union between England and Scotland was significant, yet notably fragmented. On the one hand were the Jacobite "Cavaliers," who, supported financially by France's Louis XIV, championed the cause of the "Old Pretender," James Francis Edward Stuart, also known as the "Chevalier de Saint George." He was the son of James II and had been excluded from the English throne by the Act of Settlement of 1701 due to his Catholic faith. An notable attempt was even made to land the "Chevalier" in Scotland in 1705, an endeavour ultimately foiled by adverse weather conditions and the vigilance of the English navy. The implications of a successful landing and subsequent Jacobite uprising were profound. A victorious campaign to restore the Stuarts to the throne would not only have plunged the country into a protracted and devastating conflict but also risked reversing the political and religious progress made since the Glorious Revolution. Such a scenario would have likely seen the re-establishment of the type of monarchical governance practised by James VI and Charles II, characterised by direct royal intervention in governance ("government by the pen"), which many feared would undermine the parliamentary system and rekindle the divisions and turmoil of Charles II's reign.

After a number of twists and turns, including serious resistance in Scotland, the Treaty of Union was passed by the Scottish Parliament on 16 January 1707, and received royal assent three months later. The Hanoverian succession was accepted by both countries. The Parliament of Great Britain was to sit at Westminster. Although the Jacobites would later exploit the situation, their efforts were doomed to failure. The era of the Stuarts was over.

2. France's Support of the Jacobites:

Long before his accession to the throne in 1644, the young James II Stuart also held the title of Duke of York, and since 1660, that of Duke of Albany (Scotland). Despite commercial rivalries with the Netherlands, his eldest sister, Mary Stuart (on her mother's side, she was the granddaughter of Henri IV of France and a cousin of Louis XIV), became Princess of Orange after her marriage to Count William of Nassau, Prince of Orange.

James II Stuart married twice: first Anne Hyde, with whom he had two daughters, Mary and Anne of York, and then Princess Mary of Modena. Mary and Anne of York were both Queens of England. The first, Mary, was initially promised to Louis of France, known as the Grand Dauphin, son of Louis XIV, but ended up having to marry William III of Orange-Nassau, her first cousin, with whom she produced no surviving children. William III thus entered the dynastic race for the throne of England. Anne, for her part, married George of Denmark and had no children who reached reigning age.

The invasion of England by William III, who was both James II's nephew and son-in-law, forced James II to flee England, and effectively excluded any Catholic claimants from the English throne .

James II, former Duke of York, succeeded his brother Charles II in 1685. As we have seen, he quickly alienated public opinion with unpopular measures:

- Violent repression of the rebellion of the Duke of Monmouth (illegitimate half-brother of James II);
- Creation of a standing army;
- Inclusion of Catholics in the army and universities;
- Closer ties with the papacy and the arrival of an apostolic nuncio in London;
- Dissatisfaction of the Whig party, which campaigned for the King's impeachment.

The religious question, deeply entangled with political concerns, became a flashpoint due to England's contrasting stance with France on continental policy and the ongoing conflict between the Netherlands and France since the middle of the 17th century. The Dutch War of Independence against Spain, and later, conflicts against France, had positioned the Netherlands as a bulwark of Protestant resistance against Catholic hegemony, led by France under Louis XIV.

The imprisonment of the Archbishop of Canterbury in April 1687, for opposing James II's Declaration of Indulgence, which sought to extend freedom of worship to Catholics, underscored the deepening religious strife. While this act did not result in judicial repercussions, it highlighted the unresolved religious tensions within the kingdom. For the king's opponents, the Protestantism of his two daughters was of great reassurance. However, the birth of James Edward, son of James II and Mary of Modena, a Catholic princess, prompted them to react decisively. The historical memory of the Civil War, and a residual loyalty to the monarchy, restrained them from immediate violent actions. However, the persecution of Protestants in France, particularly after the revocation of the Edict of Nantes in 1685 by Louis XIV, paralleled the anxieties felt in England and galvanised the Whig party and other Protestant factions. These groups, advocating for state Protestantism and disillusioned with the Stuart monarchy's concessions, saw in William III of Orange, a Protestant and military leader renowned for his opposition to Louis XIV, a viable alternative to James II.

William III of Orange, stadtholder of the Netherlands and husband of Mary, Protestant eldest daughter of King James II of England, wanted at last to obtain an alliance between England and the Netherlands against France. The invitation from the English and the Whig party prompted him to make his move and attack. He landed on 15 November 1688 at Brixham (Torbay), accompanied by 14,000 mercenaries and 7,000 foreign soldiers (we have seen the importance of French soldiers in their ranks, including many Huguenot officers who had fought in France under Turenne), sailing a fleet twice the size of the Spanish armada of 1588 (53 warships and 4,000 transport ships). The armies were led by Marshal de Schomberg, former general of the Brandenburg army (the future Prussian army). Upon this news, James II rushed into exile in France, which was tantamount to an abdication, and on 28 December 1688 William of Orange entered London. A vote was taken to depose the King and install William III and Mary[47] on the throne. The *Bill of Rights* of 1689 merely supplemented the Commonwealth laws of the reign of Charles II. It marked the birth of the English parliamentary system:

---

[47] According to Du Boscq, in *La Cour de Saint-Germain, op. cit.* William sent Jacques his fine stable of horses, as well as the Queen's favourite coachman, a man who had already served Cromwell.

- Catholics were forbidden to accede to the throne;
- Free elections and the renewal of Parliament were guaranteed;
- The presence of an army in peacetime was illegal.

II. **France, Holland and England, the Inevitability of War.**

As early as 1685, William of Orange had created the League of Augsburg as a strategic move to counter Louis XIV's aggressive expansionist policies and the Catholic influence of James II. The Jacobite non-jurors, loyalists to James II, followed their king into exile in 1689 and were initially welcomed at Versailles under the protection of Louis XIV. From there, they prepared to land at Kinsale (on the south coast of Ireland) in order to stir up Catholic Ireland, which was resistant to William of Orange. However, the military efforts of the Jacobite and French forces, including those composed of Irish and Scottish troops, faced decisive defeats at the Battle of the Boyne in 1690 and in Glencoe in 1692, falling victim to an imbroglio and then an ambush (although everything had started well, the Count of Avaux declared to Louis XIV: "The only thing, Sire, that can cause us pain is the irresolution of the King of England, who often changes his mind and does not always decide for the best. He preoccupies himself with small matters to which he devotes a great deal of time, and passes quickly over those that are more essential").[48]

That same year, Louis XIV and Louvois decided to mount a large-scale operation from the French port of La Hougue, which also ended in failure.

By 1668, Charles II navigated his kingdom towards a pro-French orientation by agreeing to the Treaty of Dover, a pivotal but clandestine agreement shaped by his fiscal exigencies. In return for an annual stipend of 160,000 pounds, Charles II consented to a future conversion to Catholicism, supported by a pledge of 6,000 French troops. The sincerity of Charles's intention to convert remains a subject of historical speculation, especially after the dramatic suicide of Clifford, one of his closest advisors. This shift towards France marked the onset of a period

---

[48] Du Boscq, *op. cit.* pp. 71-72

often misinterpreted as an aspiration to mirror the absolutist governance of Louis XIV.

However, this Francophile policy soon precipitated a rift with Parliament, exacerbated by Charles's religious policies at home and his alliance with Catholic France during the Third Anglo-Dutch War. These actions alienated not only Parliament but also earlier converts to Catholicism within the realm. By 1674, the political fallout forced Charles to seek peace, leading to the diminished influence of key courtiers who had once formed his inner circle. This group, already internally divided into competing factions, included Clifford, Arlington, Buckingham, Ashley, the Earl of Salisbury, and Lauderdale. The succession of Clifford by Lord Danby introduced a new voice of dissent against the King's approach. Charles's inability to secure an heir and the subsequent focus on his brother James, Duke of York, led to the strategic marital alliance of his daughter Mary Stuart with the Protestant William of Orange. Meanwhile, Charles's continued financial arrangements with Louis XIV, in pursuit of monetary support, eventually led to the downfall of Lord Danby, who faced charges of high treason by the House of Commons. Parliament grew increasingly distrustful of Charles, with some members fearing that he might leverage the standing army to quash dissent and further his Catholic agenda.

As the succession of James II appeared imminent, divisions among the nobility became pronounced, particularly with figures like the 1st Earl of Shaftesbury (formerly Baron Ashley) leading the charge against the Duke of York's ascendancy. This period heralded the genesis of the political party system still recognised today. The Tories, initially a term associated with Irish Catholic outlaws, opposed the Exclusion Bill, deeming any attempt to bar the Duke of York from succession as unacceptable. Conversely, the Whigs, deriving their name from a term linked to rebellious Scottish Presbyterians, supported the exclusion.

Charles II dissolved Parliament in 1679, and again in 1681, the latter dissolution occurring in Oxford. Despite ruling without Parliament for an extended period, the momentum behind the Exclusion Bill diminished, partly due to the intensified pressure from the King's allies on Lord Shaftesbury. Faced with threats to his safety, Shaftesbury fled to Holland.

Meanwhile, other dissenters, including the Earl of Essex, Algernon Sidney, Lord Russell, and the Duke of Monmouth, resorted to plotting against the King and James. Their conspiracy was uncovered, leading to their arrest, execution, suicide, or flight to Holland, where they persisted in efforts to dethrone the last Stuarts. In any case, Charles II's governance, while not strictly absolutist, displayed characteristics reminiscent of the French model of a separation of powers. On 2 February 1685, Charles passed away from a stroke and was interred at Westminster Abbey without any ceremonial fanfare.

It would appear that this rapprochement with France, culminating in the Stuart dynasty's exile there, was deeply influenced by the king's personal motivations and aspirations for a military, and possibly religious, alliance which neither Parliament nor the divided nobility could endorse. Inexorably, therefore, England was not to imitate French absolutism, but to form an independent kingdom with a singular religion.

James, Duke of York's military service under Turenne against the Frondeurs and the Spaniards, followed by his expulsion from France after Charles II's strategic alliance with Spain, indicated his total opposition to his brother's policies. His subsequent alignment with Condé's Spanish forces underscored a deepening affinity for Catholic alliances, setting him apart from his brother's Anglican-leaning court. Despite his aspirations for a naval career in Spain, James's return to England after Charles's ascension was motivated by familial duty and political loyalty, despite the seeming improbability of his own ascension to the throne given the expectation of heirs from Charles. James at least showed great interest in being a father, and gave the leading role to his family, which foreshadowed future events when he fled England to protect it.

James' conduct at court initially earned him widespread admiration, contributing to his favourable reception among the populace. In 1669, James secretly converted to Catholicism but continued to attend Anglican services, at least until 1676. In the events surrounding religion, James had to take a stand and publicly declared his conversion, which his brother refused, ordering that his daughters be brought up in the Protestant faith. His marriage to Marie de Modène, a Catholic perceived as closely aligned with Pope Clement X, added further tumult to his life, casting shadows of espionage and intrigue. In 1677, after influences at court worked against him, and more particularly against his own family, his daughter Mary decided to marry William III of Orange, a Protestant prince, which he reluctantly accepted. At the same time, a wave of anti-Catholic hysteria broke out throughout the kingdom, following allegations of a "Papist plot," and factious nobles worked to suppress the king and his brother. James fled to Brussels and then took up the title of Lord High Commissioner of Scotland in Edinburgh. Upon his return to England, amid his brother's ill health, James confronted widespread opposition from Parliament, with Thomas Osborne, 1st Duke of Leeds and a former ally, now emerging as a notable adversary. The discovery of assassination plots against the royal family towards the end of Charles II's reign paradoxically elicited a wave of sympathy for the monarchy.

Charles II's deathbed conversion to Catholicism indeed revealed a latent affinity towards that faith, setting a precedent that would deeply influence the reign of his brother, James II. When James ascended the throne in 1685, he was initially met with broad approval. However, James's inclination towards ruling independently, without substantial compromise with his advisors, soon led to friction within the governmental apparatus. Despite initial support from the High Council, the Protestant majority within Parliament harboured deep reservations about a Catholic monarch. The spectre of William III of Orange loomed large over James II's reign, with his involvement in English affairs becoming increasingly pronounced. This external influence, coupled with domestic discontent, ignited revolts, notably led by the Duke of Monmouth (James II's nephew) in the south of England and by Archibald Campbell, the 9th Earl of Argyll, in Scotland. The latter was captured and beheaded.

James II's contemplation of a standing professional army was a strategy inherited from his forebears, intended as a bulwark against further rebellion. However, this proposal clashed with the entrenched English tradition of a non-professional military, stoking fears of absolutism and further alienating his subjects. Consequently, James was compelled to suspend Parliament once more, further straining relations by promoting the supremacy of Catholicism over Protestantism, including sending contentious letters to the Scottish Parliament regarding the Presbyterians.

His intent to display magnanimity was overshadowed by his clear preference for Catholicism, as evidenced by the appointment of Catholics to high-ranking positions, some of whom were notably unpopular with Protestants. This period also witnessed Robert Spencer, the 2nd Earl of Sunderland, initiating a thorough purge at court. Beginning in 1686, James II boldly exerted his authority, targeting the universities among other institutions. The continued purge into 1687 signalled an increasingly authoritarian stance, until it became apparent that William III of Orange harboured significant concerns regarding the trajectory of England's governance.

The birth of James Francis Stuart in 1688 to James II and his second wife, Mary of Modena, dramatically shifted the political and religious landscape of England. Until then, the Protestant succession, through James's daughters Mary and Anne, had provided a semblance of stability, despite the King's Catholicism. However, the arrival of a Catholic heir precipitated a profound crisis, transforming latent opposition into active ideological resistance. This shift galvanised the Protestant nobility, who, disillusioned with the prospect of a Catholic dynasty, extended an invitation to William III of Orange to invade England.

Louis XIV, observing the unfolding drama from Versailles as the political and religious clashes in England intensified, giving the continental wars a new twist, lent his support to James, even offering him aid. In 1685, the King of France revoked the Edict of Nantes, forcing the Huguenots to flee, most of them to England and the United Provinces. The alliance between James II and Louis XIV highlighted a broader European concern about the alignment of two Catholic monarchies amidst continental conflicts. For William III of Orange, opposing France and by extension James II presented an opportunity to assert himself as a protector of Protestantism and to extend his influence beyond the Dutch borders. The rhetoric against France and Catholicism intensified, setting the stage for the War of the League of Augsburg, which unfolded from 1688 onwards, and to which some also refer to as the War of the English Succession, or King William's War. For William of Orange, in order to continue to face Louis XIV on the continent, the question of England had to be dealt with as quickly as possible, and James's attitude made his task easier. When the landing at Brixham took place, most of the former loyalists defected and sided with the invaders. Despite possessing the military and financial resources to confront William's forces, James II prioritised the avoidance of bloodshed among his subjects and the safety of his family over direct confrontation. His symbolic act of throwing the Great Seal of England into the Thames River was a precursor to his attempt to flee the country, which ended with his capture in Kent. William had no interest in imprisoning James or even making him a martyr, so he let him escape to France, where was warmly received by Louis XIV, and the Jacobite court was set up in Saint-Germain-en-Laye, a place with historical significance for the English monarchy, having also served as a refuge for Charles II during his period of exile. In this way, France demonstrated that, while it had been intransigent in its politics - and we can speak of occasional opposition - it had never wanted to oppose the English kings themselves, as long as they had remained Catholic.

James's daughter Mary acceded to the throne as Mary II Stuart, and reigned jointly with her husband William III. James, for his part, was considered to have abdicated, leading to a formal proclamation that barred any Catholic from claiming the English crown and prohibited any monarch from marrying a Catholic. In 1689, in an attempt to reclaim his throne, James II turned his sights to Ireland, where the Parliament had not yet pledged allegiance to William III. With the support of Louis XIV of France, James landed a substantial force in Ireland, only to be defeated at the Battle of the Boyne in July 1690. This defeat was a critical blow to James's ambitions, leading to the Treaty of Limerick in October 1691. This treaty effectively ended James II's attempts to regain control of his former kingdoms, sealing his fate as a monarch in exile. The Treaty of Ryswick in 1697, which resolved the war of the League of Augsburg, reaffirmed William III's sovereignty over England. It necessitated France's recognition of its commitment not to endorse the royal ambitions of James II's progeny. We shall see that this was not the case, and open warfare gave way to a war of intelligence, of spies and henchmen.

CHAPTER 5

SCOTLAND'S ROLE AFTER THE GLORIOUS REVOLUTION (1688-1715)

The contest for control over the British Isles is but one chapter in the extensive saga of European conflicts that spanned the 17th and 18th centuries. This period, richly chronicled through a multitude of books and memoirs—many of which remain to be unearthed—features a well-known cast of historical figures: Louis XIV, James II and the Pretender Stuart, William of Orange, and their successors. While the confrontations and alliances formed by these individuals are no secret, being part of the official record of history, there exists another dimension to these geopolitical entanglements.

As explored in the preceding section, the realm of international politics is navigated through various means, not all of which operate in the light of day. Beyond the official narratives and diplomatic encounters, there lies a clandestine struggle, veiled in secrecy and punctuated by mysteries (sometimes remaining unsolved), with its unique characters: spies, ambassadors, diplomats, double agents, all driven, in one way or another, by the service of their country.

These formidable, extensive and influential networks were all the more dangerous because they were hidden or even transformed at the whim of intelligence games. France, England, Holland and the Court of Saint-Germain were factions that played off each other through their agents and spies. We say the Court of Saint-Germain-en-Laye, because the Stuarts, representing a faction in their own right, reigned from their place of exile, and possessed everything that makes a state within a state. In other words, this exiled Stuart monarchy, surrounded by a coterie of significant figures, became a nexus for espionage, attracting a myriad of spies and double agents. Louis XIV kept a close eye on his English cousin James II, just as James II was aware of France's policies and priorities towards Louis XIV. These relationships, which punctuated the exile and led to attempts to restore James II and then the Pretender seemed to us to correspond to a particular temporality.

The period spanning from 1688, marking the official deposition of James II Stuart, to 1715, the year of Louis XIV's demise, is rich with instances that shed light on the covert warfare conducted by the agents and spies of the principal states involved. While 1688 symbolises the beginning of an era characterised by exile and the positioning of a faction within French borders, it does not imply that the covert operations initiated precisely at that moment. Instead, it represents a key turning point that saw the Stuart faction find sanctuary in France. Similarly, 1715 does not signify the conclusive end of the Stuarts' presence in France, but rather marks the closure of a significant epoch—the reign of Louis XIV, under whom France emerged as Europe's preeminent power. The Stuart dynasty continued to exert influence over the British Isles post-William of Orange's death in 1702, albeit through Protestant queens, thereby setting the stage for the ascendancy of the House of Hanover. This broader historical backdrop serves merely as a context for our focused exploration of the intelligence battle for the British Isles from 1688 to 1715.

Between these two dates, and with what we have laid out in the previous sections, the time has come to delve into the essence of our study: the intelligence battle for the British Isles between 1688 and 1715.

I. **War Objectives.**

By the late 1670s, France under Louis XIV had emerged as the preeminent power in Europe. The Peace of Regensburg in 1684 momentarily suggested a respite from the relentless cycle of conflict. However, peace in this era often served as merely a prelude to further hostilities. In a significant move in 1685, Louis XIV escalated religious tensions by enforcing draconian measures against the Protestant Huguenots, prompting a mass exodus. This hardline stance alienated several European powers, notably William III's Holland, which championed the Protestant cause and harboured growing animosity towards France. However, Louis XIV had an ally in James II Stuart. This support disappeared with the English revolution. James II had converted to Catholicism and the English were only waiting for his death to see his daughter Mary accede to the throne. A Protestant, she had married William III of Orange. In 1688, the situation became critical when the King of England had a son, whom he had baptised into the Catholic faith. William III seized this moment of instability. Leveraging support from the Whigs and responding to an invitation from English nobles, he mounted an invasion, landing in England to assert his claim to the throne. James II, opting against a bloody conflict for the crown, fled to his cousin Louis XIV in France. Louis offered sanctuary and the Château of Saint-Germain-en-Laye for James to establish his court in exile. His supporters, the Jacobites, joined him or stayed behind in England to prepare for his return.

Following the War of the League of Augsburg in 1697, Louis XIV found himself in the position of having to formally acknowledge William III as the King of England. This recognition, however, masked a flurry of clandestine activities both at the French court—shared by Louis XIV and James II Stuart—and within their covert networks, all aimed at reclaiming the English crown that had slipped through their fingers. James II's death in 1701 at Saint-Germain prompted Louis XIV to quickly declare James's son, James III the Pretender, as the rightful King of England, earning him the monikers "the Pretender" and "the Old Pretender." Yet, William III had meticulously arranged for the continuity of his legacy; following the rule of his wife, Mary Stuart, the crown passed to her sister, Anne Stuart, who was married to a Danish prince. William III's demise in March 1702 did not occur without a final boon to the Whigs, securing their parliamentary dominance. Queen Anne's reign was unpopular and it was a relative, Sophia (Protestant), who placed her son, George I of England on the throne in 1714.

1. The English Court (1688):

Julian Whitehead, in his book on espionage within the Stuart dynasty between 1685 and 1715, helps us to answer this fundamental question.[49]

---

[49] Whitehead, Julian, *Espionage int the Divided Stuart Dynasty*, 1685-1715, 2020, 200 pages.

Each state maintained its intelligence network, which, under James II prior to 1688, saw Robert Spencer, the 2nd Earl of Sunderland, at the helm of intelligence operations within the English Court. This role, analogous to practices observed at the French court, entailed the interception and examination of correspondence through the General Letter Office and its agents. This network capitalised on the activities of ambassadors, lord-lieutenants, and magistrates to collate information. A notable success of this system was the exposure of the Rye House plot in 1683, largely attributed to the efforts of Sir Leoline Jenkins, a lawyer. Sunderland's task was to emulate the vigilance of James II's administration, which had effectively dismantled Whig conspiracies, driving their proponents into exile in the Netherlands. Thomas Chudleigh, serving as the English ambassador in The Hague, monitored these political refugees closely, with particular attention to Sir Thomas Armstrong, who lived incognito under the name "Henry Lawrence" (Armstrong was found and arrested, then executed in London). Shortly afterwards, in April 1684, Spencer replaced Thomas Chudleigh. In the "Department of the North," Charles, the 2nd Earl of Middleton, was tasked, along with Spencer, with counteracting the radical Whigs who had sought sanctuary in Scotland. As in France, the King of England used his Secret Intelligence Fund to control the risk from outside and within.

In 1685, amidst the King's surging popularity, the selection of personnel for key diplomatic posts was a matter of strategic importance. Sunderland appointed Ignatius White, succeeding Bevil Skelton, as ambassador to the United Provinces. White, an Irish Catholic whose father had fled Cromwell's regime, had aligned himself and his son with Leopold I of Austria, earning them several titles. Ignatius initially engaged in espionage for Spain, then France, and subsequently the United Provinces, until his activities aroused suspicion, leading to his imprisonment in the Bastille by Mazarin. Upon their release, Ignatius and his father were recruited by English agent Joseph Bamfield.

2. The French Court (1688):

By 1688, the French court, keenly observing developments in England, dispatched a message to Sunderland in London: "It is said at The

Hague that the English people, and even the army, are on the verge of revolution, and it is openly stated that if the Prince of Orange were to appear in England, the whole nation would declare itself in his favour."[50] England. James II, accustomed to such speculative reports—often disseminated by spies—chose to dismiss these claims.

Nevertheless, Louis XIV took proactive measures, sending the Marquis de Bonrepaus to London to consult with the English King's cabinet and offer the support of the French fleet. Additionally, Louis XIV issued an ultimatum to William III of Orange, a move that found little favour with James II. Despite these overtures, James II rebuffed any assistance from France, sceptical of Dutch ambitions. Faced with this situation, Louis turned to the Continent and prepared to attack with all his might.

As diplomatic efforts faltered, Louis XIV shifted focus to the Continent, bracing for an aggressive campaign. Bonrepaus's subsequent mission to London on September 4, 1688, with an enhanced offer of military support, was likewise declined. Even the Pope's envoys failed to sway the Pretender.[51] On 5 November 1688, William landed in England.

The alliance between France, the exiled Stuart dynasty—originally hailing from Dole in Brittany—and the Scottish Highland clans was a complex and often problematic endeavour. France's reliance on the centuries-old Auld Alliance (established in 1295 as the oldest agreement of its kind in the West) had been a strategic cornerstone against Great Britain. The Scottish Guard of the Kings of France, a revered institution, and the role of Scottish Constables are testament to the enduring connections fostered by this alliance. Despite their four-century reign over their territories, the Stuarts were keenly aware of both the benefits and challenges inherent in their relations with the Highland clans. A significant number of clan chiefs remained steadfastly loyal to the Stuart cause, motivated by either vested interests or tradition. However, the same dedication was not universal, with some clans choosing to support England instead. Scotland's rugged landscape, physical border with England, and

---

[50] D.C. Turner, London 1950, p. 412
[51] Edward Valance, *The Glorious Revolution. 1688-Britain's Fight for Liberty* (London 2006) p. 110

the staunch pride of its people presented strategic advantages. Yet, the region faced considerable hurdles: susceptibility of clan chiefs to corruption, internal divisions among the clans, and widespread poverty.

Relations between the English ruling dynasty and the Highland clans were often marked by violent conflict. The English monarchy exploited clan rivalries, elevating powerful clans like the Campbells, Gordons, and MacKenzies to positions of military leadership (Lieutenants to the King), to maintain control over the Highlands. The Stuarts, despite their longstanding ties to the region, struggled to effectively govern the Highlands, hindered by a lack of understanding of its deep-rooted cultural traditions. Moreover, Highlanders maintained connections with continental Europe, particularly through mercenary service, selling their martial prowess to other monarchs. Despite these broader engagements, it was the alliance with France that remained most significant and influential.

II. Scottish, French and English Intelligence.

1. War Interminable (1688-1715):

By the late 17th century, Scotland's population of 600,000 was primarily organised into clans. In the first part of our book, we saw that the religious policies of the Stuart kings had created a situation of civil war. Starting from late 1685, James II Stuart (James VII to the Scots) tasked his agents and spies with undermining the Duke of Argyll, a prominent leader of the Campbell clan and an ally of the government forces, aiming to neutralise his political influence. This initiative saw the alignment of clans such as Munro, Mckay, Ross, and Sutherland with the Whig opposition.

In 1688, James II Stuart abdicated and took refuge in France at Saint-Germain-en-Laye,[52] a locale with historical significance to the Stuarts due to its role as a sanctuary during earlier tumultuous periods. With the Stuart

---

[52] The day after his arrival, Jacques visited Louis XIV at Versailles with great pomp. At first, visits to Versailles from the exiled English court were frequent, as were return visits from the French court. Over time, however, as it became clear that a return of the Stuarts to England was increasingly unlikely, each court "began to regard its social obligations in respect of visits as useless and tedious drudgery."

monarch's departure, Jacobite agents mobilised the remaining loyalist supporters in Scotland, igniting a series of revolts across the nation. John Graham, Viscount Dundee, emerged as a symbol of this resistance, earning the moniker Bonnie Dundee. In a bid to solidify support, James II's operatives commenced financial transactions with the clans rallying to their cause, including the McDonald clans (Keppoch, Glencoe, Clanranald), McDonnell of Glengarry, Cameron, Robertson, McPherson, Stewart of Appin, McLean, Mckintosh, McKinnon, McLachlan, Chisholm, Drummond, Farquharson, Fraser, Gordon, Grant, McBean, McGillivray and Menzies. But dissension soon arose within the group as government agents took action.

1688-1689: Conspiracy of the Scotsman Sir George Barclay, lieutenant-colonel of James II's cavalry, aged sixty and disabled in the right hand. A former officer of Lord Dundee, he had fought at Killiecrankie (27 July 1689). After Dundee's death, he went to Ireland before returning to Scotland in 1691, where he was authorised to negotiate and act on James's behalf with the clan. However, the Jacobite revolt failed to materialise and he returned to France, where he served under the Duke of Berwick. He returned to England in 1696, with Captain Williamson, where he carried a proclamation urging English subjects to revolt against William. On his way from Richmond to London, he was joined by around forty cavalrymen. There, he intended to trap the royal carriage, drawn by six horses, in a narrow alley where it would be impossible to turn back. William, however, was aware of the plan and remained in his palace. Of the conspirators, only Barclay fled to France and all the others were arrested. He later maintained that James knew nothing of his conspiracy against William.[53]

July 1689: John Graham, Viscount of Dundee, rallied his forces and defeated William of Orange's troops, led by the clan chief Mckay, who had been made a general, at the Battle of Killiecrankie (near Pitlochry) on 27 July 1689, but was killed during the battle. Despite this, the Jacobite troops, led by Dundee's successor, a certain Cannon, who had not received the Irish reinforcements they had requested (from Tyrconnel) and who

---

[53] Du Boscq, *op. cit.* p. 209

were divided in internal wars, were decisively defeated in August of the same year at Dunkeld (21 August 1689).

1690: James II Stuart's son, he Pretender, initiated a restoration endeavour in collaboration with Louis XIV and his military commanders, aiming to reclaim the British throne through Ireland. This strategic move culminated in the Battle of the Boyne on July 12, 1690, which resulted in a decisive defeat for the Pretender's forces. Notably, the presence of Highland Scots at the court of Saint-Germain was minimal, as many chose to remain within their native Scottish territories. Both James II and Louis XIV were acutely aware of the differing martial capabilities between the English Jacobite forces and their Scottish counterparts. Recognising the formidable combat prowess of the Scottish Highlanders, they focused their military efforts and hopes on leveraging this strength.

1692: Attempted French uprising and landing in Scotland. Since the defeat of 1689, the Scots had had to swear allegiance to William III of Orange. The MacDonald clan, despite professing loyalty and awaiting directives from Saint-Germain that arrived belatedly, sought to express their dissatisfaction, significantly delaying their appearance at Fort William. The new Whig government, under the leadership of Secretary of State Sir John Dalrymple, the Master of Stair, identified Alasdair McDonald of Glencoe as a convenient target for retribution. Robert Campbell of Glenlyon was dispatched to neutralise the perceived threat from the McDonald clan. The Scottish chieftains loyal to Alasdair McDonald were summoned to Inveraray, arriving on 6 January 1692. Subsequently, the clan, seeking refuge in the Vale of Glencoe, faced increasing governmental pressure, with even the Campbell clansmen being enlisted to enforce tax collection. The resultant tensions culminated in the infamous Glencoe Massacre, where the MacDonald clansmen fell victim to a brutal massacre. This tragic event significantly tarnished William of Orange's reputation, a development France capitalised on by disseminating libels and pamphlets within London itself. Moreover, the French naval endeavour faced a significant setback on 2 and 3 June 1692, as the French fleet suffered a decisive defeat at the hands of the English navy in the Battle of La Hougue.

1696-1697: France orchestrated another attempt to land in England, positioning 16,000 soldiers near Calais in anticipation of the operation. However, this initiative stumbled at the outset, primarily due to the Pretender's hesitation to grant his approval for the action. Once the decision to proceed was finally made, the expedition was beleaguered by a series of misfortunes: adverse weather conditions, the vigilant English fleet, and notably, the Jacobites' lack of proficiency in military tactics and manoeuvring. These factors collectively ensured that the attempt to land in England ended in failure.

1703-1704: We will come back to this event later, but Anne Stuart, along with numerous English politicians and leaders, expressed a desire for the Pretender to ascend to the throne of Great Britain. However, this aspiration came with a condition: the Pretender's conversion to Protestantism, or at least a pretence of such conversion. The Pretender's refusal to conform to this requirement dashed any hopes of his restoration to the crown, prompting Parliament to select Sophie of Hanover, daughter of Elizabeth Stuart and granddaughter of King James I Stuart, as the successor.

1707: Act of Union of the Crowns. This Act effectively dissolved the Scottish Parliament, integrating it within a unified Parliament of Great Britain. Despite this political consolidation, the Act ensured the preservation of the unique identities of the Church of England and the Presbyterian Church of Scotland. Furthermore, it guaranteed the continued distinction between the legal systems of England and Scotland, specifically between common law and Scots law. Concurrently, the Act established the current flag of Great Britain and affirmed Anne Stuart's position as the rightful successor to the throne.

1708-1709: James II, died in 1701. His son the Pretender took up the mantle of the Stuart claim to the British throne. Sensing the continued unrest and dissatisfaction in Scotland, he organised a new landing attempt, with troops under his command and with the help of the Scottish clans that had remained loyal. Admiral Forbin, undoubtedly "worked" by English and Dutch spies, showed little hope in his mission (he was even begged to land the Pretender). The fleet ventured into the Firth of Forth and came face to face with the English navy. Admiral

Forbin, who was not prepared for such a naval battle, retreated. This action thwarted the Pretender's plans to set foot on Scottish soil, leaving him to contend with the stark realisation of betrayal, likely orchestrated by spies within their midst.

1710: After the Whigs and Tories clashed in Parliament over the succession to Queen Anne (the Whigs believed that Parliament had the right to determine the succession and award it to the Queen's closest Protestant relative, and the Tories believed that the hereditary rights of the Stuarts took precedence), George of Hanover, son of Sophie of Hanover (and therefore great-grandson of James I Stuart), announced that he would succeed her to the throne of England. He was officially crowned on the death of his mother Sophie of Hanover on 20 October 1714.

1713: Following the Peace of Utrecht, Louis XIV was obliged to remove the Stuart court from France, and sent them to Lorraine.

1714: George I of Hanover was confirmed as King of Great Britain, despite the less than warm relationship with his son, George Augustus, the Prince of Wales and future George II, who worked to limit his power. This familial discord presented a unique opportunity for French espionage to manipulate British foreign policy, particularly concerning Sweden. The Hanoverians' ambitions to constrain Swedish territory were well-known, and the French sought to exploit this to their advantage. George I's suspicion of the Tories led him to forge an alliance with his son George Augustus, despite their personal differences, in a strategic move to maintain influence within Parliament, allowing the Whig party to establish itself permanently in the political landscape of Great Britain. The Danes were utilised against Sweden, which seemed to encourage Sweden to accept a proposal to land its troops at Newcastle in support of the French expedition.

1715: The Whigs win the general election, and some Tory members move closer to the Jacobites. Believing in the possibility of restoring the Pretender to the throne, these Tory converts and their agents convened with the Pretender at Saint-Germain-en-Laye, planning a revolt and uprising in Scotland. This endeavour came to be known as the Mar Rebellion, a campaign infamous for its ill fortune and strategic missteps, emblematic of the challenges that consistently plagued Jacobite efforts.

The rebellion, initiated by the Earl of Mar in September 1715, saw the mobilisation of various Scottish clans. Financial incentives facilitated this assembly, with arms dispatched to support the insurrection and extend operations into the southwest. However, a lack of unified strategy led to failure in the Lowlands, while in the Highlands, preparations for conflict continued. Clans such as the Mckenzie, under the Earl of Seaforth, the "Atholl Brigade" comprising relatives of the Duke of Atholl, and other historically Jacobite clans including the McGregor, McDonell of Keppoch and Glengarry, McLean, Cameron, and a faction of the Campbell clan of Breadalbane, rallied to the cause. The English government's response featured a contingent of 1,500 men from the Argyll region to counter the Jacobite forces. Mar's hesitancy and the subsequent division of his forces led to an inconclusive clash with Argyll at the Battle of Sheriffmuir on 13 November 1715, where neither side secured a decisive victory. The Pretender's arrival in late December was poorly timed; with winter setting in, the clans dispersed, diminishing the rebellion's momentum. Ultimately, the Earl of Mar and the Pretender departed from Montrose, returning to France. At this stage, the Jacobite cause seemed to have been won.

2. Courtyards and Anterooms full of Spies:

We have a first-hand account from France that gives us an idea of what spies meant to leading figures at the end of the 17th century. The Marquis de Feuquières (1648-1711), lieutenant-general of the king's armies in 1693, a combatant and then a recognised leader, did not receive his marshal's baton, for obscure reasons that seem to us to relate to internal struggles at the court of Louis XIV, and died "abandoned, abhorred, obscure and poor [...] without reward and without friends."[54]

In response to his sidelining and the frustrations it wrought, he penned his *Memoirs*, offering not only reflections on military art but also a rich depiction of life and the undercurrents of intrigue that characterised his time. Having rubbed shoulders with sulphurous characters and men of the shadows, he gives us his opinion on what spies were like in 1693, confirming what we said in the previous section. But more than that, he

---

[54] Saint-Simon, *Op. cit.*

gives a clear and concise account of the environment in which the princes lived in their states during the period we are interested in:

> Spies come in many varieties. They are to be found in the Councils of Princes, in the Offices of Ministers, in the Cabinets of Generals, in enemy Cities, in the Flat Country [Holland], and even in Monasteries.
>
> Some offer themselves; others are formed by the care of the Minister, the General, or those in charge of detailed affairs. All are driven by greed for gain. It is up to the Prince and his Ministers to corrupt the Council of his Enemy. It is up to the General, and those who work with him for the good of business, to corrupt or train the others.
>
> In general, you should always take instructions from the spies and never open up to them. For one and the same subject, it is necessary to employ several of them who do not know each other, to communicate with them only in secret, to talk to them often about things about which you do not care to be enlightened, to make them talk a lot and say few things to them, in order to know their character of mind and their scope; to have them spy on themselves, after you have separated from them, to find out if they are not making doubles, which happens very often. And when, on the basis of the separate reports of several people, you believe that you are certain that they are telling the truth, you should still have them guarded separately; and if it is to carry out an undertaking, you should take them all separately, question them often, and see whether they agree in fact.
>
> There is also a third type of Spy, or at least people from whom you can gain certain knowledge by talking to them. These are the locals whose particular affairs attract them to the Camp or to the Towns, and the prisoners.
>
> The first must never be questioned. They should be talked to, or have them talked to, by people of spirit, who, without affecting curiosity, make them talk enough on different subjects to obtain from them knowledge of the things you want to know.
>
> The Prisoners, according to their character, may be questioned a little more or a little less harshly, but nevertheless always separated from each other, and always led to the knowledge of what we want to know, by long detours of conversation, so that they do not take any notice themselves of what they have said, and so that after being dismissed, they cannot put their General on the track, about the intentions that we may have; because in this case the General will not fail to release double spies, or defectors, to give different

notions about what was intended to be penetrated, and thus cause false measures to be taken.

There are countries where the spies that can be found in monasteries are the best and most reliable. The government of consciences is a secret empire, which is not penetrated by anyone, and which penetrates everything. The use of these kinds of Spies is infallible, either in a Place occupied by a Prince of a different Religion [the Protestants], or in a State, in the change of a domination [William III in England, James II Stuart in exile]. Women are even used, either to introduce them into a City, or to test a Camp, or to carry Letters because they are less suspected than Men.

There is no need to go into detail here about all the different uses of spies. Suffice it to say that a Prince, a Minister and a General cannot know too precisely what is happening in friendly or enemy States and Armies; and that therefore there cannot be too many Spies of all kinds and for all kinds of use.[55]

---

[55] *Mémoires de M. le marquis de Feuquière, Lieutenant-général des armées du Roi*, tome premier, A Amsterdam, 1761, 353 pages.

CHAPTER 6

THE COURT OF JAMES II AT SAINT-GERMAIN-EN-LAYE (1688-1689)

I. The Stuarts Papers.

On 13 July 1807, Henry Benedict Stuart, also known as the "Cardinal of York" and son of the Pretender and Clementine Sobieska, died. Subsequently, all the concealed documents and correspondence of the House of Stuart spanning from 1713 to 1770, previously under the guardianship of Jacobite Under-Secretary of State David Nairn in Rome, were transferred to the library at Carlton House, the abode of the Prince Regent, the future King George IV of England (1762-1830). This collection, comprising 541 bound volumes and 11 boxes of documents, offers an unparalleled treasure trove for those eager to delve into the Jacobite attempts to reclaim the throne through original documents. Currently, the majority of these documents have been digitised, making them accessible for scholarly examination.

For an extended period, these papers served as a resource for politicians covertly scheming alongside the Stuart court exiled in Saint-Germain. Presently, however, academic scrutiny has unravelled their nuances, disappointing those who anticipated groundbreaking revelations. Nonetheless, these documents afford a renewed lens through which to study Jacobitism, illustrating its immersion in the broader tumult and crises of European politics.

In the 1760s, as Jacobitism's influence diminished, there remained some politicians who perceived conspiratorial elements within the Tory party. This party, at the time, was positioning itself as a conservative force and an advocate for King George III: "Shew me a Tory," fumed John

Wilkes, "and I will shew you a Jacobite." This belief fueled speculation that unveiling the secret Stuart documents would lead to the Tories' downfall. However, this outcome did not materialise. Indeed, prominent figures within the English legal system had already expressed their allegiance to the exiled Stuart monarchy. Furthermore, Scottish author James Macpherson's publication of a British history aimed to expose the Whig party's controversial role in the early 18th century. This period also saw renewed scrutiny of the Duke of Marlborough, a celebrated Whig hero, with attempts to critically reassess his and other prominent Whigs' actions during the 1690s, such as Admiral Edward Russell, Earl of Oxford; Charles Talbot, Duke of Shrewsbury; and Robert Spencer, Earl of Sunderland, all of whom had engaged in conspiracies with the exiled monarchs James II and the Pretender.

During the Napoleonic Wars, the Whig party continued its efforts to undermine its Conservative (Tory) rivals. Both factions engaged in schemes to secure the Stuart Papers, with the first acquisition initiated by Sir John Coxe Hippisley and Charles James Fox, both Whigs, through Abbot James Waters in Rome between 1804 and 1805. Charles James Fox aimed to pen a less-than-glowing biography of the last Stuarts, bolstered by correspondences from James II that purportedly showcased the Duke of Marlborough's involvement in a collusion of interests.

The first documents of note were those belonging to Robert Watson, a Scottish radical who had sought refuge in France during the Revolution. He acquired these papers in Rome from the executor of the Cardinal of York's will, and in 1815, handed them over to Henry Brougham, a Whig lawyer and businessman. Brougham was keen on preventing these documents from reaching George IV, fearing political sanitisation. This sparked a series of scandals, highlighting the greed for money over truth among notable Whigs and Tories. By 1817, all documents had been transported to England, where they underwent examination by experts from 1819 to 1829 under the supervision of the Conservative MP Wilson Croker.

Accusations flew about individuals removing letters that could tarnish their family's reputation, but the acclaimed author Walter Scott refuted these claims. In fact, if we check the corpus of documents, we can see that some of the so-called missing letters are still present.

Hence, historians have approached the *Stuart Papers* with caution, recognising their emergence from a context of decay, offering little beyond accusations and defamation. The true significance of these documents lies not in their political content but in their historical value, offering insights into a very tumultuous era. While looking for sensational discoveries, historians encountered a complex tapestry of internal uncertainty, factional manoeuvres, betrayals, and conspiracies. This narrative has occasionally drawn from their contents to substantiate our discussion, underscoring the essence of the demonstrated phenomena.

II. Games of influence in Saint-Germain-en-Laye.

The narrative of English royalty seeking sanctuary in Saint-Germain-en-Laye stretches back to Mary Stuart in the late 16th century. This tragic Queen of Scots, having departed France to claim her throne, ultimately faced a dire fate in England. This pattern of seeking refuge in France was echoed when the widow of Charles I of England, along with her son, the future Charles II, found solace in the Louvre. Henrietta Maria was poorly received by Cardinal Mazarin, and her stay in the Louvre was unpleasant and cold. The Duke of York, James Stuart, her second son, fled across Europe, as we have written, in search of adventure and to become a warrior. He was well versed in military affairs, as his tutor for military studies and behaviour was Henri de La Tour d'Auvergne, viscount of Turenne (1611-75). Turenne was one of six Marshals promoted to the rank of Marshal General of France.[56]

By November 1673, the Duke of York, James Stuart, had been back in England for several years and had garnered the affection of its people. His conversion to Catholicism and subsequent marriage to Mary of Modena, an Italian princess from the House of Este, incited significant

---

[56] However, his judgement that "the natural dispositions of this young man allow us to hope that he will be the greatest prince and the best general of his time" proved to be wrong, even though he took part in no fewer than five French campaigns in his youth. Some have even suggested that he was the inventor of the art of signals.

controversy, especially among the London populace.[57] This marriage, facilitated by the Earl of Peterborough, was met with resistance from the English Parliament, dominated by Whigs. However, Louis XIV, recognising an ally in the Catholic Duke amidst the escalating tensions in Europe, supported the union, as did the Pope.

Once married, the couple travelled to France and were received warmly by the king. In fact, the Duchess of York brought with her an Italian retinue, including her mother, Duchess Laure (Regent of Modena), Cardinal Mazarin's niece, and was commended by Pope Innocent XI for her virtues.

After James II's exile to France in 1688, due to William III of Orange's invasion and the support of James's daughter Mary Stuart for William, Mary of Modena dedicated herself to the restoration of her husband's rights in England. In fact, Mary had remained in England and joined her husband from 21 December 1688 (Antoine Nompar de Caumont, Comte de Lauzun (1632-1723), who took her in at Whitehall Palace, dressed soberly, and escorted her to Calais).[58]

Accompanying them were two children destined to play significant roles: Prince James, known as "the Pretender," and his sister, Princess Louise. The birth of Princess Louise was celebrated by the Jacobites for her unwavering Catholic faith and loyalty to her father, King James II: "I now have a daughter who has not sinned against her father." Unfortunately, her life was cut short, leaving her brother as the sole beacon for the Jacobite aspirations. Known as the "Knight of St George," Prince James faced opposition from the Orangemen, who branded him a rebel and traitor. Despite political animosity, Horace Walpole, a staunch political adversary, couldn't help but recognise the prince's resemblance to his ill-fated ancestors:

> The Chevalier de Saint-Georges is tall, thin and melancholy. He seems like the ghost that a well-informed imagination would conjure up to represent Charles I with his misfortunes minus his faults. He has the pronounced

---

[57] Du Boscq, G. and M. Bernos, *op. cit.*, p. 156
[58] *Ibid*, p.3

features and air of fatality of the Stuarts. From the moment I saw him, I could not have doubted the legitimacy of his birth.[59]

The Pretender's valour was evident at the Battle of Malplaquet in 1709, where even Marshal de Villars commended his bravery. He led several charges, often needing to temper the zeal of the Irish regiments eager for close combat with the English guards.

However, in a bid for the throne, James was counselled by allies like Bolingbroke to conceal his Catholic faith, aiming to avoid his father's errors. Despite this, James insisted on a reign that would accommodate the Protestant faction, advocating for religious freedom. This stance placed him at odds with Louis XIV's harsh anti-Protestant policies. James's marriage in 1719, though outside this book's focus, marks a continuation of the Stuarts' undying hope for restoration in England until the mid-1740s.

In 1689, amidst the Irish conflict where French forces rallied to Catholic supporters, William prepared for direct involvement on the battlefield. Meanwhile, Marie de Modène, overseeing her court at Saint-Germain, stayed well-informed through her network of agents. She cleverly dispatched letters to her allies in England, utilising two couriers on distinct routes to ensure the messages' delivery. These letters, penned with invisible ink (lemon juice or urine), were ingeniously concealed within the couriers' garments. One was William Fuller, previously associated with Lady Melfort at Saint-Germain, and the other, a young man named Matthew Crone. Tasked with delivering these secretive communications to London and Kensington, their loyalty wavered, leading Fuller to betray their cause to William. Crone, initially elusive, was eventually captured, vehemently denying any involvement until the pressure of interrogation by William III's Secretary of State, Nottingham, coerced him into a confession. In exchange for his life, he revealed plans for a Jacobite plot to seize Queen Mary and confirmed key appointments within the Jacobite movement, namely the appointments of Lord Melfort as Secretary of State and Coordinator of Intelligence, exposing the extensive network operating from St. Germain.

---

[59] Horace Walpole, *Memoirs and Recollections*.

Intelligence Infiltration:

The Jacobites of Saint-Germain and London traded through a Protestant Jacobite, William Birkenhead, who feigned allegiance to William while meticulously surveilling the English Channel. He found a crossing point for these exchanges between Saint-Germain and London, and missives passed along this route. However, this line of communication was perpetually under threat as William's agents, like John Mackey, infiltrated the Saint-Germain court.

In January 1696, Sir George Barclay embarked on a perilous journey, utilising Birkenhead's previously scouted route, aiming to reach the English shores at Romney Marsh, specifically at the secluded residence of a Jacobite sympathiser named Hunt. Barclay's disguise was crucial for the mission, given his unmistakable appearance: "[...] he was tall, thin, with a large hooked nose and a crippled right hand, which made his distinctive appearance well known to the authorities."[60]

Tasked with the audacious objective to assassinate William, Barclay's involvement in this notorious assassination attempt at Kensington ultimately faltered. It appears the scheme was compromised by Thomas Prendergast, a Catholic gentleman from Limerick, who divulged the assassination plot to Portland, ensuring William's safety. Following the exposure of the plot, Birkenhead faced interrogation, revealing his dual role as a naval spy for the French Minister of the Navy, Count of Pontchartrain. Though imprisoned at Newgate, Birkenhead managed to escape.[61] The fallout from the foiled plot saw an extensive crackdown, with around 3,000 suspects arrested; many faced execution or imprisonment. Despite suspicions, James II distanced himself from the conspiracy, striving to demonstrate his non-involvement.

Amid their clandestine operations, the Jacobite agents from Saint-Germain encountered the expertise of Dr. John Wallis, a renowned cryptographer at the English court. The encrypted correspondence of James II, which included simplified designations such as "16" for Melfort, "110" for Middleton, "300" for James, and "302" for the Queen, proved

---

[60] According to Paul Hopkins DNB, vol 3, p. 766
[61] William Birkenhead had received £200 from Saint-Germain, as well as money through the cabinet at Versailles.

decipherable. They employed code names like "Good Farmer" for James, "Bold Britain" for the Prince of Wales, and "Mr and Mrs Churchill" for Princess Anne and her husband Prince George of Denmark.[62]

In this context, it's worth noting the efforts of Nathaniel Hooke, a figure who served the Stuart court. Despite his experience, skills, and valour, Hooke's endeavours were thwarted by Queen Anne's agents and the convoluted situation in Scotland, rendering the orchestration of any significant rebellion unfeasible.

---

[62] John Callow *King in Exile* London2004, p. 227

CHAPTER 7

ENGLAND AND HOLLAND AGAINST LOUIS XIV AND THE JACOBITES (1688-1690)

The espionage and intelligence activities in the contest for control over the British Isles, following James II Stuart's flight, saw Louis XIV leveraging the global network established by the Jacobites prior to 1688. Post this pivotal year, the court of Saint-Germain transformed into a nexus of clandestine machinations and enigmatic schemes.

From the year 1685, the French monarchy kept a vigilant eye on English political developments, given that James II Stuart, Charles II's successor, was a Catholic sovereign in a country that was absolutely not Catholic. It was his daughters, Mary and Anne Stuart, who delivered the coup de grâce, as the former was married to William of Orange, the Dutch Stadtholder and emblem of opposition against Louis XIV's ambitions. Neither Mary nor Anne were Catholics, and it appeared their Protestant faith was a strategic play to ensure their father, the Duke of York's acceptance as the monarch of England, Scotland, and Ireland. In fact, stability seemed assured with the understanding that James II would be succeeded by one of his Protestant daughters. However, everything changed in 1688, when James II obtained an heir from his wife, whom he therefore made Catholic. Moreover, James II, with his deep-rooted and unshakeable parliamentary traditions, had multiplied his provocations in religious matters, with his unabated and provocative adherence to Catholicism.

The English Whig party, known for its widespread influence and its agents in every corner of Europe, was actively conspiring against the King and appealed to the King's son-in-law, William of Orange, who jumped at the chance to nip in the bud what he saw as reverse Catholicism, and therefore an alliance with Louis XIV's France.

Despite the efforts of the Comte d'Avaux, the French ambassador in Holland, to gather intelligence on the campaign's objectives, it remained unclear whether the Dutch forces would target France or England. The situation was equally ambiguous in London, where the seasoned French ambassador, Jean-Paul de Barrillon, found himself in the dark. William of Orange's landing and subsequent march to London were met with support from his English allies, leading to James II's flight to Saint-Germain, where he established a court of devoted supporters known as the *Jacobites*.

William ascended to the English throne alongside his wife, Mary II Stuart, while Louis XIV backed his cousin in his quest to reclaim his perceived rightful throne. The same year saw France embroiled in the War of the League of Augsburg, with Ireland emerging as a critical battleground in 1689 and 1690. The French naval expedition led by James II was to be bolstered by Irish forces on the ground. However, the conflict culminated in James II's withdrawal during the Battle of the Boyne on 12 July 1690, after which he returned to Saint-Germain-en-Laye, where the effort to reclaim his throne persisted.

James II's court at Saint-Germain-en-Laye was a clear source of British influence on French society and culture. The Jacobites, who had escaped their homeland, gathered not only around the king but also spread their influence more broadly. Nonetheless, Louis XIV and his ministers were well aware that this court was under scrutiny, as it harboured double agents who, though ostensibly loyal to James, secretly relayed information to William III.

An estimated fifty thousand Jacobites sought refuge in France, yet their unity was superficial. While openly professing allegiance to James II's cause, internal divisions surfaced; Catholics attributed their misfortunes to the ill counsel of Protestants, whom they suspected of espionage.

It is important to remember that this migration to France was borne not out of a desire for comfort but from a necessity to find sanctuary, coupled with the hope of support for a potential return to their native land. Many Jacobites had lost their fortunes and longed for the day they would be recognised and compensated for their unwavering loyalty. Financial desperation led some to adopt the role of double agents, serving competing interests for monetary gain.

I. Organising dissent (1685-1702).

The revocation of the Edict of Nantes in 1685, a catalyst for the League of Augsburg's war, propelled Protestants into exile or conversion under duress. Those who were forced to re-establish themselves abroad almost all harboured a violent hatred of Louis XIV. While some, driven by conviction or caution, denounced insurgent doctrines, the stance of figures like Pierre Bayle (1647-1706),[63] remains ambiguous, possibly indirectly combating Louis XIV's France through his writings, though it is not known whether he may have been bribed by the French government. To resist Louis XIV's oppression, some Huguenots took up arms against their country or spied for France's enemies. The conflict reignited in 1688, challenging France to confront its neighbours anew in 1689. Concurrently, Waldensian refugees in Switzerland plotted their forceful return. A cadre of French Huguenots, supported by England and Holland, orchestrated refugee companies to assist the Vaudois and Savoyard troops in their invasion of Dauphiné, inciting uprisings in the Cévennes in September 1689 and across southern France, although these insurrections were swiftly quelled. In 1690 and 1691, Catinat's army prevented the invasion of France. During the League of Augsburg's war, other Protestants engaged in espionage against Louis XIV for England. Figures like Pastor Gravisset and Saint-Martin operated solo, while Blancard helmed an information network since 1689. Additionally, a spy agency emerged in Rotterdam around 1689, under the high and secret direction of Pierre Jurieu, a Protestant pastor (1637-1713), by a merchant from La Rochelle named Etienne Caillaud. Largely subsidised by England, this agency used Protestants who had remained in France for religious reasons as well as former Catholics acting for profit. It thus succeeded in having agents in

---

[63] Protestant teacher and man of letters, precursor of the philosophy of the Enlightenment. He abjured Catholicism in 1670 and fled to Geneva. He published major works commenting on the holy books.

the main French ports, and even in the ministries and at court, who provided it with information on the policies of Louis XIV and on the movements of French ships, as well as on the actions of the former king of England, James II. These supporters of the insurrection, as we shall see, remained very active until the end of the 17th century.

In 1690, as the southern regions of France braced for combat, it was a French Huguenot general serving William III of Orange who played a key role in thwarting the expedition and securing victory at the Battle of the Boyne in Ireland on 11 July 1690, solidifying William's claim to the English crown.

Following the revocation of the Edict of Nantes in 1685 by Louis XIV, a formidable coalition, often referred to as the Protestant International or the Reformed International, emerged with the primary objective of countering the policies of the French monarch. This revocation compelled a significant number of French Protestants to flee their homeland and seek refuge and support from foreign Protestant powers, notably England and Holland. This struggle transcended mere diplomatic protest, encompassing covert operations such as espionage and escalating to outright rebellion, as exemplified by the Cévennes War. These efforts were part of a broader conflict aimed at reinstating a Catholic monarch, specifically James II followed by the Pretender, to the English throne. The plight of French Protestants, who had been enduring escalating pressures since the early 1660s—embodied in the saying "patient as a Huguenot"—reached a critical juncture in 1685, marking the starting point of a transition from passive endurance to active resistance.

Pierre Jurieu (1637-1713), a Calvinist pastor, played a crucial role in this resistance, establishing a spy network for Holland and England. He asserted that "the madness of the king [Louis XIV] would serve God's plan," and his publications became tools for foreign agents and Dutch propagandists. In January 1685, Jurieu's writings reached Berlin through the Elector's envoy. Around this time, another exiled pastor, Gaultier de Saint-Blancard, who had formerly ministered in Montpellier, was dispatched to Brandenburg by William of Orange. Claude Brousson, another pastor, was notably received by William to discuss alliances that eventually led to the formation of the League of Augsburg. The whole of

Languedoc welcomed the news with joy. To support them, a lawyer from Nîmes, Pascal Mirmand, who had taken refuge in Zurich, was sent as a deputation to Holland in 1687 and supported William's plans to invade France.By July 1688, Mirmand, along with a pastor named Bernard, were in The Hague assisting William of Orange in his preparations to invade England.By November, it became evident to England and Holland that the French Protestant leadership was not only willing but capable of instigating uprisings in southern France. These acts of rebellion were intended to support the Reformed agenda in London and to counter James II Stuart's efforts to reinstate Catholic supremacy. It was Gaultier de Saint-Bernard, a mysterious figure about whom we have little information, who informed Pierre Jurieu that William was ready to help and support the rebels in the Cévennes. An operation was being planned in the region, with William desiring to keep his involvement concealed. But after some prevarication, the fighters returned home and were organised into Compagnies Franches, some of which were sent to Switzerland to fight Louis XIV.

On November 25, 1689, Pascal Mirmand addressed a gathering of expectant Protestants, revealing plans for an Anglo-Dutch fleet to conduct a coastal raid on France. The operation was set to involve ten thousand Protestant soldiers, tasked with engaging fifty thousand of the King's troops, under the protection of Allied forces. By December, Pierre Jurieu issued another urgent call for action within France, proposing that foreign forces, including Germans under the command of Marshal de Schomberg's son, with officers from Brandenburg, should swiftly engage. This call underscored the dire situation that had been escalating since 1686-1687, marked by unpredictable and inevitable conflicts. Heretics faced death sentences, with Nicolas de Lamoignon de Basville, the intendant of Languedoc, leading a harsh purge: 84 individuals executed, 300 deported to the Americas, and many more tortured or sentenced to the galleys. In the same year, François Huc from Le Vigan, a Huguenot refugee and special envoy of Schomberg, rallied with rebel leaders in the Cévennes, spearheading the Gévaudan militia's resistance.

In early 1692, the English contemplated an amphibious operation in Saintonge and Poitou, yet the year's military engagements in Europe yielded mixed outcomes for the allies. Despite Tourville's defeat at La Hougue, the French captured Namur and triumphed over William III at Steinkerque. On August 29, aiming to outmanoeuvre Louis XIV in the realm of propaganda, Schomberg orchestrated the publication and dissemination of a manifesto throughout Dauphiné under the auspices of William III of Orange, proclaimed "King of England." The declaration appealed to both Protestant and Catholic residents, exhorting them to abstain from engaging in military conflicts.

Pierre Jurieu, Head of an Espionage Network for Holland and England (1690-1713):

We have highlighted a figure named Pierre Jurieu, a French Huguenot pastor and fervent pamphleteer, born in 1637 and dying in Rotterdam in 1713, who emerged as a significant figure among the Huguenot refugees. Engaging deeply with both the refugees and political figures from nations opposed to France, his intellectual prowess and pastoral duties placed him at the heart of resistance against Louis XIV's policies. Recognised by influential circles, Jurieu, alongside Etienne Caillaud, was entrusted with establishing intelligence networks within France to surveil its ports. However, the failed attempt to land in England in 1696 put Jurieu under the threat of disrepute. Lord Portland, William of Orange's envoy to France, disapproved of Caillaud's conduct in Paris, highlighting the precarious nature of their espionage efforts. The death of William of Orange further destabilised the "Jurieu network," with Lord Manchester (Charles Montaigu, 1st Duke of Manchester, a Whig ally of William of Orange since 1688) criticising the network and suggesting the establishment of an alternative secret operation. Caillaud's defence sheds light on the realities of a spy network:

> Their knowledge is too limited for this trade, because the original intention was to have a man travel there. I leave it to you to think whether this would be of great service, because if you don't arm at one time, you can do it at another. So you have to have people on the spot, and it will be very difficult for them to do that. I know from experience what it's like; it's not a one-year

job. It takes several years to put it [the spy network] on the footing where I've established it.[64]

The necessity for spies to be deeply embedded in the countries they were tasked with surveilling was increasingly recognized by 1706. Criticisms regarding inefficiencies and financial oversights began to mount, particularly from the English Secretary of State Charles Hedges (1650-1714), who pointed out delays and instances of overpayment. We also know that the minister Torcy was suspicious of Caillaud and regularly informed the plenipotentiaries. Amidst this backdrop, the announcement of France's plans to invade England and Scotland was made by Etienne Caillaud, who had started to gain prominence, especially as Jurieu's health declined. To gather intelligence from Saint-Germain-en-Laye, the network led by Jurieu and Caillaud employed an individual known only as Marsault, (about whom we have no information, as the name was probably just a patronymic), who sent the news before it officially reached the court in Versailles.

II. Military Operations (1702-1713).

1. Choosing the Sites of Military Engagement:

Despite the Treaty of Ryswick in 1697 largely neglecting the plight of French Protestants, the refusal of Louis XIV to engage with the English ambassador Pembroke on what he deemed an internal affair only intensified the Huguenots' resolve. Entering a new, more violent phase of their struggle, they were led by fervent preachers and self-proclaimed prophets into what would become known as the Camisards' Revolt during the War of the Spanish Succession (1702-1704).

The revolt was sparked on 24 July 1702 when Abraham Mazel and Esprit Séguier led an armed group into the home of Abbé François de Langlade du Chayla (1647-1702), inspector of missions in the Cévennes on behalf of Intendant Basville, and killed him. News of this act of

---

[64] Dedieu, Joseph, *Le Rôle politique des protestants français (1685-1715)*, Paris, 1920. Letter from E. Caillaud to Blathwayt, Rotterdam, 30 June 1702, BM.M. Addit. Mss. N°21552, fol. 46. Pp. 237-238.

resistance spread quickly, being reported in the gazettes of Brussels and Bern, with English agents keeping a watchful eye on developments, though England had not yet decided to intervene. Command of the royal troops tasked with quelling the revolt fell to Lieutenant-General Victor-Maurice de Broglie (it should be remembered that not all Protestants were aligned against Louis XIV, but rather a determined subset led the resistance against the Camisards).

In addition to operations on the ground, there were actions of influence, and it was Jurieu, Schomberg's son, Henri de Massué, Marquis de Ruvigny and now Lord Galway (a French diplomat and Protestant in the service of England), and Henri-Armand de Bourbon-Malauze, Marquis de Miremont[65] who became more actively involved in the struggle.

The year 1702 not only marked the death of William III but also the ascension of Anne Stuart, James II's second daughter, to the English throne. This period saw a flurry of espionage activities, with English agents deployed to France, influencing the Camisard rebels and tipping the scales in their favour. Concurrently, Louis XIV orchestrated efforts to incite uprisings outside France, a strategy mirrored by other European nations within French borders. A pivotal, albeit enigmatic, player in this international intrigue was Nicolle, who established a comprehensive spy network in Guyenne and the Vivarais. On 11 December 1702, Nicolle reached out to Baron d'Alès, a refugee in England, urging him to lead the Camisards and seek intervention from Queen Anne. Though the Baron d'Alès received the message positively, he hesitated to engage in what he perceived as a doomed venture. Instead, he forwarded Nicolle's letter to the Lord Justice of Dublin, who, in turn, informed Rochester, the Lord Lieutenant of Ireland, and Lord Nottingham. The involvement of Henri-Armand de Bourbon-Malauze, Marquis de Miremont, particularly caught the spies' attention. His correspondences were intercepted and scrutinised, leading to the effective neutralisation of the revolt.

In January 1703, the Camisard rebellion, led by Jean Cavalier (1681-1740) and Abdias Maurel, also known as Catinat, intensified with the

---

[65] Henri-Armand de Bourbon-Malauze came from a collateral branch of the Bourbons of France, and was a staunch Protestant (his brother was killed at the Battle of the Boyne in Ireland).

formation of armed groups comprised of peasants and farmers. In response, Louis XIV dispatched Lieutenant-General Maurice de Broglie alongside thousands of troops and Catholic militias to quell the uprising. The conflict was marked by brutalities committed by both sides, complicating any potential intervention from Protestant nations due to the geographical and diplomatic distance from Languedoc. Nottingham informed the Marquis d'Arzeliers in June 1703: everything that was being said was known through spies. Jean Cavalier himself knew all about it.

However, in February 1703, Miremont and Nottingham had initiated covert negotiations with the Protestants in the Cévennes, pondering the feasibility of an English intervention. Despite Lord Aglionby's reports to Whitehall highlighting the operation's risks, the urgency of the situation escalated. With Marshal de Montrevel succeeding de Broglie, a harsh crackdown ensued against anyone found bearing arms. Jean Cavalier was defeated in a pitched battle, and on 1 April, women and children were burnt alive in an assembly (Moulin de L'Agaut massacre). The violence persisted, reaching a critical point on 20 September. Faced with relentless atrocities, Miremont urgently called for military support from the allies. The rebels in the Cévennes were religious, like the English against James II. The English were even offered a foothold in the Bordeaux region in exchange. The English government bribed a peasant called Moïse Billand, but he got nothing in return.

2. Hybrid Warfare, the Cévennes Revolt:

But on 25 August 1703, an Anglo-Dutch fleet was finally poised for action, consisting of forty English and five Dutch ships under the command of Admiral Cloudesley Shovell (1650-1707).[66] This force was bolstered by an additional fifty-three Dutch vessels, including twenty warships. Their mission: to deliver five French officers and spies to support the Camisard rebellion. However, delays ensued, and a critical miscommunication thwarted the operation's progress, leaving the Camisard leadership uninformed of the intended landing—a mishap likely

---

[66] An officer from the ranks and a British folk hero, until the naval disaster at Les Sorlingues (a storm) in 1707.

orchestrated by Louis XIV's intelligence network. In September, Marshal de Montrevel wrote to Minister Chamillart that the revolt was being "led and supported by foreign countries and that, despite all the precautions taken, the Camisards were receiving frequent help and instructions." Further complicating the situation, he also mentioned revelations from an English spy disclosed the presence of sixty-four captains, both English and French expatriates, covertly operating within Languedoc. They were reportedly biding their time, awaiting a grand uprising planned for the spring, which would coincide with a significant landing of a mixed force composed of British and exiled French troops.

The battle of the spies raged on: On 5 June, reports indicated that a group of five individuals departed Holland for Pont-Saint-Esprit, with their arrival anticipated on the 14th. Their mission was to rendezvous with Protestant sympathisers in the Vivarais region, then travel via Geneva to Bellay and Valence, ultimately dispersing in disguise. The orchestrator of this plot was Sieur de Belcastel, a nobleman from the Cévennes living in exile. Meanwhile, Sieur de Villeneuve from Switzerland ingeniously smuggled 260,000 écus using hollowed-out crutches carried by individuals feigning disabilities, with the operation's liaison being the distinctively tall and lean Englishman known as Cutz. This infiltration posed a significant threat to the royal forces, potentially leaving them vulnerable to attack from multiple fronts. Marshal Montrevel, alert to the looming danger, tightened security across key passages and halted all riverine traffic along the Rhône, extending vigilance to the areas of Orange, Montélimar, Valence, and Grenoble. On the 16th of June, five men were apprehended in Pont-Saint-Esprit, among them a suspect fitting Cutz's description. Despite his vehement denials, an Irish officer in Montrevel's entourage recognized him from England. Ultimately, two of the detainees were released, while three, including the alleged Cutz, underwent interrogation and torture before Cutz's eventual release. Another alarming report concerning Sieur de Lubières, former governor of Orange, causes Montrevel to live in anguish once again.

On the 1st of September, a dramatic arrest unfolded in Pont-Saint-Esprit, capturing five individuals including a cleric and a local Catholic from Nîmes, leading to the detention of two significant figures. Saurin-

Jonquet, a 33-year-old Protestant from The Hague with a military background in the Galoy regiment and subsequent service to England, found himself entangled in clandestine operations. He was the recipient of a covert communication from Clignières, representing Sieur Van der Ruisen, extending support from the Dutch and the Queen of England to the Camisard rebels. Their request was specific: an accurate assessment of the rebels' strength, preservation of religious edifices and personnel, and upholding of the Protestant faith. Parallel missions were entrusted to others, including Jean Peytaud, a 48-year-old native of Boucoiran with three decades away from home, who transitioned from cavalry service to a lieutenant's role in the Mirmand regiment. Peytaud had the privilege of meeting Heinsius, the grand pensionnaire of Holland, who assured them of support in case of arrest. The mission extended to Louis Teissèdre, aka La Roque, Théophile Vignaud, Antoine Fontanes, Sallien (or Saillens), and Antoine Peytaud, culminating in a strategic assembly on 9 June. They were to assume military ranks, with Jonquet, sidelined by illness, remaining in Geneva. Three agents—both Peytauds and Teissèdre—proceeded to Vivarais for reconnaissance. The Camisards' reputation preceded them, branded as murderers by locals. An ensuing arrest in Privas saw Teissèdre's death during an attempted escape, while Antoine Peytaud managed a narrow escape. Saurin-Jonquet, having departed Geneva, found himself arrested on the 8th of September. Alongside Jean Peytaud, who faced a similar fate, both were subjected to intense interrogation by Bâville in Ales. Under pressure and manipulation, they disclosed the whereabouts of Vilette and provided details on La Farelle, the woman responsible for supplying a passport, as well as a pastor named Olivier. The directives from the Allies were clear: gather intelligence, supply arms and ammunition, explore the feasibility of a coastal raid in Languedoc, incite action in Vivarais and Dauphiné, avoid church arson but target tax offices for destruction, and reject any offers of amnesty. Jean Peytaud implicated the Marquis de Rochegude, leading to Peytaud's death sentence and execution. Saurin-Jonquet, on the other hand, languished in the prison of Pont-Saint-Esprit until the Peace of Utrecht brought his release in 1713. Rochegude, detained for five months at Saint-Hippolyte, ultimately gained his freedom due to a lack of concrete evidence linking him to the

Camisards. This outcome proved to be a significant blow to the Refuge, as the correspondence from Arzeliers lamented the situation.

The preserved secret letters between Danckelmann and Darassus shed light on the intricate underground connections among the émigrés, the Allies, and the Camisards. Danckelmann, a Protestant noble from Brandenburg, had encountered Darassus, a refugee and recent convert, two decades prior. After a four-year sojourn in Brandenburg, Darassus departed, but Danckelmann believed his Protestant faith remained intact and confided in him. Regrettably, Darassus exploited this trust, betraying the confidences of the Elector of Brandenburg, to whom Dankelmann was allied. As a result, the royal government was alerted to their plans.

The machinations of diplomatic emissaries persisted unabated. In early October 1703, the Duke of Savoy rallied a considerable number of exiles to his cause. As Montrevel fortified the coastlines, he also redeployed troops to combat the Camisards, finding himself ensnared between two fronts: the necessity to thwart the Camisards' advance toward the coastline and the imperative to deter naval incursions. In the same month, Duke Amédée of Savoy severed diplomatic ties and his alliance with France, a strategic move that rendered the Dauphiné and Vivarais regions potential support zones for the Cévennes insurgents. The strategies previously devised by Mirmand and Miremont were revisited, envisaging that the Waldensian militia from Wurtenberg would aid the Duke of Savoy, thereby engaging French forces in Piedmont, while a contingent of 8,000 to 10,000 troops would unite with the forces in the Cévennes. Although Pastor Arnaud and Hill were privy to these plans, funding reluctance from the Netherlands and England posed a hurdle, and by 9 October, France exerted pressure on Switzerland.

The enthusiasm of Holland and England waned, leaving the refugees to face the repercussions. The initiative proved to be largely tokenistic. Montrevel received commands to dispatch eight battalions and a dragoon regiment from Gévaudan to Dauphiné, bolstering Vendôme, who had made strides into Piedmont to strategically encircle the Duke of Savoy. Confidential informants heralded the approach of 45 English vessels to the Mediterranean. An influx of three thousand troops was anticipated in Dauphiné, accompanied by arms and financial aid.

The strategic landscape in 1704 showed marked improvement over the previous year, according to a circulated pamphlet. Admiral Showell's reconnaissance revealed the Languedoc coast was more accessible to naval forces than had been previously assessed.

On 25 May 1704, Tobie Rocayrol, a merchant from Lyon and agent for the British embassy in Turin, alongside Pastor Sagnol de La Croix, embarked on a mission to Languedoc. They navigated through Nîmes, engaging with Camisard leaders Rolland, Joani, and Castanet, whose morale had been bolstered by David Flotard and his secretaries, Elie Marion and César Malplech or Malplet, sons of the former pastor of Chamborigaud. Rocayrol conveyed a crucial message from La Bourlie, revealing plans for two English frigates and tartanes to sail from Villefranche, carrying 500 soldiers and vital ammunition. These were to make landfall near Aigues-Mortes or Agde, signalled by smoke by day and fires by night, indicating the Camisards' location while ostensibly transporting salt to the Duke of Savoy. In light of Cavalier's negotiations with Villars, Montrevel's successor, the Camisard leaders resolved to persevere without him. Rolland, sequestered in his mountain refuge, faced challenges descending to the plains due to Villars' strategic measures. Despite this, he dispatched an emissary to dissuade Ravanel and Catinat from aligning with Cavalier's course. Bâville's vigilant efforts in Avignon led to the arrest of several individuals, including Rouvière, dispatched by a refugee pastor to encourage Cavalier to hold firm and converge with 3,000 Protestant allies from Dauphiné. Among those apprehended was also a carrier of encrypted communication, captured on the ferry from Avignon to Villeneuve.

By the time of Rocayrol's arrival, the French court had already taken measures to obstruct all correspondence, leaving the Camisard movement isolated. Despite a contribution of 100 gold louis from Flotard, the support arrived too late to sustain the insurrection, which could have been decisively supported earlier. The Allies' efforts, though well-meaning, ultimately only extended the conflict through a combination of promises and half-measures.

In the aftermath, the Allies began planning a coordinated intervention, but their efforts were marked by indecision and a lack of resources.

Reports emerged of five English frigates departing Villefranche with three tartanes, but their destination, whether Languedoc or Portugal, remained uncertain. Since a failed attempt in September 1703, subsequent plans lacked both financial backing and a unified strategy. Refugees such as La Bourlie, Miremont, and Belcastel had numerous plans, yet urgency was required as negotiations between Villars and Cavalier were advancing. By late May 1704, communications indicated a split between Cavalier and Rolland, and soon after, hostilities resumed. Meanwhile, the Prince of Monaco alerted the French court to the arrival of 45 refugee officers in Nice, bolstering the forces there. In response, Louis XIV directed Villars to prepare for a potential Anglo-Dutch raid on Provence's coasts, leading to the landing of arms and equipment at Villefranche. With additional English reinforcements arriving, La Bourlie's plan, supported by a financial injection of 3,000 gold louis, was set into motion, with Hill in Nice responsible for its execution.

The execution of the project, despite extensive planning, was hasty and faced significant challenges from the outset. On June 20th, when Hill convened the refugee officers in Nice, the gravity of their situation became apparent. The prospect of capture and execution by royal forces deterred many from participating, reflecting the perilous stakes involved. The composition of the troops, a mix of mercenaries, adventurers, and devout religionists, lacked cohesion and shared purpose, further undermining the operation's integrity. The incongruity within the ranks, highlighted by the presence of a defrocked Benedictine among Protestants, sowed discomfort and mistrust. Leadership under Sieur de Meirol and Sieur de Portes wavered due to a lack of conviction and the logistical hurdle of insufficient funds to settle outstanding balances and repay merchant financiers. An initial naval engagement involving one of the ships destined for Villefranche ended inconclusively after a skirmish with three French galleys. For Hill, it was a desperate attempt.

In a bid to monitor the expected flotilla, the Camisard leadership dispatched their forces, disguised as harvesters, to the coastline and the Camargue to rally a cavalry contingent. However, the vigilant oversight by Villars and Bâville, who scrutinised the harvesters and apprehended several Camisards, rendered the operation unfeasible.

Nevertheless, on 24 June 1704, between eight and nine o'clock in the evening, the five English frigates and three tartans set sail in favourable winds, taking 510 soldiers with them. However, their departure was almost immediately marred by an encounter with three French ships under the command of Rouvray. This unforeseen confrontation forced the fleet to retreat to port, but a break in the weather allowed for a second attempt at departure. The French, hindered by the weather and tactical challenges, failed to maintain pursuit, with Roanès's galley notably unable to continue the chase. However, on 25 June, bad weather forced the captains of the tartanes to cut the rope that allowed them to be towed by the frigates. On the 27th these tartanes reached Corsica and disappeared. Despite efforts to regroup, involving a search through Corsica, San Remo, and a return to Villefranche, the mission was ultimately deemed a failure.

In the aftermath, the Camisard leaders, now in exile, grappled with concerns for their homeland and the daunting prospect of reigniting their resistance. Despite the operation's failure, subsidies continued to find their way to Languedoc, facilitated by figures such as Hill and d'Arzeliers, albeit diminished by opportunistic intermediaries. By the end of 1704, a glimmer of resilience emerged as Abdias Maurel, known as Catinat, alongside other determined individuals, made their way back to the Midi.

The years between 1705 and 1710 were marked by a series of ill-fated ventures by the alliance, driven by fervent religious factions and disillusioned émigrés. They aimed to reignite conflict within France, courting disenchanted Catholics and leveraging internal discontent. A notable scheme during this period was the so-called League of the Children of God. Orchestrated by individuals such as Noah Vialas, a Protestant from Geneva, and an officer named Belcastel from England, the conspiracy aimed to seize control of Nîmes and Montpellier unexpectedly in 1705. The audacious plan involved capturing key figures like Bâville and Berwick, the latter succeeding Villars, executing Bâville, and delivering the rest to waiting English vessels at Sète. This required a force of 10,000 men. However, the plot was exposed, leading to a slew of arrests and executions, much to the dismay of figures like the Marquis de Miremont and La Bourlie. Subsequent attempts by Ravanel, Catinat, and another by Abraham Mazel in 1709, similarly culminated in failure and the deaths of their leaders. In a turn towards reconciliation, Berwick offered an amnesty.

Amid these turbulent times, in early 1706, Cavalier formed an infantry regiment with ambitions of making landings in the west or south of France, yet none bore fruit. On April 25, 1707, an endeavour to infiltrate France through Catalonia saw Cavalier's Camisard regiment suffer heavy losses at Almansa, leaving him injured.[67] Cavalier later participated in a doomed expedition by the Duke of Savoy against Toulon, which also ended in failure.

On the 24th of July 1710, an impressive fleet comprising 26 English and Dutch warships, led by Admiral Sir John Norris, executed a strategic landing of 2,000 troops on the shores of what is now known as Sète's Lazaret. Commanded by M. De Seissan of Béziers, a Catholic who had aligned with the British army, this force quickly took control of Sète and proceeded towards Agde, catching the French authorities off guard. In response, Bâville and the Duc de Roquelaure mobilised a modest contingent to confront the invaders, marching towards Frontignan, Balaruc, and Mèze. Concurrently, the Duc de Noailles, the commander in Roussillon, rallied 1,000 grenadiers, 900 cavalrymen, and 12 cannons from Le Boulou towards Agde. A significant engagement unfolded on the outskirts of Sète on the 29th of July, after which the English forces decided to withdraw, leaving behind 100 casualties and 160 prisoners. Remarkably, this incursion was marked by its lack of violence or looting, with the English promptly releasing the captured prisoners. Was this an attempt to join forces with the Camisards, who were now just a handful on the verge of extinction? Not very likely, especially as Seissan claimed to have created a diversion, arresting Noailles and facilitating Archduke Charles' victory over King Philip of Spain at Lérida. Notably, the Midi Protestants remained undeterred by these events.

The War of Spanish Succession drew to a close with the signing of the Treaty of Utrecht in 1713. Queen Anne of England intervened, requesting

---

[67] With the French forces commanded by the Duke of Berwick and the Anglo-Dutch forces commanded by a French leader, this was 'probably the only battle in history in which the English troops were commanded by a Frenchman and the French by an Englishman' [after Henry Morse Stephens and James Fitzjames, Dictionary of National Biography, London: Smith, Elder and Co, 1885-1900].

King Louis XIV to grant clemency to 136 galley slaves imprisoned on religious grounds. Heeding this request, Louis XIV pardoned the prisoners, who were subsequently exiled to England.

CHAPTER 8

SECRET NEGOCIATIONS AND THE WAR OF THE GRAND ALLIANCE (1692-1697)

This period should be seen in the context of the war of the League of Augsburg. During this era, King Louis XIV of France found himself somewhat isolated as he faced a formidable coalition led by William III of Orange, who held dual titles as the Stadtholder of Holland and the King of England. For William III to be universally recognised in his roles, it was imperative for Louis XIV to acknowledge the 1688 English Revolution and cease his support for James II Stuart. French historians François Bluche and Lucien Bély have characterised this conflict as largely psychological, highlighting how William III strategically leveraged the Huguenots within France and the widespread distribution of pamphlets to an unprecedented extent. This period marked a significant shift in diplomatic strategies, as secret agents operating on behalf of both sides played instrumental roles in the manipulation of public sentiment and political manoeuvring, culminating in the Treaty of Ryswick in 1697.

I. Jacobite Machinations (1692).

During his exile, James II maintained a cadre of loyalists within England. In 1692, Jacobite forces mobilised regiments in Lancashire under the direction of an operative named Parker. Collaboratively, Louis XIV, along with Minister of the Navy Pontchartrain and James II, formulated a strategy aiming for an Anglo-French incursion directly into England—leveraging perceived disenchantment with William III—rather than Ireland as previously attempted.

Simultaneously, France exercised caution. In that same year, French officials apprehended Jones Simpson, a Scottish rogue playing both sides, who had ingratiated himself with the Jacobite movement. The chief of police, La Reynie, documented the arrest on 19 March 1692 and proceeded to the Bastille alongside Abbé Eusèbe Renaudot. Renaudot, a proprietor of the Gazette and a fluent English speaker, was instrumental in interrogations involving secret operations and oversaw the spy network operating in England for France. Simpson then provided "a very long account in Latin of what he has done since the revolution in the affairs of England, but which can be reduced, in substance, to a few marks of his zeal for the King of England, his master, which he says he has given with others, his faithful servants, on other journeys he says he has made for that purpose in France."[68] He also states that he comes from the supporters of King James, "whom he says are more numerous than is thought in England."[69] In the end, the Jacobites know better than to deal directly with King James II, for St. Germain, we know, is a veritable nest of spies. Simpson said that he would therefore prefer to speak to the French minister to find out "whether the King would like to make a raid in England or suffer one to be made by another prince."[70] The investigators asked him what proposals he had, but he replied that he had none, but only wished to know whether Louis XIV wanted "to make a treaty or not with his friends who had sent him."[71] His overtures raised suspicions, yet the French government capitalised on Simpson for their clandestine missions. However, the failed naval engagement at La Hougue in 1692, culminating in the loss of fifteen French vessels, marked the cessation of these particular schemes.

Enticing English and Scottish Officers to the Jacobites Cause:

In 1693, Camille d'Hostun de La Baume, the Count of Tallard (1652-1728), was appointed by Louis XIV's cabinet as the ambassador extraordinary to London. Embarking on this mission, Tallard was not merely a distinguished figure transitioning into diplomacy; he was a

---

[68] François-Albert Duffo, *Lettres inédites de l'abbé E. Renaudot au ministre J.-B. Colbert* (Années 1692 à 1706) Lettres inédites de J.-B. Racine à l'abbé E. Renaudot (Années 1699 et 1700) (1931)
[69] *Ibid.*
[70] *Ibid.*
[71] *Ibid.*

consummate double agent, tasked with navigating the intricate webs of espionage that spanned the courts of Versailles, Saint-Germain, London, and Amsterdam. His military career, initiated among English gendarmes within the French gendarmerie, provided him with fluent English skills and close ties to British military figures who had deserted following the 1688 revolution. The Count of Tallard was therefore well aware of the spy business. Tallard's ambassadorship coincided with the political ascension of Earl Robert Harley, initially a Whig party member who had sided with William of Orange before switching to the Tory party for higher political aspirations, assisted by a secretary. Harley's activities attracted the attention of French operatives, including an individual named Mesnager and a physician known as Helvétius. Tallard's intimate familiarity with English Catholic aristocrats, cultivated during his military service and subsequent engagements in London, positioned him as a pivotal figure in these espionage dynamics, which he regularly reported back to the French crown. In fact, as we shall see in the 1710s, it was this backdrop of political and intelligence manoeuvring that set the stage for the Count of Tallard's protected status amidst the tumult of the War of the Spanish Succession. From his early interactions with English gentry to his diplomatic endeavours in London, Tallard epitomised the archetype of a military man adeptly transformed into an influential diplomat and spy.

II. The Marlborough affair and the Fiasco of the Bay of Camaret (1694).

Historian Eveline Cruickshanks[72] posits Jacobitism as a blend of conspiracy and ideology. Anchored in the aspirations for James II's restoration, Jacobites clung to the hope and nostalgia for a lost legitimacy, making conspiracy an intrinsic element of their movement. This entailed extensive and clandestine organisational efforts to orchestrate their attempts at restoration post-1692.

---

[72] Eveline Cruickshanks (ed.), *Ideology and Conspiracy: Aspects of Jacobitism 1689 - 1759*, Edinburgh, 1982.

William III, on the other hand, expanded his influence network, facing challenges in monitoring the myriad activities across Europe. He confronted both whimsical schemes and tangible conspiracies, navigating through the unreliable and precarious nature of intelligence sources. Lord Portland, William's confidant, established an anti-Jacobite network post-1688 but struggled to enlist capable agents, with Jones Simpson exemplifying the mediocrity of recruits. This period was marked by ministers' shortsightedness and their offices' inability to retain crucial intelligence.

John Churchill, Earl of Marlborough, found himself ensnared in the intricate web of intelligence and espionage during the era. Despite his alignment with William III in 1691, his continued communications with the Jacobites led to his arrest for treason in 1692. Yet, by 1694, Anglo-Dutch forces targeted Brest, aiming for a significant military advantage. Vauban, dispatched by the French government—likely alerted by an unidentified informant—successfully repelled the Anglo-Dutch troops at Camaret on the Crozon peninsula on June 18, 1694, inflicting heavy casualties. Marlborough, implicated once again for allegedly informing James II of the impending attack in May of that same year, is associated with the contentious *Camaret Bay letter*, purportedly urging secrecy to James II with only his wife, Mary of Modena, to be informed. In fact, as we have said, Marlborough had enemies in Parliament, some of whom displayed eagerness for his downfall. He was exonerated soon afterwards, for not only did the French seem to have been warned through other channels, but Marlborough retained command of British forces on the Continent, with which he won many victories over Louis XIV. Winston Churchill himself later considered the letter to be a forgery. However, ultimately Marlborough did not escape his enemies, falling victim to a Whig plot in the 1710s.

III. Assassination plots (1695-1696).

1695: A spy is imprisoned for trying to kill William of Orange, but the investigation reveals that he is working for both countries at the same time. He would kill anyone if they gave him money. Louis XIV cannot let this dangerous man go free (after a Bastille prisoner, "Constantin").

Jean Alexandre Van der Burg entered the Bastille in 1695. He had served twenty-five years in the king's armies, was a cavalry captain and received a pension. According to the police, he killed a peasant and had to leave the kingdom. In Holland, he slipped into the entourage of William III, the leader of the coalition against France. He suggested to Barbezieux, Secretary of State for War, that the King of England should be killed, which led him to the Bastille at the behest of Louis XIV, whose "greatness and probity" never allowed him to use "similar means to get rid of his enemies." In a report in 1714, d'Argenson noted "his inclination to betray both parties and to take credit for the most execrable attacks." He was not released until 1715.

Parallel to Van der Burg's narrative, the Jacobite faction harboured its own dark ambitions against William III, viewing him as a usurper whose throne was seized by force. Despite the era's conventions eschewing violence against sovereigns, plans to eliminate William materialised early on, with the imprisoned agent Simpson admitting to such designs in 1690. Further attempts were made in 1692, culminating in the execution of the agent Sieur de Grandval, who implicated not only French officials but James II and Colonel Parker in the conspiracy. In 1693, a proposal was made to James II to kidnap him, and it was another affair that took place shortly afterwards, in 1696, that brought these clandestine efforts to light.

In that tumultuous year, amidst the unyielding conflict with Louis XIV's France, England and Holland found themselves at a critical juncture. Louis XIV seized this opportunity, urging the Jacobites to instigate an uprising. However, the Jacobite efforts in England, under the direction of Sir John Fenwick, suffered from ineffective leadership. Fenwick's inability to sustain a prolonged armed resistance led James II, from his exile in Saint-Germain, to appoint Sir George Barclay as his successor. Barclay, a loyal officer to James II, was charged with the recruitment of soldiers within England and established an extensive network in London for this purpose. He held a secret commission from James II, couched in deliberately ambiguous terms, empowering his adherents to take over strongholds and engage in various hostile actions against the reigning William III. This cautious phrasing reflected James

II's reluctance to overtly endorse violence, even if his directives suggested otherwise.

Captain John Parker, previously of the Duke of Monmouth's regiment in France, emerged as a notable figure in the clandestine struggles against William. Elevated to lieutenant-colonel in the cavalry at St Germain, Parker bore injuries from the Battle of the Boyne, where he had accompanied James to Ireland. His undertakings, often shrouded in controversy, were driven by an unwavering sense of loyalty and honour, as noted by his great-nephew Onslow: "He never shrank from any attempt, however futile and even reprehensible, in the service of his king, being inhabited by a strange notion of loyalty and honour." Despite being apprehended in London on charges of plotting William's assassination—an allegation seemingly contradicted by his presence at a public bowling game—he managed to escape, only to be arrested and then escape once more, even as a substantial bounty of £400 hung over him. In a twist of fate, during a visit to London with the Duke of Berwick in the fall of 1696, Parker found himself betrayed by Berwick's mother, Arabella Churchill, possibly in an attempt to distance her son from the conspiracy. Once again, Parker fled to France, where his actions were met with disapproval from James and the Duke of Berwick

The latter, in his Memoirs, wrote: "Barkley, whom I saw three days after my arrival, confided in me, and although I was not as confident as he in the success of the affair, I did not feel obliged, in honour, to dissuade him.... Barclay saved himself, and if I had delayed my departure from London I should have run a great risk."

By 1698, Parker found himself under suspicion once more for his alleged presence in London on conspiratorial activities, though the subsequent legal actions failed to secure a conviction. Following James's death, Parker openly discussed his role in various plots, much to the dismay of James's widow. Her complaints led to Louis XIV ordering Parker's imprisonment in the Bastille, where he spent two years before being released with restrictions to reside in Châlons, away from St-Germain. Disenchanted with his Jacobite endeavours, Parker sought a new role under Queen Anne through the mediation of his wife, Marie Millenges, and English agent Caillaud. Despite authorisation to return to

St. Germain and remarrying Anne Balustrode on 10 September 1711, Parker's final years were marked by financial hardship. In a letter from 30 September 1716, he lamented his poverty and reaffirmed his unwavering loyalty to the Pretender through the Duke of Mar and the Chevalier de Saint-Georges.

In early 1696, as influence operations resumed and French forces poised themselves for departure from Calais and Boulogne, a separate faction plotted an audacious attack against William III, targeting him during a hunt in Richmond Park. This plot, known as the "Assassination Plot," was to precipitate a widespread revolt.

Entrusted with overseeing these plans was the Duke of Berwick, a son born to James II and his mistress Arabella Churchill. Berwick's clandestine journey to England was unimpeded, and upon meeting with the conspirators, he was led to believe the aim was to abduct, not kill, William—a deception to mask their true intentions. Despite the risks, Berwick seized the opportunity to visit his mother before returning to France to report to Louis XIV. Before leaving to prepare for the landing, he pledged to serve as ambassador extraordinary should his father reclaim the throne. In his later years, elevated to a Marshal of France, Berwick reflected on these events in his Memoirs, explicitly denying any intention to assassinate William. Nonetheless, the extent of Louis XIV's and James II's desires for Berwick's involvement in such a dire plot remains a matter of historical speculation.

Unfortunately, in the twilight of their plotting, the conspirators, poised for action, were apprehended or met their demise. The investigation, spearheaded by William himself, unearthed further participants in the intricate schemes aiming to restore the monarchy.

Among them was Sir John Fenwick, who attempted to extricate himself by casting aspersions on English ministers, thereby revealing internal rivalries within the Whig party. His defence strategy, however, sealed his fate, leading to his execution. The peace treaties of 1697, marking the conclusion of the War of the League of Augsburg, hinged on Louis XIV's formal acknowledgment of William III as the legitimate King of England. This acknowledgment essentially served as an admission of the 1688 revolution's legitimacy. Notably, English diplomats subtly suggested Louis XIV's complicity in assassination plots against William.

To understand what was happening in 1696, we have to go back to the Protestant spy networks set up by Etienne Caillaud in 1689. These networks were instrumental in intercepting the correspondence of Berwick, showcasing the tangible dangers spies faced, with many being captured and hanged by French authorities. As negotiations for the Treaty of Ryswick gained momentum, French Protestants sought to enter discussions with Louis XIV, hoping for concessions or recognition. Despite their efforts and the perilous work of their spies, their appeals were ultimately disregarded, leaving them active but unacknowledged as the treaty was finalised by the end of 1696.

IV. The Treaty of Ryswick but the Struggle Continues (1697).

The Treaty of Ryswick, signed on 4 February 1697, marked the conclusion of the War of the League of Augsburg. It was a negotiation among French plenipotentiaries (Callières, Harlay de Bonneuil, and Verjus de Crécy), the Dutch, and the English. While the Habsburg emperor preferred to continue the hostilities, both William III of England and Louis XIV of France were inclined towards peace.

William was accompanied by his right-hand man, William Bentick, the 1st Earl of Portland. Of Dutch origin, Bentick had previously undertaken several diplomatic missions, some of them confidential, to the English kings Charles II and James II. He acted as an intermediary between Holland and the English conspirators, and advised William after the landing at Torbay (5 November 1688). For his actions during the Glorious Revolution, he earned his title of 1st Earl of Portland. Despite his fervent opposition to Louis XIV during the War of the League of Augsburg and his dedication to his sovereign, Bentick's intense zeal rendered him somewhat unpopular.

William Bentick, tasked with gauging Louis XIV's commitment to peace, hailed the French monarch as the preeminent ruler of his era during their discussions. He secured an assurance from Louis that he would refrain from engaging in conspiracies against William. William, for his part, made his agreement to the peace contingent upon the concurrence of other parties, a stance that Louis leveraged to renege on prior concessions. The peace, formalised in October 1697, was celebrated in England as it signified the global acknowledgment of the 1688 revolution, yet it was met with disdain in France, where ceding what was deemed the "true King of England" was seen as a disgrace.

As for the Protestant spies in France, they seemed abandoned to their fate by the foreign powers. The latter, forgetting the double collaboration of the French Protestants, abandoned them to their fate. Although the French Protestants were dropped by William III at the time of the Peace of Ryswick (1697), they continued to serve England in the fight against Louis XIV. And they still used the same means: espionage and insurrection. In 1698, Blancard's intelligence agency was still in operation, and Caillaud's lasted until 1722, demonstrating that intelligence and espionage remained long-term activities.

Bribing Plenipotentiaries:

But it is also through financial data that we are able to paint a picture of another kind of shadow war, that of secret gratuities and subsidies. These seem to have been very active between 1697 and 1699. While the war may have drained the state's treasury, the funds allocated for these undercover financial operations, although substantial, represented a smaller fraction of the overall financial expenditure.

The Franco-British rivalry extended its reach into the courts of Europe, most notably in Sweden, where financial incentives played a crucial role in swaying influential figures.[73] Despite the challenge of tracing these transactions today due to the deliberate obfuscation by involved parties, certain actions hint at the exchange of money for political favours.

The autonomy afforded to specific ministers catalysed acts of betrayal, shifts in allegiance, and the acceptance of bribes. This dynamic was

---

[73] Charles XII of Sweden had devised a plan to support the Pretender, his cousin Germain, and to dethrone George I. To this end, George I met with the Count of Sparre, the Swedish ambassador, in a cottage in the Bois de Boulogne. Charles XII's death in battle put an end to this conspiracy.

notably exemplified in Sweden through the figures of Chancellor Oxenstierna and Count Nils Bielke (1644-1716), Governor of Pomerania. Both wielded considerable influence, deploying agents and familial networks to champion their respective causes. Oxenstierna, in particular, was instrumental in advising the London court on engaging Swedish diplomats Gyldenstolpe and Akerhielm. Amidst this backdrop of political manoeuvring, France and William III of England expended substantial sums in efforts to sway these key players, albeit with divergent objectives. London sought to extricate Sweden from French influence through Oxenstierna, while Louis XIV aimed for him to continue as a mediator. Notably, Oxenstierna and his spouse were persuaded with precious jewellery from Louis XIV, while the Swedish minister Wrede accepted watches from William III. Gyldenstolpe, dubbed "the Fox," navigated these overtures adeptly, justifying his acceptance of gifts from both realms by invoking Sweden's state interests and the fluid nature of political allegiances.

The undercurrents of the financial intelligence war were deeply intertwined with the diverse backgrounds of the politicians involved. The consolidation of Louis XIV's dominion over his territories simultaneously enriched the monarchy at the expense of the aristocracy, significantly diminishing the wealth and influence of the high nobility. This economic stratification was exemplified by figures such as Gyldenstolpe, who found himself ensnared in debt, and Bielke, a Swedish plenipotentiary who indulged in an opulent lifestyle. Similarly, Oxenstierna was burdened with the financial upkeep of a large family across his extensive lands and residences. In certain instances, entire courts were swayed with substantial sums, a strategy employed in July 1712 when the court of the Elector of Brandenburg was enticed with an offer ranging from two hundred to three hundred thousand pounds, because in Berlin it was the ministers themselves who were bought.[74] This was a period when direct financial incentives were utilised to secure the loyalty of ministers within a court. Such transactions enabled some to leverage their newfound wealth for social ascension, as seen with Jean Gaspard Hatzel (born in 1669), the

---

[74] This situation corresponds to the time when the authority of the King of Prussia was disappearing from the country.

royal syndic of Strasbourg, who utilised his financial gains as a springboard towards ennoblement.

In England, the 1st Earl of Strafford, Thomas Wentworth, experienced financial duress, leading to his involvement in negotiations overseen by the French minister Torcy, which included discussions over territorial exchanges for sixty thousand pistols related to Bavaria. Strafford received the proposal with indifference, and took the opportunity to ask for an even greater sum.

The French ambassador to London, Duc d'Aumont, undertook covert operations to support the Pretender. John Hay of Haystoun relayed in a detailed letter the negotiations between the Duke and his contacts, revealing a reluctance from d'Aumont to fully meet a financial demand, a decision criticised given the plan's significance. This operation, involving forty-seven individuals, ultimately did not proceed as intended.

This episode is illustrative of a broader context where corruption was not only widespread but normalised within diplomatic circles. It was a period where diplomats were routinely engaged in financial negotiations for political leverage or vital intelligence: "The peace [of Ryswick] was to be attributed to the 17 million which had been distributed in London to win the minds of those who had the most influence over the reigning princess [Anne Stuart]."[75]

---

[75] Correspondence between Baron Karg von Bebenburg, Chancellor of the Prince-Bishop of Liège, and Cardinal Paolucci, Secretary of State, 1700-1719: 1712-1719, Institut historique belge de Rome, 1968, 1364 pages.

CHAPTER 9

THE WAR OF SPANISH SUCCESSION (1699-1702)

In 1697 at Ryswick, Louis XIV acknowledged the Glorious Revolution, thus legitimising the reign of William III and his wife, Mary. However, while accepting the revolution was one matter, accepting the succession was a wholly different one. This is exactly what England did until the Treaty of Utrecht. In 1701, the *Act of Settlement* imposed the Hanover dynasty, with Electress Sophie. The death of James II upset all these plans, as Louis XIV recognised his son as King of England.

To ensure internal stability and maintain the allegiance of its subjects and European nations, England imposed an oath on parliament members, clergy, and universities, among others. Despite initial lack of opposition from Holland and the Emperor, the political scene shifted with the death of William III in 1702, leading to Anne Stuart's ascension to the throne with parliamentary support.

England's quest for stability continued with the Regency Act of 1706 and the Act of Union in 1707, further consolidating the nation's political framework. The Dutch were enlisted to support the Protestant succession, if necessary, by military means, culminating in the "Treaty of the Barrier" in 1709, which established a "barrier" for defence.

The 1710s were a challenging decade for France, marked by significant military setbacks on the continental stage. The prolonged conflict and its demands on resources strained Louis XIV's capacity to sustain support for the Pretender, James III. The culmination of these challenges was evident in 1714 when George I ascended the British throne, his succession ratified by Parliament without formal opposition.

All these events were supported by the fervent operations of diplomatic and espionage networks.

I. Geopolitical Espionage (1699-1701).

Espionage operations throughout Europe often involved individuals who, while not formally part of established networks, operated on the fringes or were coerced into becoming double agents. Their precarious position made them especially vulnerable; once suspected of espionage, they lacked the protections afforded to more prominent figures like diplomats or trusted advisors. For these individuals, caught in the web of espionage, the consequences of discovery were severe and immediate.

An illustrative case from 1699 involved two sailors engaged in espionage who attempted to set fire to ships in a port. Upon their arrest, it became apparent that they were seen as too dangerous to be left unattended, leading to their swift incarceration (after Constantine at the Bastille).

The same year, Mathias du Wal and Marc Linch, Irish sailors who initially served James II Stuart, found themselves imprisoned after proposing to William III's ministers a plan to set French ships ablaze in Brittany's ports. When apprehended, they claimed their offer was merely a ruse to mislead, and subsequently proposed to target English ships "even though the peace was made in common."

Conversely, the French espionage efforts were orchestrated by notable yet controversial figures, exemplified by Jean-Baptiste de Poussin, a distinguished diplomat and Knight of the Orders of Saints Maurice and Lazarus. Dispatched to London as a clandestine emissary, and later to Copenhagen and Hamburg between 1701 and 1714, Poussin played a pivotal role in establishing French intelligence networks abroad. At the dawn of the 18th century, England was not heavily infiltrated by foreign agents, with Italians predominantly occupying this niche. Poussin set up an extensive network aimed at gathering intelligence within England around 1700-1701. To achieve his goals, Poussin enlisted the cooperation of Charles Davenant (whom we will talk about later) managed to eliminate passages unfavourable to France from the publication *The True Picture of a Modern Whig* (1701). Despite his alignment with the Tory party,

Poussin's activities eventually led to his expulsion from London, but he nonetheless continued to undertake significant missions across Northern Europe.

During the War of the Spanish Succession, Protestant spies notably employed insurrection as a strategic tool to further their objectives. In addition to established networks, there existed another espionage office, the details of which remain obscure, that aimed to operate in The Hague under English auspices. One of the most vivid illustrations of using insurrection as a means of espionage and political manipulation is the Camisards revolt in the Cévennes.

II. Charles Davenant (1656-1714), English Intellectual Spy for France (1701-1702).

At the dawn of the 18th century, among English intellectuals engaged in espionage, Charles Davenant stands out. An economist, Tory parliamentarian, and double agent for France, Davenant exemplifies the sort of erudite individual co-opted to disseminate slanted information on behalf of a foreign adversary, France in his case.

As the progeny of the esteemed English poet Sir William Davenant (1606-1668), Charles's academic journey commenced at Oxford, though he departed without a degree. Following in his father's footsteps, who had established a theatre, Charles took on the role of director and engaged with legal professions. His ventures extended into trade and agriculture, culminating in his election to Parliament in 1685, where he served as a legal commissioner. The exile of James II Stuart in 1688 cost him this position, yet he remained in England, endeavouring to reclaim his prior roles during the mid-1690s. In 1695, leveraging his proximity to legal spheres, Davenant devised "political arithmetic," a compendium of essays on commerce, law, and finance. His foray into the public intellectual sphere was marked by frequent critiques of the English monarchy, establishing him as a formidable figure in theoretical and literary circles.

In 1696, amidst a climate where his allies were increasingly under political scrutiny, Charles Davenant found himself isolated, confronting his critics. Initially aligned with the Tories, he soon garnered support from the Whigs, who were in William III's camp. It was at this point that Torcy,

France's Minister of Foreign Affairs, seeking to diminish England's influence in the unfolding War of the Spanish Succession, dispatched an agent to court Davenant, aiming to align him with Louis XIV's perspective. Concurrently, in 1698, Davenant realigned with the Tory party, which had secured a parliamentary victory. By 1701, cognizant of how the English revolution had adversely impacted his position and facing persistent overtures from Torcy, Davenant found himself increasingly open to French influences.

In March 1701, Charles Davenant handed over to Louis XIV's emissary, Poussin, a manuscript of his political analysis, "The True Picture of a modern Whig," which notably lacked any passages critical of France. By August 1701, this sanitised version was in circulation. Parliamentarians quickly grew suspicious of Davenant, accusing him of being on the French payroll and leaking information to serve Louis XIV's agenda. Although Poussin was exposed, he evaded capture in time, leaving Davenant's duplicity unconfirmed. To quell the growing rumours about his loyalty, Davenant ambiguously positioned his publications to avoid direct criticism of France or William III's policies, subsequently releasing two essays that rebuffed claims of French patronage. He posited himself as a neutral commentator, critiquing only the Whigs' aggressive stance. In appreciation of Davenant's contributions, Torcy, through Poussin, rewarded him with a diamond, ensuring his continued cooperation.

Louis XIV's acknowledgment of James II Stuart's son as the rightful heir to the English throne prompted William to banish Poussin, who had been closely associating with Charles Davenant. This move effectively severed Versailles' remaining ties with the English intellectual scene, significantly impacting Poussin's standing and reputation. In the wake of these developments, Davenant, labelled a "Poussineer," lost his parliamentary seat by the end of 1701. Attempting to clear his name, Davenant released "Tom Double Return'd out of the Country" early in 1702, critiquing the Whigs and distancing himself from French emissaries, aligning with Minister Torcy's new strategy of curtailing the recruitment of foreign intellectuals for France's influence campaigns.

In 1702, the succession of Queen Anne to the throne resulted in the political decline of Pembroke, a Tory MP of that era. Amidst these changes, Charles Davenant, a distinguished intellectual, secured a position within a new ministry as the secretary of a commission tasked with negotiating the union between Scotland and England. Between 1703 and 1705, he was involved in probing arms trafficking between France and the Netherlands. After fulfilling various political roles, Davenant passed away in London in 1714.

CHAPTER 10

INTERNATIONAL INTRIGUES (1702)

In their quest to reclaim power, the Jacobites established solidarity groups and influence networks across Europe. Those arriving first at Saint-Germain were marked by their escape and defeat, yet later arrivals leveraged these circumstances to their benefit. Thriving in adversity, these individuals—ranging from generals and negotiators to statesmen, bankers, and merchants—distinguished themselves in various arenas.

One such individual, Lord Melfort, James's initial minister, fell out of favour due to the mistrust of Abbé Eusèbe Renaudot, leading to his downfall. In 1702, a letter from Lord Melfort to his brother, the Duke of Perth, was intercepted by agents of William. The letter revealed well-known information that Mme de Maintenon acted as a liaison between the courts of Versailles and James II, particularly with his wife Marie de Modène. It also outlined plans for a French invasion of England. William capitalised on this intelligence, making it public to rally opposition against France. Following his disgrace, Lord Melfort was succeeded by Lord Middleton, who appeared to be engaged in his own duplicity:

> He was an atheist by profession and in effect, if there can be such a thing, at least an outspoken deist. A few months after the death of James, he went to see the Queen one morning, and as if distraught, told her that the prince had appeared to him during the night, declared with great effusion of heart that he owed his salvation to her prayers, and protested that he was a Catholic. The Queen was credulous enough to give in to her joy. Middleton made a retreat which he ended with his abjuration, and began to devote himself to the sacraments. The Queen's confidence in him knew no bounds; he governed everything at Saint-Germain. He was offered the Garter, which he refused out of modesty, but for all that his revenues from England were no less faithfully handed over to him. More than once the Scottish project, first proposed to Saint-Germain, had been rejected by him and despised by the queen he

governed. When he saw himself fully established, he gradually left devotion and gradually returned to his first way of life without any loss of credit. This time, like the previous ones, he was part of the whole secret; but, as our court entered into it effectively, he did not dare to contradict it, but he went along softly. This was the only real mentor that the queen gave to her son, the king, for the Scottish expedition.[76]

James II's demise in 1701 led to Louis XIV's swift acknowledgment of his son as James III of England, defying the commitments made at the Treaty of Ryswick in 1697. This act marked the commencement of a series of conflicts, starting with the War of the Spanish Succession and heralding a crisis era for France. William III's death in 1702 saw his daughter-in-law, Anne Stuart, ascend to the throne, aligning with the parliamentary stipulation made upon William's accession. Anne, a Protestant, was connected to the Hanover line, ensuring a continuation of Protestant monarchy.

However, from 1705 onwards, covert operations surrounding the Pretender, intensified. In this context, a French agent named Roger journeyed to Rotterdam to assess England's potential invasion plans and the condition of the Dutch forces.

By 1708, plans for a landing were in motion, yet despite being the focal point, the Pretender had little control over his destiny. As we have said, Lord Middleton was a sulphurous character, and he was soon suspected of treason. The Pretender went to visit Louis XIV at Marly on Friday 20 April. Saint-Simon attended the meeting:

> I was curious about the interview: it was a very fine day; the king, followed by everyone else, went out ahead. As he was about to descend the steps of the terrace, and we could see the courtyard of Saint-Germain at the end of this alley of perspective, which advanced slowly, Middleton alone approached the king with a very remarkable air, and kissed his thigh. The King received him graciously, spoke to him three or four times, each time looking at him fixedly, to the embarrassment of another, and then advanced down the aisle. As they drew nearer to each other, they greeted each other: then the two kings detached themselves at the same time, each from his own court, doubled their pace a little, both fairly equally, and, with the same

---

[76] Saint-Simon, *Mémoires*, T. 6, Chap. IX

equality, embraced each other closely several times. Sorrow was painted on the faces of all these poor people.[77]

These international intrigues were significantly bolstered by propaganda, adept at swaying public opinion in various nations. Between 1702 and 1709, Charles Davenant (1656-1714), a distinguished economist, politician, writer, and Tory party member, came under scrutiny for allegedly being influenced by French agents to further France's interests while divulging English secrets. His 1694 publication, "An Essay on the Ways and Means of Supplying the War," critically examined England's war financing strategies against France, ongoing since 1689. Davenant's engagement extended beyond political undertakings with Queen Anne, collaborating with Abbé Dubos, a media specialist known for his incisive critiques of England's foreign policy missteps. Both Davenant and Dubos were instrumental to Minister Torcy's strategy, with Davenant disseminating pro-French narratives during his tenure in the Netherlands as the Inspector General of Imports and Exports. His increasing significance to Torcy was further solidified when Queen Anne appointed him secretary of a commission tasked with negotiating the union between Scotland and England in September 1702. By November 1703, his publication, "An Essay on Peace Abroad and War at Home," was translated and leveraged by Abbé Dubos for press circulation under Torcy's directive.

As we have seen, spies are everywhere. A police report dated 1703 tells us that an English double agent living in Paris was secretly working with England:

We have in Paris a certain Pain, an Englishman, living in the Rue de Guénégaud, at a barber's, in the Étoile d'or, who has relations with Englishmen of the Court of Saint-Germain, who live on King William, with Halton, his physician, through whom they maintain a great correspondence with England. The King has ordered me to write to you to seek out this man and urge him to reveal to you in confidence everything he knows about this matter, assuring him that this will in no way harm him, even if he were

---

[77] *Ibid.*

involved in some evil plot, and that on the contrary, if he openly declares everything he knows, he may, by this means, find protection and reward.[78]

I. The Duke of Marlborough's Spying Priest.

On the 11th of May, 1707, an individual presenting himself as a clergyman, known in official reports as "Manicamp," was apprehended in La Fère, France. This supposed clergyman was actually Jean Albert d'Archambault, Comte de Bucquoy, born in 1650 in France and dying in 1740 in Hanover. His official record paints him as a multifaceted figure who traversed the paths of military service, monastic life as a Trappist monk, academia as a schoolmaster, and the founding of a religious order in Paris. However, his inclination towards vocal opposition against despotism soon veered towards espionage, rendering his biography elusive and his life's narrative as yet undocumented. D'Archambault's ability to seamlessly transition between diverse roles—military officer to clergyman—cast a veil of suspicion and ambiguity over his true intentions. His capture, occurring amidst his association with a company of musketeers, quickly led to accusations of espionage on behalf of the Duke of Marlborough. Consequently, he was escorted directly to the Bastille, under the scrutiny of Chancellor Phélypeaux de Pontchartrain. The French Minister of State, d'Argenson, became fascinated by the affair and himself reconstructed the life of the "Abbé de Bucquoy": "[...] He changed state according to his needs and his views; [...] he went from adventure to adventure, or, to put it more accurately, from chimaera to chimaera; thus, we can say that the story of his life is a tissue of knavery and lies."[79]

Saint-Simon, acquainted with individuals who had interacted with the circle of the Abbé de Bucquoy, recounted to Bernaville, the governor of the Bastille: "The person we are complaining about came here about four years ago, and Dom jacques remembers seeing him there under the name of Du Bucquoy."[80] Through thorough investigation, it was unveiled that the Abbé de Bucquoy was entrenched in espionage for hostile nations,

---

[78] Letter from Torcy, 20 June 1703.
[79] Ravaison, Archives de la Bastille, t. XI, p. 336.
[80] Archives de la Bastille, Bastille 10577, letter from Saint-Simon to Mme transmitted to Bernaville, quoted by Ravaison, t. XI, pp. 344-345.

engaging in duplicitous activities. He endeavoured to simultaneously convey strategic military information to both Marshal de Vendôme and Marlborough, thereby positioning himself as a staunch adversary of Louis XIV. It emerged that he was indeed harboured and shielded by a French ambassador stationed in Switzerland, who was himself critical of French policies—a fact corroborated by a dispatch from Pontchartrain.

But on 5 May 1709, Jean Albert d'Archambault escaped from the Bastille and took refuge with his protector in Switzerland, making him a key figure in the resistance to the arbitrary rule of Louis XIV. His tale, emblematic of resistance and intrigue, caught the attention of a journalist residing in the United Provinces, "Madame Dunoyer," who took upon herself the task of chronicling his adventures.

II. The Pretender: my Enemies are my Friends.

"We call an ambassador an honourable spy."[81]

While James found solace in the companionship of loyal supporters, such as the Bishop of Rochester and the notable Skelton, previously the guardian of the Tower of London and England's ambassador to France, it is imperative to delve deeper into the intricate political strategies surrounding the figure of the Pretender to the English Crown. It is accepted that to achieve political objectives, the notions of friends and enemies are useful and effective, especially in times of war, and particularly when the courts of Europe are populated by a world of spies, ambassadors and diplomats. The Pretender lived in a world of fears and hopes: Queen Anne's reign was marred by her precarious health, the political climate in London was tumultuous, and the Jacobite faction found encouragement from within the political arena, bolstered by figures sympathetic to James's cause, such as Harley and St. John.

The English Whigs, allied with the Protestants, watched the Pretender's every move at Saint-Germain, especially when he travelled. Lord Middleton was The Pretender's chief minister, and he made no secret of the fact that the spies he used were double agents:

---

[81] Hugon, Alain, *Rivalités européennes et hégémonie mondiale, XVIe - XVIIIe siècle*, Ed. Armand Colin, 2002, 202 pages.

The notice you give of the spy will be kept as secret as possible, and although the person marked has always passed for a very honest man, whether it is him or someone else will be the same, and the Archduke will know all the more.[82]

Madame de Maintenon herself deplored all the intrigues being played out at Saint-Germain, and tried to dissuade Louis XIV from getting too involved in these manoeuvres. Madame de Caylus tells us more:

> She suffers impatiently from some of the secrets they keep in their affairs, for no plans for their establishment have ever been carried out which were not as well known in England as they were imagined to be in Versailles; but this is no fault of Their Majesties: they are surrounded at Saint-Germain by people who betray them; one of the queen's ladies for whom she has shown particular benevolence, who takes from her pockets the letters that Madame de Maintenon writes to the king, copies them when the queen is asleep and sends them to England. This woman is called Madame Strickland, mother of the little Abbé Strickland, worthy heir of his mother, who sought a cardinal's hat.[83]

The year 1708 was therefore the year of the planned landing in England, and Middleton was responsible for it. His manoeuvres towards his prince and against his enemies were viewed with suspicion, and the failure of the attempt was blamed on him. Middleton was clearly regarded as a traitor. The Pretender, who suspected Middleton but had no one else to turn to, informed the French minister Torcy, who obviously benefited from Middleton's double-dealing. Torcy replied:

> I would be very unhappy to say anything against a minister whom I have always esteemed, believing him to be as loyal to Your Majesty as he is capable of serving her well. It therefore seems to the King that as Your Majesty has only this one minister, and needs him in such difficult times, it is appropriate to expect greater clarity in the advice given, and not to discard a man of confidence on the basis of such obscure insinuations.[84]

---

[82] Archives of the Ministry of Foreign Affairs, Paris, Correspondance politique, England 242, fol. 96, 30 September 1712, Châlons-sur-Marne.

[83] Madame de Caylus, *Souvenirs de Madame de Caylus,* Ed. Mercure de France, 2003, p.72

[84] Archives du ministère des Affaires étrangères, Paris, Correspondance politique, Angleterre 243, fol.68, letter from Torcy to Jacques III Stuart, 28 January 1713.

We have seen that in 1708, Marlborough (John Churchill) himself was playing a double game, having to imagine every possible scenario in order to remain at the forefront of military and political affairs. And isn't this also a family affair? We will show that the actions taken by the English general proved that he himself believed that the restoration of the Pretender was possible, and that the family affair perhaps went beyond purely political issues. Finally, we will see that, in the end, it was money that had the last word.

The correspondence between Marlborough and his nephew, Berwick (the natural son of James II and Arabella Churchill, and a general under Louis XIV) reveals a clandestine alliance amidst the military confrontations on the European continent. As Marlborough led his troops through northern France, he found himself in proximity to the French forces commanded by Berwick. Through their letters, Marlborough expressed not only familial bonds but also an assurance of his allegiance to the Pretender, suggesting a nuanced balance between personal loyalty and national interests. These communications, veiled in secrecy, highlighted Marlborough's concern over potential interception by governmental spies, particularly cautioning against frequent exchanges that might arouse suspicion: "you must not send me your trumpet often, lest it make a noise and give occasion for jealousy."[85] In the body of some letters, the Pretender was referred to as "Mr Matthews," and his mother Arabella as "Mrs Matthews." Marlborough stated that the attempt to restore the Pretender was made under his auspices, with the help of politicians, both Tories and Whigs: "We made an attempt which did not succeed."[86] Marlborough's declaration of his desire for peace prompted Berwick to relay this message to Minister Chamillart. Recognizing the importance of this communication, Chamillart utilised the information to his advantage, and the response to Berwick was crafted by the ministers orchestrating the diplomatic efforts. Despite Marlborough's deep involvement in these negotiations, he was aware of the manipulation yet continued to participate. The correspondence ceased once Berwick left the

---

[85] Legrelle, Arsène, *La Mission de M. de Rébenac à Madrid et la mort de Marie-Louise, reine d'Espagne (1688-1689)*, 1894, 154 pages.
[86] *Ibid.*

region, and the Duke of Burgundy, under Torcy's direction, took over the continuation of dialogue. Torcy observed: "The Duke of Berwick was an excellent channel for conducting these negotiations. I doubt that the Duke of Marlborough would dare to open up to you, Monseigneur, as he would have done with himself. It is easier to reveal one's weaknesses to a nephew than to a prince, whose esteem one wishes to earn, even though he is an enemy. Besides, there are things which M. de Berwick could deal with, and which it would not be appropriate for you to write about. I would hope for peace if the enemies, without changing the essentials of their plan, wanted to change the order of it."[87] Efforts to engage Marlborough persisted until 1709, involving Boufflers and the covert operative Henriquez, who aimed to negotiate based on the intelligence provided by Marlborough. The proposition of substantial financial rewards began to raise eyebrows.

The Duke of Marlborough's network was well-informed, including knowledge about François de Salignac de La Mothe-Fénelon, the Archbishop of Cambrai, who was not only a renowned man of letters but also served as a confidential advisor to the Duke of Burgundy (1651-1715). Known for his intellectual and diplomatic acumen, Fénelon was also the secret counsel for the Duc de Chevreuse and had previously been a mentor to the Duke of Burgundy during his formative years.

During the same period, Camille d'Hostun, Comte de Tallard, found himself detained in England. Previously serving as a lieutenant-general in the King's armies and as the extraordinary ambassador to London in 1693, he later commanded French troops as Marshal of France at the Battle of Blenheim, a battle marking a significant defeat for Louis XIV's forces. Following this defeat, Tallard was imprisoned in Nottingham, England, until November 1711. Throughout his captivity, he was visited by the French diplomat and explorer Aubry de la Mottraye (1674-1743), who was known for his involvement in numerous extraordinary embassies and maintained close contact with notable figures such as Mary Wortley Montagu (1689-1762), the wife of the British ambassador to the Ottoman Empire, Sir Edward Wortley-Montagu (grandson of the 1st Earl of

---

[87] *Mémoires de Monsieur de Torcy : pour servir à l'histoire des Négociations, 1757*, vol. 3, Ed. Kessinger Publishing, 2009, 276 pages.

Sandwich). Tallard's imprisonment led him to cross paths with the British minister Robert Harley, who experienced betrayal by his secretary: "He told me that Mr de Harley's second secretary had been arrested in England, his Amsterdam correspondent having discovered that, after reading them to Mr Harley, he had included in Mr de Tallard's letters to France a memorandum of the most secret information he had learned about the affairs of state." This episode not only confirmed Tallard's role as a double agent providing intelligence to the French government from within his English confinement, but also highlighted a breach within the British government itself. The discovery of this espionage in Holland indicated that Tallard's correspondence had been intercepted and scrutinised, demonstrating the reach of French espionage into the political machinations of England and beyond, all the way to Amsterdam.

III. John Drummond (1676-1742), merchant, trader and spy for King William III:

The Court of Saint-Germain, widely regarded as a hotbed of espionage, also featured agents working for a certain John Drummond, who initiated his role as a double agent in 1704. The Pretender, faced with the challenge of keeping vital information confidential, especially regarding preparations for the Scottish expedition—a matter already known to the English court—frequently found his efforts undermined by informants whose identities remained cloaked in secrecy. John Drummond was one such informant.

Drummond, a Scottish merchant and banker, ventured into politics leveraging his activities as an informant and subsequently served in the House of Commons in London from 1727 to 1742. Born into the Perthshire aristocracy through his mother Elisabeth Ramsay, daughter of Sir Gilbert Ramsay, 1st Baronet of Bamff, he embarked on a career in commerce in Holland in 1691, focusing on textiles and wool. Despite his expatriation and claims from the Dutch that he had adopted Dutch nationality, Drummond consistently affirmed his allegiance to Queen Anne. In 1697, he partnered with a Dutchman, Jan van der Heiden, to deal in luxury commodities such as coffee, chocolate, and wine. His connections expanded in 1704 during a visit to England, where he was introduced to

Harley, then Speaker of the House of Commons, by his chaplain, Dr. William Stratford.

In 1709, John Drummond's personal and professional trajectories intersected significantly when he wed Agatha Vanderbent, the sister of an Amsterdam agent connected to the Elector of Brandenburg's family. This union not only cemented Drummond's status within the affluent Dutch merchant circles but also entwined his destiny with the intricate world of espionage. Subsequently, Drummond juggled multiple ventures, developing a robust network of informants across the continent to serve the interests of Harley. In exchange, Harley secured Drummond's financial prosperity by assigning him the lucrative role of overseeing the government's tin procurement from Cornwall. Drummond's network proved particularly adept at infiltrating the court of Saint-Germain, ensuring he received regular briefings on maritime activities and port conditions. His foray into English political circles facilitated connections with key figures in the banking sector, including an influential banker named Buys, who bridged Drummond's association with the States General. Aiming for greater influence, Drummond also endeavoured to forge relationships with James Brydges, the paymaster general of the English forces, the Duke of Marlborough, and Prince Eugène, sharing a mutual appreciation for the arts with the latter. Thus, Drummond and his wife cultivated a wide-ranging network encompassing distinguished personalities and influential allies. His enterprise was characterised by a complex web of affiliations—personal, political, and financial—at a time when England and the United Provinces shared a deep connection.

By 1710, John Drummond had accumulated enough capital—specifically £5,000 from his commercial ventures—to secure a position within Parliament. His ascent coincided with the establishment of a Tory government in London, positioning him as a pivotal figure in the intelligence networks between England and the Dutch, and marking him as a principal informant for Robert Harley, 1st Earl of Oxford, and Henry St. John, Viscount Bolingbroke. The following year, Bolingbroke's entrusting of his ailing half-brother to Drummond's care in Holland served to strengthen their bond. Yet, Drummond's fate was intricately tied to Robert Harley's political ascendancy, which saw him embedded within the circle of Heinsius in the United Provinces. Tasked with a critical espionage role, Drummond was to mitigate the influence of Marlborough's loyalists. Despite his significant contributions, his sensitive role barred him from establishing a rapport with Lord Raby (Strafford), the new ambassador in The Hague. Between 1711 and 1712, Heinsius dispatched Drummond to London to promote Anglo-Dutch trade relations. During this mission, he encountered Mrs. Masham, who had succeeded the Duchess of Marlborough in the royal household. She revealed the English ministers' reluctance to strengthen ties with Holland, aiming instead to pursue peace negotiations with France.

In May 1712, John Drummond, despite the formidable reputation of his company, found himself in financial straits, facing a debt of 100,000 florins—a sum not easily dismissed. Drummond had believed his extensive network would protect him from such fiscal woes. His dual identity complicated matters further: in England, he was perceived as a Dutchman, whereas in the Netherlands, he was viewed as an Englishman. This ambiguous status even led to accusations of him being a double agent for the Stuarts. The fallout from this financial debacle was severe. Drummond's erstwhile allies could offer no assistance, leaving him abandoned by the Tories—whom he had anticipated would support his political ambitions. Ironically, Drummond's effectiveness as a spy and double agent rendered him untrustworthy as an official negotiator, forcing him to return to commercial pursuits in the Netherlands. His relationship with Strafford deteriorated, especially after 1712, making him a casualty in the political tug-of-war between Harley and Bolingbroke, despite his ambitions to advocate for the Hanoverian and Protestant cause.

To sum up, John Drummond's influence on the political landscape of the 1710s was substantial, positioning him as an essential figure in bridging the gap between financiers and politicians for the English government. As a spy and agent with a keen business acumen, he became an invaluable asset to those he served. While this account concludes in 1715, it's worth noting that Drummond pursued further ventures before his death in 1742, seemingly without financial resources.

Figure 1. James II (1633-1701), by Nicolas de Largillière, 1686.

Figure 2. Louis XIV, King of France, by Hyacinthe Rigaud.

Figure 3. 'Antoine Rossignol, maître des comptes,' in Charles Perrault's book, *Les Hommes illustres qui ont paru en France pendant ce siècle*, Paris, 1696. Anonymous engraving.

**Figure 4. King William III and his wife Queen Mary,
Engraving from R. White, Private Collection of S. Whitehead, 1703.**

Figure 5. John Wallis, by Sir Godfrey Kneller, Bt (died 1723).

Figure 6. The Château Neuf de Saint-Germain-en-Laye and its gardens, seen from the right bank of the Seine (1664 - 1665), by Adam Frans van der Meulen.

Figure 7. The White Rose of York, symbol of the Jacobites.

Figure 8. James Drummond,
2nd Duke of Perth (1674-1720) - National Galleries.

Figure 9. The Battle of the Boyne, 1 July 1690, by Jan Wyck.

Figure 10. Portrait of Queen Anne of England, in a tinted engraving from an atlas commissioned by Augustus the Strong, King of Poland and Elector of Saxony, 1707.

Figure 11. Marlborough first duke, by Godfrey Kneller, 1705.

Figure 12. James Francis Edward Stuart c.1703, attributed to Alexis Simon Belle.

Figure 13. Antoine de Guiscard (1658-1711), Private Collection.

Figure 14. Destruction of the Soleil Royal
at the Battle of La Hougue 1692, Adriaen van Diest, 1700.

Figure 15. The Abbé François Gaultier (d.1723),
by Alexis-Simon Belle (1674-1734), National Trust.

JACOB DE BUCQUOY,
Geb: te Amst: 26 Octb: 1693;
BUCQUOY des Zeemans Gids, in Wiskonst wel bedreeven
die's Waerelds kusten en zyn Reistocht heeft beschreeven.

Figure 16. Jean Albert d'Archambaud,
Count of Bucquoy, known as Abbé Bucquoy, Dutch engraving.

Figure 17. Nicolas Mesnager (1658-1714), by Hyacinthe Rigaud.

Figure 18. John Campbell, 2nd Duke of Argyll (1680-1743).

Figure 19. Depiction of the Battle of Sheriffmuir in November 1715, by John Wootton (1686-1764).

Figure 20. 'Bonnie Prince Charlie,' by John Pettie, 1893.

CHAPTER 11

NATHANIEL HOOKE (1664-1738) AND THE SCOTTISH EXPEDITION (1703-1708)

At the court of Saint-Germain-en-Laye, a confluence of royalty, espionage, and diplomatic negotiation unfolded, with figures such as Nathaniel Hooke emblematic of the numerous, albeit lesser-known, spies dedicated to the Stuart cause.

In the wake of James II's death in 1701, a period of cautious expectation ensued, marked by strategic discussions among the court's women—most notably, Mary of Modena overseeing her son the Pretender's interests while liaising with Madame de Maintenon. Prior restoration efforts were largely subdued, confined to espionage aimed at collecting valuable intelligence. The subsequent death of William III of Orange in 1702, given his lack of direct heirs, reignited Stuart hopes. The Bill of Rights (1687) had previously designated Anne as the successor due to her Protestant faith. However, Anne's lack of an heir shifted attention to Electress Sophia of Hanover, James I's granddaughter, further estranging the Stuarts from the British crown—a development that unsettled both British political factions, such as the Duke of Marlborough, and the Scottish people, who outright rejected the Hanoverian option.

Nathaniel Hooke[88] embarked on his scholarly journey at Trinity College, Dublin, in 1679, where his nascent religious inclinations veered towards Protestantism.[89] His academic pursuits led him to Glasgow in

---

[88] For the record, Nathaniel Hooke's family descended from a Norman knight who took part in the conquest of Ireland at the beginning of the 12th century.

[89] Here too, the origins of Hooke's family are significant: the character's open Protestantism originally stems from the strong links the family maintained with

1680, though he quickly transitioned to Sidney Sussex College, Cambridge, in 1681. Opting to leave Cambridge without a degree, Hooke aligned himself with Archibald Campbell, a leader of the Argyll forces, marking his entry into the tumultuous political scene of England as William of Orange began to assert his influence. Hooke's foray into espionage commenced around this period.

In the thick of the Monmouth Rebellion in 1685, Hooke disembarked with the Duke of Monmouth at Lyme Regis, assuming the role of the Duke's "personal chaplain." As Monmouth's forces pressed into Somerset in early July, Hooke, alongside Henry Danvers, was dispatched incognito to London to foment an insurrection. The rebellion's collapse saw many conspirators pardoned during the General Pardon in March 1685; however, Hooke, determined not to capitulate, was not among them. Faced with the untenability of his predicament by 1688, Hooke ultimately conceded and was granted pardon

Post-1688, Nathaniel Hooke aligned himself closely with James II Stuart, turning into one of his staunchest advocates. Following the king's deposition, Hooke ventured back to Scotland, joining forces with Viscount John Dundee to persist in the struggle. His efforts, however, led to his arrest in Chester in May 1689, culminating in a stint in the Tower of London. Come February 1690, Hooke found liberation and swiftly made his way to Ireland, integrating himself into the Jacobite army. He experienced firsthand the crushing defeat at the Battle of the Boyne. France became Hooke's refuge post-Ireland, where he assimilated into the Galmoye regiment, mingling with the Irish nobility and fellow exiles. It was during this exile that he embraced French citizenship, a strategic move allowing him legal employment, land acquisition, and, potentially, titles of nobility on par with French peers. Hooke's proficiency in French earmarked him for missions beyond military confines, dispatching him to various European courts. His journey later saw him align with the Sparre regiment, a melting pot of German soldiers and Swedish officers, and a haven for political refugees.

Cromwell's network, and then because his father (a wealthy merchant) was expelled from the Anglican Church.

In 1702, Nathaniel Hooke rekindled his ties with the Duke of Marlborough and prepared to mount a major operation in Scotland. The subsequent year marked the inception of meticulous planning by Hooke, who was concurrently appointed to a command within the Immers regiment, engaging in the War of the Spanish Succession alongside French forces in Flanders and Moselle. From 1703 onwards, Nathaniel Hooke kept up regular correspondence with clan chiefs in Scotland, the court at Saint-Germain and French secretaries of state.[90] It is this wealth of information that enables us to illustrate our comments in a factual manner and to lift the veil on the background to the preparations for the Scottish expedition.

As early as February 1703, Hooke, in a detailed memorandum to the French Foreign Minister, Marquis Colbert de Torcy, advocated for an invasion of England to reinstall the Pretender to the throne. The rationale was strategic: approaching via Scotland not only posed a direct challenge to England's northern defences but also promised to secure more favourable trading privileges for France. Following exploratory discussions with Dutch traders in Holland, the feasibility of the venture appeared promising.

At this point, the English cryptographer John Wallis was replaced as official cryptographer by William Blencowe (1683-1712). He was to serve Queen Anne by taking over the work of his predecessor. They were helped by the fact that Louis XIV, an ageing king, no longer attached much importance to the issue of intelligence. Even though the networks were still active and firmly established in Europe, missives from the King of France, which had previously been difficult to intercept, were now found and decrypted, uncovering the Stuarts' plans for restoration through the intermediary of the Jacobites. Nathaniel Hooke was to pay the price, as his attempts to intervene in Scotland were all thwarted by English intelligence services. What is more, Europe was united against Louis XIV, and he appeared to be isolated. For its part, Great Britain began its unification efforts and did everything in its power to achieve this. The balance of

---

[90] *Correspondence of Colonel N. Hooke, agent from the Court of France to the Scottish Jacobites, in the years 1703-1707* n.e, 1870, compiled by William Dunn Macray, two volumes.

power was therefore shifting, and the Jacobite cause was going to suffer more than ever.

I. <u>Nathaniel Hooke Strategy.</u>

Hooke's network expanded as agents across various locations were compensated for their contributions. Prior to embarking on direct confrontation, it was crucial to secure the success of the endeavour by fostering division between the Whigs and Tories. Moreover, engaging simultaneously against France's triple adversaries—England, the United Provinces, and Austria—would have been extremely perilous. Consequently, a delicate political strategy was employed, leveraging the capabilities of spies and agents:

- Separate the United Provinces from England and the Emperor;
- For the Tories: a return of the Pretender to the throne, in response to Hanoverian ambitions, made possible by the position of the Whigs;
- Influence Queen Anne, who had a real sympathy for Anglican culture and disliked the Whigs.

I posit that the Tories would like to reject the succession of Hanover and recall the King of England after the death of his sister, as the only means of supporting themselves against the Whigs; but that they do not dare to discover their design until they see the last faction cut down and disunited ; and that, on the other hand, the Whigs, suspecting the design of the Tories, and feeling them to be more powerful than themselves, would rather throw themselves into the arms of anyone than be under the domination of their enemies.[91]

But we also had to play the commercial game:

- To re-establish trading privileges for Scottish merchants, such as the colony of Darien in Panama (created in 1695 by William Peterson, a Scottish merchant), an operation supported by Sir MacLaine, a Scottish merchant established in the colony;

---

[91] Macray W.D. (ed.), *Correspondence of Colonel... op. cit*, Memorandum given to M. de Torcy, 18 February 1703, vil 1, p.1

- Play on the commercial disagreements between the English and the Dutch.

1. Scotland's Role:

And it's all based on a particular geographical area, Scotland:

- Taking advantage of Jacobite pretensions to land in Scotland ;
- Create a rear base for operations on British soil;
- To use the clans (most of whom were attached to the Stuarts) to make use of their strong warrior skills: "Scotland is divided into mountains and flat country. The Montagnards are robust, brave, intrepid, hardened to fatigue, living on little, always armed with rifle, shield and sword;"[92]
- Increase the sense of injustice at England's expense in terms of taxes, as war would lead to higher taxes in the Highlands;

The present state of Scotland provides an almost infallible means of putting England in the necessity of making peace or of becoming almost useless and even at the expense of the Allies. [There are two ways of using Scotland, one is to have the succession of Hanover rejected, the other is to throw in a small body of troops with the consent of the principal members of the nation who will favour their descent. [...] I am not a Scotsman, and I have no relatives in Scotland; I do not claim any part in the execution of the undertaking that could be made on that side; but having some particular knowledge of this kingdom, I am convinced that the opportunity presents itself to make the most beautiful move in the world for the service and glory of the King.[93]

2. Scottish Jacobites:

Nathaniel Hooke thus suggested deploying his covert operatives to gain comprehensive intelligence about the country. A key figure among these spies was Thomas Leviston, a French national of Scottish descent,

---

[92] MACRAY W. D. (ed.), Op. Cit, *Summary Memorandum on Scottish Affairs*, 2 February 1704, vol 1, p. 48
[93] *Ibid.*

tasked with compiling and dispatching detailed reports: "Sieur Leviston, a Scot of Scottish origin, of a family established in France since the reign of François Second and whose father, who bears the same name, now lives in the land of Sauvigny, in the bishopric of Toul, having been a page to the late Mon. The Marquis Tilladet, entered the company of cadets in Strasbourg in 1683; he was made lieutenant in the Beauvaisis regiment [...], then captain, [...] after losing the Marquis de Tilladet and the Marquis de Vielbourg, his colonel and friend, he resolved to travel, and in 1698 he went to Scotland to see the Viscount of Kilsyth."[94]

Ultimately, the Scottish forces alone would not suffice to muster the required manpower for military endeavours, necessitating significant augmentation in both material and human resources.

Yet, what distinctly emerges from Nathaniel Hooke's accounts is his disdain for the Saint-Germain-en-Laye court, a milieu where spies mingled with courtiers eager to secure wealth or even nobility. Hooke's insights, particularly valuable in this regard, reveal that the Irish who journeyed to visit James II Stuart—termed "wild geese" and numbering eight hundred and eighty—spanned a broad spectrum of social strata but shared a profound connection with the Catholic faith, a point that Hooke found jarring due to his own extreme religious convictions. Additionally, he notes that the Scots, though fewer in number at ninety-seven, were predominantly of aristocratic stock. His narrative provides a meticulous depiction of the Saint-Germain court.

Hooke's intimate understanding of court dynamics empowered him to identify key figures for alliance or appeal. An illustrative example is Lord Charles Middleton (1640-1719), the Secretary of State at the court, who managed James II's correspondence. Hooke engaged with him at an early stage, fully aware of the need to exercise caution around influential figures like the Drummond brothers, Dukes of Perth and Melfort.

The first man of importance to be sent to Scotland was Simon Fraser, 11th Lord Lovat and Marquess of Beaufort (1667-1747), who, after facing accusations of treason, regained the Stuarts' favour through Nathaniel Hooke's intervention. Financial matters were overseen by Lewis Innes

---

[94] MACRAY W. D. (ed.), Op. Cit, *Abridgment of Mr. Leviston's Memoirs*, 6 February 1704, vol 1, p. 78.

(1651-1738), Principal of the Scots College and the Queen's chaplain, and his brother, Thomas Innes (1661-1744), a historian influential in the Saint-Germain circle. The Scots aristocracy depended on the Scots College, established in 1326 to prepare future Catholic missionaries for Scotland. Likely under the Duke of Perth's aegis and harbouring archives along with a Stuart legitimacy charter dating back to the 14th century, the College was a hub of espionage and conspiracy serving the Stuart cause. Lewis Innes maintained communications with Hooke, the Scottish clergyman James Hall, and Thomas Nicholson, the Bishop of Edinburgh.

Securing allies for the Scottish expedition naturally entailed leveraging local support. The aristocracy's well-documented allegiances simplified this task, offering them a source of prestige. However, the evolving Scottish nobility landscape, with the rising prominence of the lesser nobility or Lairds, necessitated a nuanced approach. These families were strategically aligned with Scotland's influential clans, capable of financing and sustaining military forces. Anne Drummond, Countess of Erroll, hosted French operatives and clandestine agents, including Nathaniel Hooke, at her Slains Casle . Her son, Charles Hay (died 1717), who ascended to the Earldom and the title of Grand Constable of Scotland, was a fervent Jacobite, thus becoming a crucial informant.

The Gordons played a significant role too: George Gordon (1649-1716), 1st Duke of Gordon, alongside his wife and son, the Marquess of Huntly, were integral to the discussions. George's military background, including his service in France in 1675, and his steadfast Catholic faith, alongside his previous military setbacks, initially made him hesitant. Nonetheless, Hooke's persuasion in 1705 led him to commit to the cause.

William Keith, 9th Earl Marischal (1664-1712) and his wife Mary Drummond were among those who engaged with Nathaniel Hooke, welcoming him to Dunottar Castle. William's inheritance of the Marischal title of Scotland bestowed upon him the prestigious duty of ensuring the king's protection.

Another vital informant for Nathaniel Hooke was Sir George Lockhart of Carnwath (1673-1731), a well-known Jacobite figure who had a seat in the Scottish Parliament and kept his allies apprised of developments. Hooke made contact with him in 1707, uncovering his strong connection with James Hamilton, 4th Duke of Hamilton (1658-1712). Although Hamilton had previously been mentioned as not overtly supportive of the Jacobite cause, his Catholic faith and ownership of lands with Stuart-supporting populations made him a strategic ally. Hooke engaged James Hall, the Scottish priest, to facilitate this alliance. Despite the complexities of their interactions, suspicions of Hamilton's dual allegiances quickly arose.

Discussion also turns to Lord Lovat's adversary, John Murray, 1st Duke of Atholl (1660-1724), who initially championed William of Orange and held significant roles during Queen Anne's reign. His fall from grace, largely due to Lord Lovat, swayed him and the Murray clan to align with the rebellion.

Among the more obscure operatives were individuals like John Ker (née Crowford) of Kersland (1673-1726), whose duplicity earned him notoriety. Charles Flemming (died 1745), associated with the Errol family, served as an intermediary between France and Scotland starting in 1705. Other notable figures included William Johnstone, Marquess of Annandale; William Livingstone, 3rd Viscount of Kilsyth; David Murray, 5th Viscount of Stormont; and John Campbell, 1st Earl of Breadalbane, who was distinguished as the sole Jacobite among his kin.

3. The Simon Fraser Case, 11th Lord Lovat, Soldier and Double Agent:

Simon Fraser, Lord Lovat, exemplifies the quintessential Scottish aristocrat, clan leader, warrior, and scholar. Born in 1667, he was steeped in the perpetual conflict amongst the clans, a reality further underscored by his brother's death at the Battle of Killiecrankie in 1689.[95]

As the successor to his father, he soon found himself embroiled in disputes with the McKenzie and Murray clans. In a strategic move intended to precipitate an armed clash, he pledged allegiance to William III of Orange and Mary II. The situation escalated when John Murray,

---

[95] There was also a case of Protestantism in the ranks of the Jacobites, since after the battle the Earl of Dunfermline, a Protestant, had recovered the body of John Graham de Claverhouse, Viscount of Dundee (1640-1689), also a Protestant, in order to give it a decent burial (Protestants were buried at night in unconsecrated ground).

Duke of Atholl, laid claim to the Lovat title on behalf of his son, prompting Simon Fraser to take up arms against the Murray clan, a conflict that culminated in his audacious kidnapping of the clan chief's daughter, whom he later married. By September 1698, Fraser faced accusations of rebellion, leading to a relentless pursuit by Murray and government forces, resulting in the devastation of his lands. This ordeal fostered a deep-seated animosity within him, fueling his involvement in the Scottish factional strife as a formidable leader of his clansmen. Despite Archibald Campbell's (1658-1703) counsel to seek redress directly from London, Fraser's situation was further complicated when the Murrays arranged for their eldest daughter to wed Alexander McKenzie, effectively bestowing the Lord Lovat title and Simon's lands upon McKenzie. The endorsement of the Murray clan by Queen Anne in 1702 was the final straw, driving Simon Fraser to seek refuge with the Stuarts in Saint-Germain-en-Laye.

Simon Fraser's engagement in the political machinations surrounding the restoration of the Pretender saw him caught between Lord Middleton's call for patience and James Drumond, the 4th Earl of Perth's urgency for immediate action. Fraser was presented with a choice that would align him with either faction. His decision to convert to Catholicism marked his commitment to Middleton's cause, paving the way for a direct appeal to Louis XIV. His fluency in French enabled him to discuss the proposed Scottish expedition with the king, who gave his blessing and dispatched Fraser to Scotland in 1703. Subsequently, Fraser's mission extended to London, where he engaged in covert operations against James Douglas, 2nd Duke of Queensberry, (1662-1711), a supporter of the union of Scotland and England, and also to tarnish the reputation of his long-standing enemy, John Murray. By presenting documents ostensibly from Mary of Modena, James II Stuart's wife, Fraser attempted to implicate the Murray clan in insurrectionary activities. Despite the ingenuity of his ploys, Fraser's efforts bore no fruit, leading to his return to France under a new identity. The revelation of Fraser's duplicity to Louis XIV resulted in his exile to Bourges, followed by a stint in the Saumur prison for misconduct, from which he was released in 1714 through the intervention of James Fraser of Castle Leathers (1670-1760). Fraser's subsequent sojourn in London to settle his legal status—ambiguous as it was between that of a spy and a free agent—also afforded him an opportunity to gauge the evolving political landscape in England, with an eye towards exploiting it to his advantage.

The year 1715 marked the outbreak of the second Jacobite uprising, known as the Mar revolt, triggered by the Hanoverian succession to the British throne. Simon Fraser, once a staunch supporter of the Jacobite cause, dramatically shifted his allegiance to George I of Hanover, committing to mobilise his Scottish followers in support of the new regime. His action culminated on 12 November when he seized control of Inverness. After this date, which is not part of our time frame, Simon Fraser changed sides again and ended up in the Tower of London in 1747, where he was beheaded on 9 April.

The first comment that can be made about the endeavours leading up to the Jacobite uprising is that they were characterised by a lack of cohesion among its proponents. The Court of Saint-Germain, home to the exiled Stuart monarchy, was rife with internal divisions, host to a plethora of factions each with its own network of spies and informants. Moreover, the aspirations of the Scottish exiles often clashed with those remaining in Scotland. Nevertheless, Nathaniel Hooke had this to say, indicating that Louis XIV and the French government frequently circumvented the Saint-Germain court to engage directly with the Scottish cause: "If the Court of Saint-Germain continued to oppose it, the King could make use of the Scots independently of it."[96]

Make no mistake about it, the Stuarts were primarily seen as English by France, who labelled them as "the English of Saint-Germain." Despite the numerous (548, to be precise) meetings between Louis XIV and the exiled court from 1689 to 1715, scepticism regarding the feasibility of restoring the Stuarts grew within France, compounded by the considerable financial investments already made by Louis XIV in the late 17th century. Worse still, Hamilton no longer hesitates to assert that they have been forgotten.

---

[96] MACRAY W. D. (ed.), *Summary Memorandum on Scottish Affairs 2 February 1704, vol 1, Op. Cit,*, p. 48.

II. Intelligence Preparation in Scotland.

The inception of the project was facilitated through Marie de Modène, the Pretender's mother, Mme de Maintenon, and Simon Fraser, also known as Lord Lovat. It's been suggested that Lovat, rather than Nathaniel Hooke, was the driving force behind the initiative. Lovat's persuasive oration garnered support from Louis XIV, who offered him accommodations in Paris and financial backing. However, this meeting did not unfold as anticipated, much to the king's dissatisfaction. Despite this, Hooke harboured doubts about Lovat's reliability, appointing Jacques Murray as a trusted agent to assess clan support in the Highlands, including the Stewarts of Appin, Strath, the McGregors, and McLeods. Murray's investigation in the Lowlands revealed that backing for the Jacobite cause was largely nominal. Concurrently, Lovat's allegiance shifted, prompting Sir John McLean of Duart's dispatch to monitor Lovat's manoeuvres in Scotland.

By 1704, it became apparent that Lovat was primarily self-serving, focusing on his own interests and landholdings. Furthermore, he conspired against his adversary, the Murray clan's leader. This betrayal, along with the defection of other agents who actively undermined the project's preparations, signalled a significant setback for the cause.

Upon discovering Lord Lovat's duplicity and his own personal ambitions diverging from France's objectives, King Louis XIV expressed his profound and personal disappointment and frustration. The notion of orchestrating a Scottish uprising now seemed ludicrous, marred by the lack of fidelity from the involved parties. In this context, Nathaniel Hooke was compelled to recalibrate his strategies without forsaking his overarching mission.

It appears Simon Fraser, upon recognizing the Scottish clans' reluctance for rebellion, contemplated acting independently, much to the chagrin of the Saint-Germain court which concluded that the Scots were averse to taking up arms. This situation reignited old court disputes, casting Nathaniel Hooke into a maelstrom of accusations, including an alleged assassination plot against Middleton. On the British front, the situation seemed resolved with Queen Anne becoming privy to the French machinations in Scotland, thanks to Fraser's defection. Authorities were dispatched to detain and question the insurgent clan leaders, leading to the Duke of Atholl being stripped of his positions and influence at court. Hooke, witnessing the diminishing prospects of the Jacobite cause, reverted to his military obligations with the Sparre regiment, which was destined to become the Royal Swedish regiment. However, as the geopolitical landscape began to shift, a new window of opportunity emerged, breathing life back into the once-dormant scheme.

1. Scottish Strategy:

In 1704, Nathaniel Hooke rejuvenated the seemingly stalled initiative. Amidst the Sparre Regiment's engagements, Hooke kept a close watch on the political scene, noting occurrences that might favour his cause, such as the defeat at Blenheim in August and Marlborough's victories in Alsace.

Hooke returned to France in January 1705, seeking to rally political backing from Marshal de Villeroy. He observed: "The breach between Scotland and England is widening every day and the Scots are so united that the Duke of Gordon, the only lord who could dispute the command with Duke Hamilton, has made the latter say that he is ready to yield to him, and that he will join him with all his vassals, who are in large numbers, as this affair is becoming more general every day."[97]

Indeed, the English Parliament had labelled the Scots a threat to national stability, with Queen Anne assigning the Duke of Argyll as her representative in the Highlands—an appointment unpopular with the other clans.

Despite Lord Middleton's reservations about the expedition's viability, Hooke found an ally in the Duke of Perth, who affirmed the clans' readiness for uprising, albeit strictly under the leadership of the Dukes of Gordon and Hamilton. From her castle at Slaines, the Duke of Perth's sister called for military aid. An emissary was dispatched to validate these claims among the clans, which appeared genuine. Hooke thus resolved to appoint an agent to facilitate negotiations with the Scots:

---

[97] MACRAY W. D. (ed.), *Op. cit*, Mémoire donné à M. le Maréchal de Villeroy, 10 mars, 1705, vol 1, p. 158.

A man of confidence to them with precise and extensive instructions. Provided that this man knows the genius of the Scottish nation, that he has a binding and moderate spirit, that he is not prejudiced in his favour by any faction and that he seeks only the service of the King [...] and he will bring back with him to France deputies of the nation fully instructed and authorised to put the finishing touches to the treaty, on reasonable terms and which will not cost the King much.[98]

2. Nathaniel Hooke Named Emissary for Scotland:

The task of selecting a suitable envoy to venture to Scotland proved to be a complex affair. Tensions arose when the Duke of Perth discovered he was not the preferred candidate for this crucial role, leading to feelings of discontent. The individual ultimately chosen for this mission, James Carron—a Scot previously engaged in royal assignments in Scotland—presented a conundrum due to revelations about his reluctance to continue serving France. Nevertheless, he embarked on the diplomatic mission. The decision-making process was further complicated by a palpable sense of anticipation and delay; the Saint-Germain court's Stuarts awaited news from Scotland, while the Scots looked towards France for guidance.

By 1705, Nathaniel Hooke found himself reenlisted with the Sparre regiment, still awaiting a response from Torcy, the Minister of Foreign Affairs, regarding proposals for a Scottish expedition. This silence from France prompted Hooke to seek intervention from the Duke of Perth to communicate with Torcy. Eventually, it appeared that both the French government and the court at Saint-Germain leaned towards nominating Hooke himself for the mission to Scotland—a decision he approached with hesitance, given the court's reputation for leaks and the Scottish nobility's distrust: "The Highlanders are wary of us; their trust lies solely with the French court."[99]

---

[98] Ibid.
[99] Ibid. , p. 147

3. Secret Letters Relating to the Scottish Project:

From 1705 to 1708, Nathaniel Hooke was immersed in the intricate preparations for his journey to Scotland, a period marked by intense correspondence with Scottish allies. The paramount challenge was maintaining the confidentiality of the operation, amidst concerns that every letter sent was subject to interception and scrutiny. The task of ensuring the secure delivery of these letters fell to individuals like Mr. Pequet, who served as a vital conduit between Hooke and the Marquis de Torcy. The transmission of correspondence, particularly through French networks, could see a letter taking approximately five days to reach its destination.

For letters bound for Paris, a circuitous route through Rotterdam was employed, utilising merchants or bankers as unwitting postal services. Scottish correspondents addressed their letters to nondescript individuals in Rotterdam, such as "Mr. John Gordon, merchant," to obscure the true nature of their communications.

Louis XIV, recognising the importance of these covert operations, enlisted the services of M. Lefevre, the Antwerp Postmaster, to oversee the safe passage of Hooke's messages. An astonishing volume of correspondence, tallying between one hundred and twenty to one hundred and fifty letters related to the Scottish campaign, passed through Lefevre's hands. The Countess d'Errol, in her own clandestine communications with Hooke, employed lemon juice as an invisible ink, while Cardinal Gualterio's correspondence with Hooke was safeguarded through the use of a code system previously discussed, involving twenty-five code names.

The level of secrecy enveloping the Scottish mission was such that even Hooke's own wife was kept in the dark about the proceedings.

III. **Nathaniel Hooke Takes his Position in Scotland.**

In August 1705, following numerous postponements and hesitations, Nathaniel Hooke was at last dispatched to Scotland. He embarked on this critical journey equipped with an array of vital documents—including letters addressed to Scottish nobility, financial resources, and even blank passports granting him unfettered passage across borders. Additionally, he carried bills of exchange, enabling the conversion of funds into English pounds. Notably, Hooke possessed a royal commission which safeguarded him by ensuring his status as a prisoner of war, should he find himself captured at sea, for example. Hooke's orders were clear:

- Ensure Scottish motivation;
- Mobilise and arm minds;
- Confirm France's support and promise material aid;
- In this context, offer the services of training officers to discipline the Highlanders;
- Learn about Scotland's intelligence links with Ireland and England;
- Ensure that there are geographical points capable of hosting a major military undertaking;
- Ask for envoys from Scotland to come to France;
- Do not sign treaties or conventions on your own.

Upon his arrival, Hooke discovered the widespread knowledge of his mission, likely due to leaks from foreign agents at the Court of Saint-Germain. Over a month and a half, he traversed the territories of his allies, collecting crucial intelligence, notably aided by the female aristocracy whose mobility was underestimated: Lady Anne Hay Drummond, Countess of Errol; the Duchess of Gordon; and the Countess Marischal. These influential women facilitated his connections with pivotal figures, including clan chiefs.

Hooke quickly discerned the deep divisions among Scottish factions, driven by mutual distrust among the aristocracy. He confronted a harsh reality he had previously been hesitant to acknowledge: the clan chiefs' loyalty to the Stuart cause was contingent upon monetary rewards and titles. The selection of the Scottish military leader further stoked rivalries, notably the Presbyterian Duchess Anne Hamilton's opposition to her son, the Duke of Hamilton, whose appointment was contentious.

Ultimately, Hooke recognised the insurmountable challenge of unifying the clans under a single banner when personal ambitions and suspicions held sway, questioning the feasibility of rallying the troops under a leader whose authority was not universally respected.

1. James Duke of Hamilton (1658-1712), Royal Rival Pretendant to the Throne of England:

Nathaniel Hooke set out to engage with James Hamilton, the Duke of Hamilton, whom he envisioned as the commander of the Jacobite forces. Notably, Hamilton, through his lineage traced back to Mary Stuart, held a claim to the English throne. Despite Hooke's awareness of this lineage, he perhaps did not fully anticipate the complexities that would arise.

Their clandestine meeting at Holyrood House revealed significant obstacles. The Duke, burdened with considerable responsibilities, hesitated to lead a potentially losing battle that could end in his imprisonment or execution. His aspirations for the English throne, grounded in his ancestral claim, made the prospect of seizing it through military conquest an unnecessary risk when a more legitimate path might open upon Queen Anne's demise. While Hamilton expressed loyalty to the Stuart cause, his strategic patience until the Queen's death suggested a preference for legal succession over rebellion. Recognizing these complexities, Hooke concluded that involving the Duke as the military leader would be imprudent. This realisation led him to abandon the notion of Hamilton leading the Jacobite army.

2. Negotiations:

Subsequent to his deliberations, Nathaniel Hooke gained confidence in the willingness of the Scottish populace to rally for their cause, even though a leader had yet to be designated. He conducted a military assessment, revealing potential forces comprising 12,000 infantry, 5,000 cavalry, and 8,000 Highlanders. These forces, augmented by an additional 5,000 French soldiers, were poised to advance towards England. The Viscount of Stormont expressed willingness to lead the Highlanders, albeit for financial compensation. The Scottish aristocracy displayed eagerness to forge treaties with France, seeking assurances for their forthcoming operations. However, Hooke was not authorised to finalise any such agreements independently. Thus, he advocated for the dispatch of Scottish representatives to France for formal treaty signings. Consequently, the

Scottish nobility selected delegates, among whom the Earl of Panmure, the Earl Marishal, and Lord Kenmure, were to travel to France.

Hooke then journeyed to the Highlands to galvanise the aristocracy, navigating the linguistic barriers of Scots or Gaelic with varying degrees of success.[100] He managed to secure commitments from numerous clans, highlighting the feasibility of their mission, yet underscored the need for financial resources, conspicuously scarce in the Highlands. By 18 September, Hooke returned to France buoyed by the Scottish nobility's allegiance.

Reporting to Torcy on 17 October 1705, Hooke detailed his findings on Scotland's readiness and advocated for a French commander to lead the uprising. Eagerly anticipating the arrival of the Scottish delegates, Hooke's optimism waned as delays ensued, attributed by the Countess of Errol to protracted negotiations with clans. Furthermore, the French military's necessity to focus on continental engagements following the defeat at Blenheim (13 August 1704) added to the complexities of launching the Scottish venture.

During the same period, the Whigs secured a majority in Parliament, a development that was at odds with Hamilton's political stance. Moreover, there was a serious consideration for the unification of the English and Scottish crowns. On 12 December, two envoys arrived bearing news. Among them was Charles Fleming, designated as a deputy to France. Unfortunately, his mission to return to Scotland with messages from the court was thwarted by the English navy, leading to his capture during the return voyage. By 11 January 1706, Fleming made his way back to the court at Saint-Germain, delivering news that, despite being incomplete, buoyed the Pretender's spirits, bringing him seemingly closer to his aspirations.

The year 1706 saw Queen Anne enact legislation that found little favour with the Scots, catalysing discussions of rebellion within the nobility. The Duke of Hamilton's alienation from English politics nudged him towards a definitive commitment to the Jacobite cause. Hooke, informed of these developments, learned of concerted efforts by his

---

[100] The names of some of Scotland's peers "are harsh and difficult to pronounce for those who are not accustomed."

Scottish allies to forestall the union of the two kingdoms. Tensions escalated, with certain clans taking up arms and various Scottish factions uniting in opposition to the union (comprising Jacobites, Episcopalians, Presbyterians[101]). Hooke saw in this unity an opportunity to leverage. The acceptance of the union would not only relegate Scotland to a mere province within the Kingdom of England,[102] but would also, by endorsing Sophie of Hanover's ascendancy to the English throne, eliminate the Stuarts from the succession line altogether. Essentially, the ratification of the union served as a rallying cry for mobilising Scotland. Although Daniel Defoe was dispatched to advocate for the Union, his efforts bore little fruit. Nonetheless, as France's influence on the continent waned, the Scottish project was once again deferred.

By March 1706, France showed indifference to Scotland's entreaties, a situation that deeply affected the Duchess of Gordon, prompting her to personally appeal to Torcy. Additionally, Charles Fleming, still present in France, submitted a memorandum that similarly failed to elicit a response. The defeat at Ramillies in May of the same year further exacerbated matters, leading Louis XIV to disengage from Scottish affairs due to other pressing concerns and a lack of interest. Nathaniel Hooke, like many exiled Scottish and Irish nobles, was actively involved in these tumultuous times, participating in battles as a member of the Sparre regiment and encountering Marlborough, who was unwavering in his resolve. As 1707 unfolded, France's situation on the continent deteriorated, bringing the Scottish dilemma back to the forefront amidst tactical impasses. This rejuvenated focus on Scotland served as a strategy to counteract continental setbacks.

IV. **A Last Opportunity.**

The initiative experienced a revival, albeit in the context of dwindling finances (the so-called "years of misery"). The French government, driven

---

[101] Hostile to the Hanoverians, but resolutely anti-unionist.
[102] In the end, Queen Anne had laudable reasons for integrating Scotland into the kingdom: raising the standard of living, defending the territory as her own, pacifying the region. Conversely, the Scots would lose their parliament and be subject to the same taxes.

by desperation, contemplated further debt to carve out a strategic advantage by invading England via Scotland. The Pretender had matured, impressing Louis XIV with his potential for kingship. The king found favour in Hooke's proposal, and eventually consented, instructing Chamillart that he had: "the honour of representing to him that to set the Scottish nation in motion it will be necessary to begin by bringing them arms, munitions and a sum of money."[103]

In February 1707, amidst plans to transport arms to Scotland and deploy Hooke alongside agents to liaise with the clans—actions taken with utmost confidentiality and in defiance of the Court of Saint-Germain—the operation was abruptly halted. The official rationale provided was the need for preliminary discussions with the Scottish nobility before proceeding, though it's speculated that the resources designated for Scotland were actually redirected to support the campaign in Flanders.

Hooke was thus poised for another journey, the timing of which remained uncertain. By February of the same year, he had received initial directives from Chamillart stipulating that French support would be confined to the provision of equipment, ammunition, and weaponry, without the inclusion of troops. The responsibility for troop mobilisation, aiming for a force of 25,000 to 30,000 men, was assigned to the clans, who were also tasked with nominating a unified commander-in-chief. Charles Fleming was instructed to stay behind in Saint-Germain to avoid arousing suspicion among the Scots due to his departure. Jacques Murray and his brother Robert were selected to accompany Hooke on this mission.

Yet, the endeavour once more veered off course. Hooke was taken aback by a letter from Lord Lovat (Simon Fraser) in Angoulême, which not only lauded his undertaking but also proposed Lovat's services anew. Hooke chose not to respond.

The Pretender entrusted Nathaniel Hooke with a letter to be delivered, exhorting the clans to unite behind their cause. Once again, the Duke of Hamilton would be approached, as such a figure should not be overlooked in such an undertaking, not least because of his extensive network of influence.

---

[103] MACRAY W. D. (ed.), *Op. Cit*, Hooke, *Mémoire des choses nécessaires pour mon voyage*, 31 January 1707, vol 2, p. 111

1. Jacobites Disunity:

By March 1707, Hooke found himself back in Dunkirk, facing neglect and the commandeering of the ships meant for his passage. In a moment of frustration, he penned a missive to François de Callières, a recognized diplomat at the French court (1645-1717), illustrating a spy's diminishing patience with the dawdling of his superiors. This correspondence highlights the precarious existence of agents who are at the mercy of covert operations and their unpredictable nature:

> I blame you for having persuaded me to make this journey [...] since they think so little of me and my safety, if it pleases God that I return, I will think more of myself than I have done in the past, since they despise a bold and affectionate zeal, I will try to moderate it in the future as many others do.[104]

By April 17th, Hooke, accompanied by Jacques Murray, set sail for Scotland. There, the Duke of Hamilton and other nobles eagerly awaited to formalise an agreement with France. Welcomed by the Countess d'Errol at her Slaines castle, Hooke soon learned of Hamilton's waning commitment to the Jacobite cause, having drifted towards alignment with the English government. This disillusionment revealed the absence of the unity Hooke had previously perceived among the Scottish nobility. Secret negotiations between Saint-Germain's court and Scotland came to light, marred by espionage and document forgery, rendering the situation perplexingly opaque. The swift shifting of clan loyalties, previously deemed steadfast, played into the hands of the English government, which aimed to sow discord and confusion—a strategy that proved effective. English spies infiltrated even Saint-Germain, hinting at intricate power dynamics and conspiracies. Amidst these revelations, Hooke, though personally implicated in the ensuing chaos, pursued his mission with unwavering determination.

What remained for Hooke to do was to play the game of secrecy, deception and manipulation. However, the task of securing the allegiance of a Scottish nobleman was fraught with negotiations that often led to further delays. For every ally won, another was lost, culminating in the

---

[104] MACRAY W. D. (ed.), *Op. Cit,* To M. de Callière, 22 March 1707, vol.2 p.174.

Marquis of Drummond and the Earl of Brodalbain proclaiming themselves as representatives of all Highland clans.

The mantle of Scotland's most influential lord shifted from the Duke of Hamilton to the Duke of Atholl, necessitating a delicate balance of power to maintain harmony between them. During Hooke's visit to a Highland noble's residence, the host shared that "his vassals were continually urging him to give them permission to rise up [...] reproaching him that the nobility were allowing the country to be sold off and ruined while the people asked nothing better than to take up arms in their defence."

2. Memorandum but no Treaty:

Despite engaging in discussions aimed at formalising a treaty, the lack of unity hindered any definitive action. The proposal that France would contribute 5,000 troops was a point Hooke couldn't commit to, a stipulation that rankled the Scottish nobility.

Despite the complexities and disagreements, a consensus emerged that the situation's intricacies made formal treaty negotiations unfeasible. Instead, it was determined that a memorandum, once endorsed by the Scottish nobility and dispatched to France, would be an adequate compromise. Hooke set off to collect signatures: Lord Drummond and his brother the Marquis, representatives of all the clans, Lord Kinnaird, Lord Moray of Abercairney, the lairds of Strathearn, the Earl of Strathmore, the Earls of Wigton and Linlithgow, Lyon of Aucherhouse, Lockart of Carnwath, the Earl of Panmure, the Lord of Pourie representing all the Lords of Angus, the Lord of Coxton, the Earl Moray of Darnaway, the Laird Grant, the Earl of Errol, Lord Saltoun, the Earls of Caithness, Eglintoun, Aberdeen, Buchan, Mernes, the Lord Keith, the Earl Marishal, the Lord of Boyne. While not all nobles signed the memorandum, many pledged their support, expressing concerns over its premature commitments without any concrete promises from the monarch. This memorandum, bearing the weight of Scottish hopes, was carried back to France by Hooke, alongside Jacques Murray, in June 1707.

Upon their return, Charles-Honoré d'Albert de Luynes, Duc de Chevreuse, a trusted adviser to Louis XIV, and the Marquis de Torcy were briefed on the developments, although Pontchartrain's reservations led to his exclusion from these consultations. On 11 July 1707, the memorandum was read at the King's Council. After four years of travels, marches in the Highlands, numerous prevarications and meetings, preparations for the military operation for the Scottish project could finally begin.

V. A Secret Military Strategy Prepared.

The memorandum sent to the Ministry in Versailles contained various clauses dealing with equipment, supplies, food and the number of men. The demands were very substantial:

- Food: according to Hooke, the Scots eat porridge;
- Country accommodation: the Scots didn't want to talk about shelters or tents because, in their words, they didn't want to get into the habit so as not to become "effeminate;"[105]
- Ammunition, gunpowder: stockpiled in strategic locations;
- Uniforms: the fabrics were chosen by the clan chiefs to ensure that the soldiers could withstand the elements and sleep outdoors;
- Officers: no pay for the moment, but subsistence. Remove officers who are not Jacobites when the time comes;
- Strongholds: plans of the main strongholds were given to Hooke;
- Manpower: regular troops of the nobility, 3,000 men / with reinforcements, 15,000 men / all available fighters throughout Scotland, 40,000 men;
- The commander-in-chief for operations: the clans demand that the Pretender himself come to Scotland to take command of the troops;
- The commander of the expedition and landing: the Duke of Berwick, half-brother of the Pretender ;

---

[105] HOOKE Nathaniel, *The Secret History of Colonel Hooke's negotiations in Scotland, in favour of the Pretender, in 1707 : including the original letters and papers which passed between the Scotch and Irish Lords and the Court of Versailles and St. Germains*. n. e., London, 1760, Memoir of the Scottish Lords, 1707, p. 83.

- French landing places: the Firth of Forth, the Edinburgh estuary, Kirkcudbright, in the south of Scotland and close to Ireland, the town of Montrose, in the east of Scotland).

1. Operational Plan:[106]

On 1 August 1707, the Duc de Chevreuse, M. de Callières and Nathaniel Hooke met at the Hôtel de Luynes (on the Faubourg Saint-Germain in Paris) to draw up the first plans, which they called the *Enterprise of Scotland*.

- Period of operations: in September, as most of the British troops were in Spain and Portugal at the time (operations in Catalonia);
- Human reinforcements: Irish brigades, 6 battalions, 1 regiment of dragoons, embarked on 20 frigates with 20 to 40 guns (250 men per frigate).;
- Places of embarkation: preparations would be made discreetly in Dunkirk, Brest or Rochefort, within two days;
- Ammunition: to last for at least 6 months, weapons for 30,000 men, 1 field artillery train (6 batteries and 4 mortars), bombs, cannonballs and grenades, gunpowder for all the troops;
- Money: 600,000 francs to start the war;
- Choice of disembarkation point: the Firth of Forth, to reach Edinburgh more quickly;
- Alternative plan: the Scottish forces would retreat behind the River Tay, reputed to be impassable.

In the strategy for the forthcoming expedition, it was naturally evident that deception would play a crucial role, with the Pretender even adopting the alias 'Knight of St George.' The consensus was that financial constraints would not hinder the operation given its significant political potential. However, the financial reality fell short of expectations, with the

---

[106] HOOKE Nathaniel, *op.cit*, Memoir of the Scottish Lords, 1707, *Plan of the Operations of Scotland,* 1708 p. 83

2. Submission of the Plan to Louis XIV:

The next day, the proposals and plans conceived during these discussions were promptly forwarded to Chamillart, the Minister of Foreign Affairs, for approval. Over the summer, a palpable sense of anticipation and impatience grew among the Jacobites as they awaited a response from Versailles: "Secrecy is necessary in great affairs, but too much mystery ruins everything."[107]

As the days turned into months without any forthcoming updates, Hooke attempted to pacify the Scottish nobles with promises, despite receiving no new information himself. Meanwhile, an undisclosed English informant tipped off the London government, leading to the arrest and subsequent detention of Robert Murray until December 1707. Murray's imprisonment, however, did not seem to compromise the plan. Efforts to unmask the informer included anticipating an English delegation at Saint-Germain, suspected of harbouring a diplomat with connections to double agents. Despite these suspicions and a comprehensive search through the Post Office's correspondence, the source of the leak remained undiscovered.

In August 1707, the Lord of Boyne visited Saint-Germain to engage with the Pretender and Charles Fleming directly. Following this visit, Chamillart, alongside Nathaniel Hooke, requested an audience with Boynes, who reiterated the details of the Scottish preparations and expressed a desire to personally thank King Louis XIV for his support.

On September 27, 1707, Nathaniel Hooke meticulously refined and dispatched the plan to Chamillart and King Louis XIV, emphasising the eager anticipation of the Scots. By December, when Lord Boyne met with the King, there was a palpable recognition of the Scots' fervour, though the monarch hesitated, mindful of previous misfortunes. Ultimately, persuaded by the Dukes of Chevreuse and Beauvilliers, along with Madame de Maintenon, Louis XIV embraced the Scottish endeavour. This

---

[107] MACRAY W.D, *Op.cit*. The duchess of Gordon to me 5 August 1707, vol 2 p. 444

decision allowed Lord Boyne to assure Scottish nobles of France's impending logistical efforts.

3. Final Preparation for the Scottish Expedition:

The closing phase of planning for the Scottish expedition was marked by Hooke's final missive to Torcy on October 7, 1707, suggesting the culmination of preparations and the necessity for strict confidentiality. However, the subsequent absence of correspondence may hint at alternate reasons, perhaps the deliberate destruction of records during tumultuous periods such as the French Revolution. The strategic discussions held in Fontainebleau involving Hooke, Chamillart, Duc de Chevreuse, and Pontchartrain, remain partially cloaked in mystery. Nonetheless, the historical defence archives provide a glimpse into the operation's latter stages, allowing us to piece together the narrative of this audacious scheme.

Only 5,000 men had been assembled at Dunkirk, with twelve battalions from various regiments, detachments from the Irish Brigades, and promises of reinforcements from the Pope. The armament comprised five ships of the line, each armed with fifty guns, alongside two transport ships and twenty-six frigates, with twenty to thirty guns each. However, more thought had been given to ammunition: 100,000 pounds of gunpowder and 20,000 bayonets were being transported. Despite meticulous planning, the expedition, originally set to be led by the Duc de Berwick, experienced a change in leadership to the Comte de Gacé, due to Berwick's apparent disillusionment with the venture. The fleet's command fell to the Comte de Forbin, selected by Chamillart, yet Forbin harboured deep reservations about the mission's feasibility:

> I knew the situation of Scotland, and I knew very well that everything was impossible there [...] I cannot see without expressing my feeling that we lose six thousand men who would be needed elsewhere,

because if I land them in Scotland, you can in advance consider them as lost.[108]

In March 1708, preparations saw Charles Flemming dispatched to Scotland, tasked with orchestrating the logistics for the French landing in the Firth of Forth, strategically avoiding the English fleet stationed in the North Sea. The meticulous compilation of intelligence on the English fleet's composition and positioning underscored the operation's detailed planning. The Pretender, seizing the opportunity for action under the guise of a hunting trip in Anet (north-west of Paris, in the Eure region of Normandy), covertly travelled to Dunkirk.

However, internal discord between Forbin and Gacé, attributed to personal rivalries, threatened the expedition's cohesion. Moreover, reports to Chamillart of English naval presence near the Channel and in Holland urged a swift departure. Even as Louis XIV began to question the expedition's viability, the arrival of the "Chevalier de Saint-Georges" on 18 March 1708 marked a decisive moment, allowing the fleet to finally embark on its mission.

VI. *Sic Transit Gloria Mundi:*[109]

The expedition to Scotland, conceived with high hopes, ultimately culminated in failure, a result of a confluence of adverse factors. Queen Anne, forewarned by intelligence of an impending French fleet aimed towards England, took comprehensive measures to prevent its passage across the Channel. Additionally, a storm wreaked havoc on the French fleet, scattering its ships. The remaining vessels pressed northward, only to be pursued by English forces. In a navigational blunder, Forbin missed Edinburgh, sailing past it to Aberdeen, necessitating a retreat. The preparatory phase had been marred by procrastination and waning enthusiasm among the key figures involved, further hampered by protracted and fruitless negotiations dating back to 1703.

---

[108] FORBIN Claude de, *Mémoires du Comte de Forbin (1656-1733)*, Mercure de France, Paris, 1993, p. 424-425.
[109] *So passes the glory of the world.*

Chapter 11

On 21 March 1708, the French flotilla's arrival at Edinburgh was met with a formidable English naval presence. Attempting to reach Aberdeen for a landing, as the Pretender and the Comte de Gacé advocated, was thwarted by Forbin's refusal, leading to the fleet's return to Dunkirk by 2 April 1708. The journey back saw the capture of two French vessels, carrying Lord Middleton's sons among others, exacerbating Scottish resentment towards France for the botched effort.

Forbin bore the brunt of the blame for the fiasco. The Duke of Berwick criticised his lack of initiative and perceived cowardice, arguing that Forbin, as the fleet's admiral, had an obligation to disembark the troops regardless of the location. Despite his defence, evidence against him was compelling, leading to his disgrace.[110]

Historians later posited that the operation might have been a diversion intended by Versailles, with the destruction of Nathaniel Hooke's correspondence possibly serving to obscure the true intentions behind the mission. Hooke's silence from October 1707 onward hints at a broader understanding or complicity in the operation's real purpose, suggesting that the apparent failure may have concealed a more complex strategy at play.

Subsequent accusations targeted Lord Middleton, alleging his clandestine communication with the English government via a Versailles-based spy. This alleged betrayal illuminated for England the tangible threat of an incursion from the north, leading to the enactment of stringent treason legislation aimed at Jacobites.

Queen Anne, in a bid to quell potential insurrections in Scotland, exercised restraint, possibly influenced by the Duke of Hamilton's shift away from the rebel cause and his efforts to shield his Scottish allies from harsh reprisals.

Reflecting on the Scottish Expedition spearheaded by Nathaniel Hooke—a figure seemingly lifted from the pages of espionage fiction—it's evident that a myriad of factors conspired against the venture's success. Despite a commitment spanning five years and receiving

---

[110] In his defence, he had not wanted him to go ashore because he did not want his death to be blamed on him, which would have been even worse. But Chamillart and Ponchatrain's orders were also contradictory, which is also understandable.

accolades for his endeavours, Hooke faced disappointment. Although the Scottish aristocracy extended an invitation to revisit the initiative, he demurred.

For our purposes, the preparations for the Scottish Expedition are a real textbook case for those who want to understand in detail the behaviour and role of spies and double agents in the war between the English, French and Dutch for the British Isles. Finally, we gain a fuller understanding of the extent of the intelligence work that went into ensuring the success of such an action, which, had it succeeded, could have dramatically altered the course of British history by reinstating the Stuarts and reintroducing Catholicism to the realm.

Nathaniel Hooke Retires from the Scene:

The subsequent year, 1709, saw Nathaniel Hooke respectfully declining the Scottish aristocracy's renewed appeal for engagement, passing the baton to McLean who presented the concept afresh to the Pretender and Louis XIV. However, financial constraints and a dearth of resources led to inaction. It wasn't until 1715 that the Pretender embarked on another endeavour with the support of the Scottish figures previously discussed, culminating in the Mar Rebellion's defeat at Sheriffmuir by the Duke of Argyll. Following this, the Pretender sought refuge in Rome in 1719.

In 1708, in recognition of his dedicated service, Hooke was honoured with the title of Brigadier-General in the French military and bestowed the title of Baron of Ireland. His military engagements included participation in the Battle of Malplaquet on September 11, 1709. By 1711, his expertise in intelligence and espionage summoned him to Dresden, continuing his covert activities until the culmination of the Treaty of Utrecht in 1713-1714.

While Hooke was not directly implicated in the Mar Rebellion, he remained in constant contact with John, Earl of Stair, the British ambassador in Paris. On 18 March 1718, Hooke was elevated to maréchal de camp (major-general of the army), and on 1 January, 1720, his French naturalisation was officially recognised (with registration in April 1721).

At the end of his life, Louis XV honoured him with the title of Commander of the Order of Saint Louis. He died on 25 October 1738.

Letters:

Hooke's correspondence from 1703 to 1707, partially transcribed by his nephew Nathaniel Hooke, was donated to the Bodleian Library in Oxford. It was then edited by William Dunn Macray for the Roxburghe Club in 1870-1871. Parts of his writings had already appeared in the works on the Scottish and Irish Revolutions of 1707, 1708, and 1709, published at The Hague in 1758, and in James Macpherson's Original Papers (1775).

Family:

In 1704, Hooke married Eleanor Susan MacCarthy Reagh (known as Lady Hooke from 1708). She was lady-in-waiting to Queen Mary II. She had a son, James Nathaniel Hooke (1705-1744), the 2nd and last Baron Hooke.

CHAPTER 12

A GEOPOLITICAL CRISIS IN FRANCE AND RENEWED PLANS FOR ACTION IN SCOTLAND (1709-1710)

Engulfed in a relentless series of defeats, France faced demands for concessions it deemed untenable, notably the insistence that Philip V relinquish the Spanish crown. The diplomatic front was manned by key figures: Prince Eugène of Savoy leading the imperial forces, the Duke of Marlborough at the helm of the English contingent under the auspices of Anne Stuart, and the Grand Pensionary of Holland, Heinsius, spearheading negotiations with France. In a bid to break the deadlock, Colbert de Torcy proposed a diplomatic mission to Holland to affirm Louis XIV's refusal to dethrone his progeny from Spain. The allies, wary of French motives, envisioned the proposal as a stratagem for France to regroup its forces. This culminated in a draft that recapitulated French concessions and stipulated Louis XIV's compliance in removing his son from the Spanish throne, paired with an offer of a two-month armistice. The proposition was spurned, leading to Torcy's return and the subsequent collapse of talks.

I. Financial Constraints Undermine the Jacobites Strategy.

On June 12th, Louis XIV issued a rallying cry to the French populace, urging support for renewed war efforts. This period also saw a reshuffling within the ministry: Voysin succeeded Chamillart as War Minister, finance was entrusted to Desmarets, Colbert's nephew, and Torcy ascended as Foreign Minister. Despite the adversity, the maritime powers' perception that their campaign was in Austria's defence, and the Battle of Malplaquet, attested to France's resilience. However, France grappled with a mire of challenges: spiralling debts and disarrayed politics. Torcy's diaries, unearthed in 1884, shed light on the era's complexity, revealing his roles as a diplomat and chronicler of confidential correspondences. Louis XIV was deeply engrossed in clandestine affairs and intricate machinations, indicative of a government grappling with desperation.

Maximilian-Emmanuel, Elector of Bavaria and a French ally, found himself displaced following the Allied triumph at Blenheim in 1704, his tenure in Brussels concluded. The subsequent Allied occupation of Germany and the Spanish Netherlands further isolated Maximilian. In 1709, his envoy, Monasterol, clandestinely facilitated a meeting with Torcy, during which Maximilian advocated for a French offensive along the Rhine in 1710.

On November 7th, a significant meeting took place at Marly, where Maximilian, Elector of Bavaria, conferred with King Louis XIV, discreetly, without revealing his identity to the court, but directly engaging with the monarch. The subsequent day, Torcy recorded the King's satisfaction with this clandestine encounter. By November 12th, Maximilian revisited Marly, subsequently consulting with Torcy, expressing his desire to participate in any peace preliminaries, aiming to reclaim the Netherlands as per the treaties of 1701 and 1702. This ambition was underscored by the Dutch's non-hostility towards him and with the assent of Philip V of Spain, despite the latter's limited territorial hold over Luxembourg, Namur, Nieuport, and Charleroi.

On November 13th, King Louis XIV showed favour towards Maximilian's propositions, deciding to dispatch an envoy to the Spanish monarch to propose the cession of the Netherlands. D'Iberville, a seasoned agent of Louis XIV with a prior diplomatic stint in Geneva, was chosen to accompany this mission, receiving his briefing on November 17th.

The diplomatic ballet continued on November 19th when Hermann de Petkum, representing a northern prince, the Duke of Holstein-Gottorp, and acting as a mediator among the warring factions, engaged Torcy. The Duke of Marlborough's interception and decryption of Petkum's communications with Torcy, executed by William Blencowe, underscored the tense espionage undercurrents of these negotiations, as noted by Winston Churchill in his autobiography.

Torcy bestows the title of Vicar General of Holland to Maximilian of Bavaria. In return, Maximilian sends a ring to Torcy via Monastero, which he does not accept. During discussions on 20 November, Petkum conveyed his mission's endorsement by the Grand Pensionary of Holland, Marlborough, and Prince Eugène, aiming to validate specific peace articles with Torcy. The Dutch, represented by dignitaries including Buys and Van der Dussen, sought peace, prompting Louis XIV to dispatch Petkum back to Holland laden with French assurances. Despite ostensibly acquiescing to the allies' conditions, Louis XIV's actions belied a parallel preparation for war. The strategic deliberations expanded to include Switzerland's role by November 25th.

On 26 November, Petkum expressed frustrations to Torcy regarding France's diplomatic posture. Torcy, acting on Louis XIV's directive, communicated to Holland through Petkum the proposal to suspend military operations over the winter. A clandestine directive received by Torcy on November 30th concerned the Duke of Orléans, referred to cryptically as M.L.D.D.O., hinting at the delicate matter of the Duke's aspirations to the Spanish throne. This period also saw Spain attempting to distance itself from France's orbit, signalling to the Dutch and English their welcome return to trade in Seville.

II. Attent to Destabilise Queen Anne for a New War in Scotland.

In 1709, the culmination of strategic planning and espionage efforts saw the Enterprise of Scotland finally coming to a head, primarily orchestrated by Nathaniel Hooke at the Stuart Court in Saint-Germain.

Often mentioned, but rarely discussed in detail, the Enterprise of Scotland, which began in 1703 (and which we have analysed), was one of the many attempts to restore the Stuart dynasty to the throne of England, Ireland and Scotland. Nathaniel Hooke (1664-1738), whose role in the Stuarts' espionage services we have already seen, was an Irish military officer and diplomat in the service of France. As early as 1703, he proposed a project to bring together the interests of France and the Jacobites in order to form an alliance against England. His aim was to ensure the restoration of the Pretender, James Edward Stuart, but also to help the Scots, threatened by a definitive union with England, to gain lasting independence with the support of France. Nathaniel Hooke's correspondence with the French Secretaries of State, Scottish Jacobite peers and the nobility exiled at the Court of Saint-Germain, bears witness to the issues at stake in this military expedition and the negotiations undertaken to bring the project to fruition.

Very quickly, the Pretender found himself compelled to go into hiding, and was allowed to serve in the French army under the name of "Chevalier de Saint-Georges." In 1709, when the allies demanded that Louis XIV expel him from France, the latter pretended to accept and let him return to the armies, still more incognito. The Duke of Burgundy, Louis XIV's grandson, vouched for him and was instructed "to be careful not to name the King of England, and to give the general officers, and even the Duke of Vendôme, cause, by your example, to know him only by the name of Chevalier de Saint-Georges; I am well aware that it is not possible for those who have seen him for a long time to confuse him with the others, but this precaution seems necessary to me."[111]

On the bloody day of Malplaquet (11 September 1709), Marshal de Boufflers praised his good conduct in battle, as did the English: "M. de Kelton (Skelton, brigadier in the service of France) says that all the English among the enemies show infinite respect for the King of England, are delighted that he is in the army and that he is acquiring glory and that Milord Marlborough and the English lords have drunk to his health and call him the Prince of Wales, which is properly to recognise him as the true successor to the crown of England."

Despite the efforts made to hide him, the Pretender was clearly visible to everyone, but especially to the English, who ultimately had a real admiration for him. The Baron de Breteuil, who was at the time the introducer of the embassies, said that the Pretender's incognito was a real example:

> The King of England, being a volunteer under the name of Chevalier de Saint-Georges in the army of Monseigneur the Duke of Burgundy, was there in such perfect incognito that at the table of Mgr de Bourgogne, where he

---

[111] Mémoires de Torcy, *op. cit.*

usually ate, he was seated on a stool like the other courtiers and officers of war, while Mgr de Bourgogne and M. the duke of Berry, his brother, were seated in an armchair and the king at home had the officers who came to see him seated as a private lord would have done in his tent.[112]

1. The Pretender Refuses to Abandon Hope:

On 6 December 1709, Torcy was received by the Pretender at Saint-Germain to discuss a new expedition to Scotland. Berwick, The Pretender's half-brother, disagreed: "She (His Britannic Majesty) confided to me in secret the sorrow she felt at seeing that the Duke of Berwick, whose zeal and attachment to her she knew, persisted in saying that this expedition should not be attempted unless the King gave twenty thousand men to undertake it."[113]

Simultaneously, a novel approach to negotiation emerged when Victor-Amédée II, Duke of Savoy, extended a mediation proposal to the Spanish envoy in Genoa, entrusted to his agent, known as the "Jew Sacerdoti." The Duke aimed to exchange Briançon, prompting the Duc de Beauvilliers to caution Louis XIV against engaging with the unpredictable Duke. Torcy suggested augmenting Sacerdoti's efforts by dispatching an additional envoy to Turin while rejecting the Duke of Savoy's demands.

On 11 December, discussions within the Council touched upon Scottish discontent with the Act of Union with England. Reflecting on the failed expedition of 1708, exacerbated by the English monarch's illness, Torcy cryptically noted, "God knows what occurred." Louis XIV hesitated on sanctioning another expedition, citing the necessity of concealing any such plans from the Pretender. Contrarily, Torcy argued the feasibility of both secrecy and James's involvement, given his evident motivation, despite potential feelings of betrayal. The omnipresence of espionage within the Saint-Germain court was well recognised by Louis XIV and his ministers.

By 15 December, the King sanctioned a new Scottish expedition, viewing it as the sole strategy capable of transforming "the face of affairs." He meticulously documented the operational blueprint, including the

---

[112] Saint-Simon, *Mémoires, op. cit.*
[113] Mémoires de Torcy, *op. cit.*

deployment of forces, naval and troop details, commanding officers, and weaponry, emphasising the criticality of extensive preparation for such a monumental undertaking. Acknowledging the challenge of maintaining secrecy with a substantial force, Louis XIV favoured a smaller contingent to enhance operational discretion, albeit with concerns over the Pretender's possible reactions:

> They wanted to hide the project from him so that it would not be discovered by the spies of Saint-Germain; but they feared that, when it came time for the prince to leave, he would say that he did not want to attempt the venture with a smaller number of troops than the Scots had requested.[114]

Louis XIV was cognisant of the pressing inclination among his ministers (Desmarets, Beauvillier, and Torcy) towards concluding a peace treaty due to the dire state of the kingdom's finances.

On 18 December, discussions within the Council revolved around the capture of a Piedmontese adjutant to Prince Eugène, intercepted at sea en route from Italy to Catalonia with letters from the imperial ambassador in Barcelona to Vienna. The revelation that England sought possession of Minorca and the establishment of Protestantism, intended to be concealed from the Dutch, presented France with an opportunity to sow discord between its adversaries.

2. Louis XIV loses Faith in the Jacobite Cause:

On 22 December, the Scottish affair was still being discussed. Torcy recounts:

> The King held a Council. As it began, His Majesty said that the King of England and the Queen his mother, speaking to Madame de Maintenon about the enterprise in Scotland, had said that they knew that the lack of secrecy at Saint-Germain was feared, but that they would both be pleased if His Majesty were willing to make the preparations for this enterprise, to prevent them from knowing about it and to warn the King of England the day before that he would have to leave to embark.[115]

---

[114] *Ibid.*
[115] *Ibid.*

Mme de Maintenon acted as an intermediary between Saint-Germain and Versailles, since the queen mother, Marie de Modène, was a friend (Torcy also notes that the king wanted to bring together all the Foreign Affairs papers in one place. This was the first attempt to create a Foreign Affairs archive).

On December 29, in response to Maximilian's proposal for a German offensive, Louis XIV communicated the excessive risks involved. Instead, he extended an invitation to Compiègne for a hunting retreat.

1st January 1710: During the Ceremony of the Order of the Holy Spirit, Torcy conveys to Maximilian through Monasterol that the planned military operation in Germany will not proceed. Louis XIV designates Marshal d'Estrées to helm the Scottish expedition, instructing him to maintain utmost secrecy and collaborate closely with Voysin and Minister of the Navy Pontchartrain. In this period, Louis XIV exhibited occasional indecision, necessitating vigilant oversight by Torcy to navigate the monarch's fluctuating directives. To appease the allies, Versailles feigned a diplomatic distancing from Madrid, strategically disassociating from Philip V's agents.

3 January 1710: The King engages with Bergheick, Philip V's minister in the Netherlands, prior to Bergheick's detention in Ghent as mandated by the Act of Capitulation of Mons. He played the Versailles game with Madrid.

5 January 1710: Louis XIV talks to Voysin and Torcy about the Pretender, and about shipping him off to Scotland "without telling him the secret." The King knew that in order to know the Pretender's attitude and the situation in England, he needed to know exactly what was happening at Saint-Germain. Torcy advised that Brigadier Hooke, a Jacobite agent, should be sent to Great Britain.

> The king paid attention, discussed the pros and cons, and finally concluded that if anyone found out that he had left, it would be enough to expose the secret.[116]

On January 6, Hooke was briefed by Marshal de Villars on the perils of the planned Scottish expedition, highlighting the stringent scrutiny

---

[116] *Ibid.*

faced by those landing in Scotland. The plan necessitated passage through Holland aboard Norwegian vessels, delaying arrival until May, which was deemed too late. Torcy noted the rumours that were spreading:

> I was informed in the evening that rumours were beginning to spread of the King's intention to make an expedition to Scotland...[117]

The French and Spanish discuss the Netherlands. The Spanish say that Bergheick can cede the four places in Flanders to the Dutch (these places are in the hands of the Bourbons). Some ministers did not trust him. Louis XIV wanted to know exactly what Madrid was saying, and worked with Bergheick.

14 January 1710: Torcy also noted that Louis XIV wanted to know Bergheick's secret. This was done at the King's dinner: the Flemish agent was to hand over the four strongholds in Flanders to the Dutch on behalf of Spain, by deposit or loan.

15 January 1710: The King discusses what he has just learned. France wants to give these places to Maximilian of Bavaria, but Spain wants to give them to the Dutch. The King wants to wait for the return of Petkum's memorandum. Consideration is given to sending spies: a merchant from Ypres, Florisson, goes to The Hague "with the King's permission" to meet Heinsius. He returned and reported to Le Blanc, intendant of Dunkirk.

26 January 1710: The Council examines the Scottish project. Torcy reads Hooke's memorandum. The King was in favour of the operation, but wanted to meet a Scottish emissary. The Chancellor is not in favour of the expedition. Torcy receives Florisson to talk about Spain. Florisson wants a missive from Mme de Maintenon, which cannot be accepted.

27 January 1710: The Duke of Alba, the Spanish ambassador, delivers a letter stating that the King of Spain has requested that the Duke of Vendôme command his armies (Vendôme was a legitimate branch of the Bourbons). Despite what Torcy knew, the Duc de Vendôme went and won two major victories. On this day, the King is furious with the negotiations, which are not progressing, and particularly with Rouillé, an agent. Ultimately, the King accepts the article of peace, under the injunctions of Mme de Maintenon. A treaty was therefore being prepared, but who would

---

[117] *Ibid.*

be the plenipotentiaries to discuss a shameful peace? Marshal d'Uxelles, Abbé de Polignac (a friend of Torcy)?

19 February 1710: The situation in France is catastrophic, there is no more money and the army is in bad shape. A letter is sent to Petkum, so that the allies do not sign the preliminaries too quickly.

At the end of February 1710, the Elector of Bavaria learns of the forthcoming peace. He is worried and comes to Paris.

2 March: He meets Torcy and tells him that he expected to lose his country, but asks for a territory instead.

4 March 1710: Maximilien meets Torcy and then the King in secret. Louis XIV remained vague. Bergheick then proposed exile to Spain to take command of the armies, and announced that Philip V would be prepared to compensate him by giving him Sicily.

The plenipotentiaries set off for Holland, where they were to obtain a division of the Spanish inheritance. The Dutch would have to accept in order to protect Minorca, coveted by the English. Abbé Gaultier, an agent, informs Torcy that England is experiencing internal tensions. The first discussions took place on a yacht at Moerdijk, near the town of Gertuydenberg. The Dutch stuck to their guns and the French envoys felt humiliated.

26 March 1710: France is in danger because it can no longer afford to campaign. Immediate peace is therefore required. The Council takes place at Madame de Maintenon's, and secret couriers are opened. Torcy recommends asking for Naples and Sicily for Philip V, but refuses to join the allies to dethrone Philip. The Duc de Beauvillier does not want to wage war against the King of Spain, son of Louis XIV. The King did not yet want to decide.

30 March 1710: Agreement is finally reached, and Louis XIV proclaims his army ready. But the ministers did not agree amongst themselves, and the dilemma remained: to go to war and respect the condition of peace, and therefore drive his own son from the Spanish throne, or not to accept the condition and wage war against the allies. But peace is necessary.

21 June 1710: The Council meets. Beforehand, the French plenipotentiaries promised Holland a large sum of money to wage war

against Philip V. The Dutch asked for four strongholds as hostages. At the same time, the French troops deserted in droves.

Torcy meets the king secretly and tells him of the advantages of a peace, even if it is humiliating for the time being. Here Torcy comes to terms with reality and shows us his true face as a politician and diplomat: accepting humiliation, then betraying at the right moment. Louis XIV retorted that, being old, he would never see that. Torcy was close to tears but held back. But the Dutch wanted Louis XIV to wage war on Philip, and were not content with money. The two French plenipotentiaries were humiliated, and King Louis XIV felt insulted.

16 July 1710: They are recalled to Versailles.

30 July 1710: Marshals d'Uxelles and Polignac meet Louis XIV, without Torcy, who seems to have been dismissed by the King. Torcy's Diary sets up a humane king. There were many discussions, particularly about the choice of agents.

CHAPTER 13

NEGOCIATIONS AT THE TREATY OF UTRECHT (1710-1712)

I. The Pretender Retreats from the Political Stage.

The Pretender, possibly wearied by the political obscurity and the passive warfare of his incognito existence, perceived a shift in his fortunes, foreseeing a dimming political future. Saint-Simon notes observing him: "bored apparently by his sad incognito campaigns, and even more so by remaining in Saint-Germain during the war."[118]

After a period of travel within France, James returned to Saint-Germain on December 4, 1711, during a pivotal moment when the preliminaries of the Treaty of Utrecht were established. Nicolas Mesnager's announcement on September 20, 1711, dictated James's expulsion from France, a directive stemming from these negotiations. The Abbé de Polignac, opting to withdraw from the negotiations in 1713, refused to be implicated in this expulsion due to his indebtedness to James and the high expectations he held from the Pope.

Despite these political and diplomatic setbacks, plans for an uprising in Scotland lingered, only to be dismantled by French Protestant spies operating under English commission.

During 1711-1712, Marlborough faced a significant career setback, marked by his dismissal amidst accusations of duplicity. Since 1709, as we have seen, he had been clandestinely collaborating with his nephew Berwick while simultaneously leading the allied forces with notable success. The ensuing criminal charges exacerbated his financial woes, notably halting the construction of his residence at Blenheim.

---

[118] Saint-Simon, *Mémoires, op. cit.*

Consequently, Marlborough sought refuge in exile across Europe, where he was received with distinction. Liberated from his military commitments, Marlborough pivoted towards diplomacy and personal endeavours. In this context, he sought an audience with Fénelon, the esteemed Archbishop of Cambrai, known across Europe for his moral and philosophical contributions. Marlborough's request aimed at garnering Fénelon's support for peace: "he had an extreme desire to be able to have the honour of seeing him and talking to him, and he asked him not to refuse him this satisfaction, as well as not to believe that he was opposed to peace, that he ardently desired it and that he even needed rest, having passed the age of sixty-two."

Unfortunately, Fénelon declined to meet Marlborough, referring the matter to the intendant Bernières and Minister Voysin instead. Marlborough, thus rebuffed, sought engagement with the court at Saint-Germain. Given Marlborough's emerging reputation as a double agent and his intentions to align closer with the Pretender, who had limited agency, the Pretender felt compelled to defend their prior interactions:

> Since my correspondence with Milord Marlborough ceased, which is more than two years ago, I have had no dealings with either the Whigs or the Tories, other than what you know, and I can assure you that I have not made the slightest move without your knowledge since the first news I had of the present Ministry. It is true that last winter Milord Marlborough sent me some vague compliments, but I took so little notice of them that I did not even reply.[119]

In October 1712, Abbé Gaultier, operating covertly in London for the French, requested an investigation into a French individual, Saint-Hilaire, suspected of meddling excessively. Minister Torcy characterised Saint-Hilaire as emblematic of the plethora of double agents and adventurous spirits misrepresenting their significance, often believed at face value: "There are many French adventurers in the world who pass themselves off as people of importance and who are taken at their word."[120] This necessitated reassurances to perturbed English diplomats.

---

[119] James Edward Gregg, *James Francis Edward (1688-1766)*, Oxford University Press, 2004;
[120] Letter from Gaultier to Torcy, fol. 25-28, 15 October 1712.

During the 1712 Congress of Utrecht, the Italian diplomat Count Azzurini emerged as a significant figure, maintaining connections with imperial diplomats and the Grand Pensioner of Holland. His father's ties to Cardinal Gualterio, a Parisian nuncio supportive of France and thus acting as its secret agent, were notable amidst the Duke of Marlborough's retreat to the continent. At this time, the English government, under Grand Treasurer Harley (later Earl of Oxford), closely monitored conspiracies against notable figures such as Heinsius, Prince Eugene of Savoy, and Marlborough himself. Azzurini reported Harley's disdain for Marlborough, anticipating the cessation of hostilities to demand his capture. The narrative further unravels the web of double agents serving various factions, including a Spanish secretary in London, divulging all to both Oxford and Torcy. Azzurini, adept at serving multiple masters, soon entangled himself in blackmail, mirroring his father's actions of soliciting funds from the French court through a banker named Antoine. This banker inadvertently financed Azzurini's duplicity, including leaking Louis XIV's secrets. Unbeknownst to France, which had yet to grasp Azzurini's betrayal, Count d'Arco was dispatched to London, where he was to encounter a figure linked to Azzurini's father. Ultimately, Azzurini himself exposed d'Arco to the allies, while portraying himself as a staunch ally of France, albeit one funded by Versailles. Azzurini's revelations about the Marlborough controversy, including the involvement of Earl Oxford and Duke of Ormond in Stuart restoration efforts, illuminated the deep-seated intentions among England's nobility to reinstate the Pretender. These covert, unpublicized endeavours, whether disclosed at Saint-Germain or not, seemingly failed to fully convince the Pretender of their validity, likely due to Azzurini's notorious reputation as their informant. In any case, the Pretender persisted in his low-profile existence in France, removed from these clandestine machinations.

Ultimately, France, upon uncovering Azzurini's schemes through their investigation, awaited the opportunity presented by the Treaty of Utrecht to entice him into French territory for his arrest: "We believe that it would be important to lure this rascal to French lands in order to arrest him, and with this in mind, as he came to see us with a deliberate air, we proposed that he return to England by way of Calais...."[121] The revelations unearthed during the subsequent probe into Azzurini's dealings, particularly concerning negotiations with Hanover—the future source of English monarchs—were astonishing. Azzurini had exposed not only the connections between Marlborough, Prince Eugene, and Heinsius to the Tory ministry but was also doubling his profits by supplying information to both the Earl of Oxford and another party, thus exploiting the system for greater financial gain. Additionally, Azzurini feigned knowledge of conspiracies against English Protestants, misleading Heinsius by alleging his mission in England was to pave the way for James Stuart's return. This duplicity was eventually unmasked, tracing Azzurini's machinations across Europe. His arrest proceeded quietly, emphasising the necessity of maintaining secrecy around the incident. Interestingly, the English government observed the situation passively, possibly benefiting from the insights into potential Dutch plots against them, thereby turning Azzurini's downfall into an advantage: "the ministers of England, informed of the fact and curious to learn of the plans that Holland would like to form against them, will serve you well in this little manoeuvre."[122] Azzurini found himself imprisoned prematurely, to the chagrin of those who wished to extract further information from him. Amid the charges levied against them, the agents mounted their defence. Thomas Wentworth, the 1st Earl of Strafford, disclosed the involvement of a Hanoverian envoy: "he admitted before me that he had not given Azzurini any money, but that he had sent one of his letters to Hanover."[123] The father was therefore also incriminated, and was followed closely like the son by the French plenipotentiaries: "we are warned that there is an Englishman here sent by the Whigs to fetch him in Italy and take him to England."[124] Torcy even proposed that an English vessel transport him to Toulon for interrogation, where it was established that both father and son had interactions with France's adversaries, under the protection of the English Whigs. The case

---

[121] Archives des Affaires Etrangères, C.P. Holland, fol.190, the PP at Torcy, 26 July 1712.
[122] Ibid. Holland 237, fol.95-96, the P.P. to the King, 31 August 1712.
[123] Bodleian Library, Rawl. MSS. A286, fol. 212-215, letter from Strafford to Bolingbroke, copy, 13 September 1712, The Hague.
[124] Ibid. C.P. Holland 237, fol. 168, the P.P. at Torcy.

took a turn with the involvement of an English Catholic named Barnevelt, instrumental in the arrest. Both father and son faced imprisonment, the former in the Bastille until 1726, and the latter on the Isles of Sainte-Marguerite, managing to escape twice.

The Utrecht Congress was rife with espionage, with all parties engaging in intelligence activities against each other. Despite the clear goals of peace, the ultimate intentions of the involved nations remained opaque, leading to speculation about their true aims, whether they be the instigation of a new war or the pursuit of economic dominance. Holland, in particular, seemed to have more at stake, resistant to the prospect of peace between England and France. In this context, a certain Sicco Van Goslinga wanted to establish close contacts with the Earl of Strafford, in order to uncover England's true intentions:

> For some days I have been looking for an opportunity to have a talk with Earl Strafford to try to penetrate his true feelings on some obscure points both in the peace plan and in the treaty of succession...[125]

In response, and to circumvent Goslinga's influence operation, Strafford betrays the Imperials' intentions by reading a letter about them. Once finished, Goslinga repeats what Strafford has told him:

> It is all very well for you to torment yourself in order to obtain the sovereignty of the conquered country and thereby make yourself master of our trade, but we have judged it to be contrary to our interests and we will easily prevent it from succeeding, and for what it is, from the correspondence that the Duke [Marlborough] has at court, it may well be that there is some spy.[126]

Goslinga thus learnt that English policy was aimed at not leaving the sovereignty of the Netherlands to the United Provinces, from a commercial point of view. Strafford was also known for his outbursts, which had the unfortunate tendency to reveal his secret intentions.

---

[125] Algemeene Rijksarchief, The Hague, Netherlands, Heinsius 1696, letter dated January 1712.
[126] *Ibid.*

II. Jacobites Attempts to Win over the English Press (1711-1713).

The close monitoring of the Duke of Marlborough by intelligence agents across Europe hardly raises eyebrows, given his prominence on the continental stage. However, it's intriguing to highlight a case where an ostensibly minor deed, certainly his, escalated into a significant diplomatic imbroglio, driven by overzealousness, almost becoming an affair of state. It's not unusual for individuals to seek a grander role within the shadowy realms of international relations and espionage, aiming to influence events without directly betraying any side. While some were singed by their forays into this dangerous game, others faded into obscurity, though not without leaving behind tidbits that turned out to be less groundbreaking than initially thought.

By March 1713, as the negotiations for the Treaty of Utrecht were drawing to their culmination, an unidentified informant brought forward a claim that seemed to have far-reaching implications. According to this source, the Duke of Marlborough had undertaken a clandestine journey to Vienna: "a man zealous for the King's service came here a few days ago to inform us that the Duke of Marlborough, during the stay he had made at Aix-la-Chapelle, had left secretly and returned to this city with the same secrecy." This intelligence was vital, as it suggested that Marlborough might be liaising with the Emperor to perpetuate the conflict with France, just as the peace treaty was on the verge of being finalised after lengthy political manoeuvres.

Certainly, the Duke of Marlborough's role in the clandestine communications amongst Europe's diplomats and royalty cannot be overstated. His involvement is mentioned repeatedly, illustrating how just one person could exert significant influence. By 1713, Marlborough had aligned himself with George of Hanover, designated by Queen Anne as her successor, thus positioning himself as a champion for the Hanoverians, Whigs, and the Protestant cause, in addition to being a fervent advocate for continuing the war. France's apprehension was justified, especially given its recent military revival with a victory at Denain in 1712, and the potential disaster that Marlborough's actions could spell for the peace negotiations. The French Secretary of State, Torcy, reported

Marlborough's secretive trip to Vienna, but scepticism soon arose regarding the reliability of the informant, suggesting perhaps an overeagerness rather than factual reporting. This incident faded without further action, revealing the informant to be a globe-trotter, eagerly spreading news—or perhaps rumours—across Europe, capitalising on the widespread speculation of the era.

The journey towards the Treaty of Utrecht, spanning from the negotiations in 1711 to its formal ratification in 1713, was fraught with challenges, among which the influence of the press played a pivotal role in shaping political dynamics.

In England, as well as by extension in Holland, a fierce battle for dominance raged between the Tories and the Whigs, a conflict amplified by the era's press. This era witnessed the burgeoning of what can be termed as propaganda, particularly pronounced during discussions on peace and the drafting of treaties. The press took on the mantle of rallying public support by engaging deeply with foreign policy issues. According to Lucien Bély's thorough examination in his study of espionage and diplomatic relations during Louis XIV's reign, the period saw the publication of 65 pamphlets on these themes, crafted by renowned authors and polemicists.

The Tories, in particular, found strategic value in the proliferation of such pamphlets, aiming to solidify their influence within the nation—a goal they achieved with notable effectiveness. Among the distinguished contributors to this effort was Jonathan Swift, who openly acknowledged the critical role of concerted literary efforts in swaying public opinion. He remarked: "If a few active pens had not gathered to improve the good dispositions of the people, in connection with the last change, and had not continued since to overthrow the falsehood, abundantly and sometimes plausibly spread, I doubt very much whether those who are at the helm would have had reason to be satisfied with their success."[127]

Jonathan Swift's pamphlet, "The Conduct of the Allies," published on 27 November 1711,[128] serves as a prime example of the written word as a

---

[127] Coombs, Douglas, *Op. cit.*

[128] In fact, his mission was to prepare public opinion for the political changes the Tories wanted.

tool for shaping public consciousness. This pamphlet, which saw an astounding circulation of 11,000 copies within a month, brought to the forefront the issue of war expenses, suggesting a disproportionate burden borne by England compared to Holland, bolstered by John Bolingbroke's (St. John) detailed accounts which portrayed England as shouldering a greater financial load. Swift's provocations stirred the public and political spheres alike, leading the Commons on 25 January 1712 to question the equity of war expense distribution between England and Holland, particularly spotlighting the Treaty of the Barrier of 1709.

Swift's pamphlet and the ensuing political actions it spurred demonstrate the power of propaganda in influencing legislative bodies. By 1712, the Commons were quoting Swift's work and adopting resolutions to more equitably distribute the financial burdens of the war, despite the fiscal strain on the United Provinces. The discourse was propelled into the public sphere not through official publications but through the medium of pamphlets, notably "An Explanation of the Eleven Resolves of the 5th February last 1711," which gained renewed attention alongside "The Offers of France Explain'd" amidst unfolding French propositions. This sequence of events favoured the Tories, bolstering their stance in the political tug-of-war with the allies. The vigorous parliamentary debates that ensued were soon overtaken by a deluge of polemical pamphlets that took the argument beyond the confines of governmental halls into the broader public domain. Works like Thomas Burnet's "March and October, Letter to the People" and "The Humble Confession and Petition of a Whig with his Eyes open" were met with counterarguments in "The Miserable Case of Poor Old England Fairly Stated" and "The Second Representation of the Loyal Subjects of Albinia."

Throughout 1712, as diplomats and representatives engaged in covert negotiations, a significant conflict unfolded within the realm of public discourse, marking a shift in political communication. This era witnessed the eruption of a press war, with the Tories and Whigs forsaking traditional venues of debate such as political councils and governmental chambers in favour of the newspaper columns. Leveraging the power of print, both factions deployed their literary gladiators in a battle for public opinion. Daniel Defoe, wielding his pen for the Tories, launched salvos with publications like "A Defence of the Allies and the Late Ministry" and "Remarks on a False Scandalous and Seditious Libel." In defence of the Whigs, Dr. Hare, a chaplain associated with the Duke of Marlborough, entered the fray with retorts titled "The Allies and the Late Ministry Defended against France, and the Present Friends of France" and "Full Answer to the Conduct of the Allies." Not to be outmanoeuvred, Defoe responded with a piece entitled "A Farther Search into the Conduct of the Allies," further fuelling the war of words.

On 22 February 1712, Jonathan Swift, engaged by the Tories to critique the Treaty of the Barrier, published a new libel that reignited debates reminiscent of those during Marlborough's prominence. In swift retaliation, Hare produced a formidable response, extending beyond 200 pages in one instance. Diplomats and decision-makers carried these contentious publications across borders, their strategies and opinions shaped by the narratives they encountered within these pages. Of the 65 works published in this period, the Tories and the administration under Harley contributed 33, the Whigs authored 30, and dissenters accounted for the remaining 2.

Amidst these ideological skirmishes, the press chronicled several outbursts. On 10 June 1712, the Commons expressed its disapproval through a resolution condemning the dissemination of a controversial piece. In instances like these, public sentiment served as the testing ground for political concepts. Daniel Defoe, in his fervour, pushed such an idea too far, unsettling the public and transcending the intended political discourse.

The English Press Watches War Against the Jacobites:

It can be said here that literature and satire became potent tools for conveying complex geopolitical dynamics to the public, and thus an essential weapon to be wielded in warfare. John Arbuthnot (1667-1735), physician to Queen Anne and a member of the intellectual circle that included Jonathan Swift and John Bolingbroke, masterfully wielded allegory and pseudonymity to critique and comment on the tumultuous events of his time. Arbuthnot infused political discourse with fictional narratives that mirrored real-life events and personages. England was personified as "John Bull," Holland as "Nicolas Frog," Louis XIV of France as "Lewis Baboon," Philip V of Spain as "Lord Strutt," and the Duke of Marlborough was cleverly disguised as "Hocus the valet." An example can be seen in a memorandum sent by the Dutch, through an agent, on 3 April 1712, intended for the Queen, was included in Arbuthnot's short story, *Nic. Frog's letter to John Bull.*

However, it was perhaps Jonathan Swift who emerged as the leading figure in the realm of political literature during the period leading up to the Peace of Utrecht in 1712. Serving essentially as a literary agent under the Tory administration, Swift was instrumental in crafting speeches for politicians, marking his influence not only through his own writings but also in shaping the public addresses of key political figures. Notably, Swift's editorial hand was evident in the "Vote of Address of Thanks for the Speech" presented by the Queen to both Houses of Parliament, a version of which was later published as "The Humble Address."

On the other side of the literary battlefield stood Daniel Defoe, a prolific writer who, unlike Swift, operated without direct political patronage. Defoe adeptly navigated public sentiment and political waters, maintaining his independence while cautiously engaging with the political issues of the day. His nuanced stance is exemplified in a letter to the Grand Treasurer Harley in June 1712: "I am far from exciting the people against the Dutch and I do not think it is the design of the Government to offend the Dutch or to break with them, but it seems necessary and I believe it is your purpose to have the Dutch for friends and not for masters, as confederates and not as governors, and to keep us free from a Dutch tutelage as much as from a French one."[129] This careful positioning often found Bolingbroke himself providing Defoe with material for publication.

In summary, the intricate dance of espionage mirrored in the world of literature and political propaganda operated on principles of subterfuge and secrecy. This clandestine battlefield unfolded within the political sphere, where revealing one's true intentions was tantamount to tactical suicide. Authors adhered to a certain code of conduct, steering clear of accusations of lèse-majesté, maintaining a delicate balance between influence and discretion. The period spanning 1709 to 1712, leading up to

---

[129] Coombs, *op. cit.* p.234

the Treaty of Utrecht, underscores the instrumental role of the press, libels, and pamphlets in shaping public perception and preparing society for the diplomatic outcomes.

III. Abbé Gaultier, or the ideal spy at the service of the Peace of Utrecht (1710-1713).

Beginning in 1710, Abbé François Gaultier emerged as a key figure in the early Franco-British negotiations that eventually culminated in the London Preliminaries of 1711. Without his involvement as an intermediary, Gaultier might have remained a figure of obscurity. However, his significant contribution to facilitating peace between France and Britain demands a deeper examination of his espionage activities, which were crucial for France's strategic interests.

The initial negotiations of 1710, spearheaded by the Dutch diplomat from Geertruidenberg, did not yield the desired outcomes. Subsequent efforts were redirected towards England amidst the political ascendancy of the Tories. In response, France sought a reliable intermediary who could operate under the radar yet possess sufficient credibility. Their search led them to the parish of Saint-Germain-en-Laye, a place historically linked to the court of James II Stuart since the 1690s. François Gaultier, a cleric known for his regular attendance at Mass and his discontent with his superior, was selected for this mission. Given leave in 1698 to accompany Maréchal de Tallard, the French ambassador, to Great Britain, Gaultier initially communicated with French Minister Torcy under the alias M. Le Vasseur. During this tenure, he also served the Count of Gallas, the Emperor's ambassador in London. Torcy's memoirs provide an account of the directives Gaultier received from Tallard:

> He advised him to prolong his stay in London for as long as it was possible for him to remain there, to observe events wisely, to report on them in France to the minister in charge of foreign affairs, but to do so with the necessary discretion, so as not to be regarded in England and accused as a spy: thus to

write rarely, and in such a way that he could not attract an order to leave the kingdom or some other even more unfortunate treatment.[130]

Gaultier rapidly gained the trust of the Earl of Jersey, a prominent Tory aligned with the new power brokers in British politics, and was made the confessor to his Catholic wife. This connection proved crucial for advancing negotiations. Minister Torcy, recognizing Gaultier's pivotal role, offers a detailed account of him, highlighting his significance as an operative:

> Abbé Gaultier, a simple priest, without pomp or ceremony, was so much to the liking of the Grand Treasurer that, when the King had plans to send an agent of a higher calibre to England, this minister urged His Majesty to leave Gaultier in charge of carrying out his orders. In fact he carried out the orders he received exactly, explained them clearly, and was no less exact in the account he gave of the replies of the ministers of England, the commissions they gave him, the knowledge he could have of the state of this kingdom, and the dispositions of the nation. If he had to travel by sea and come to give a verbal account of some important commission, explaining it in more detail than the letters required, he did not complain about his trouble: everything was easy for him when it came to service.[131]

Following the Tories' ascension to power, Torcy counselled Gaultier to foster relations with the Duke of Shrewsbury and Abigail Masham, Queen Anne Stuart's confidante, succeeding the Duchess of Marlborough's fall from grace. Leveraging his connection with the Earl of Jersey, Gaultier initiated contact with the Duke of Shrewsbury and Robert Harley, dispatching initial reports to Torcy under the pseudonyms M. Morand and M. Rolland. Faced with scepticism over his legitimate authorization by the French minister and to dispel doubts of being a mere opportunist, Torcy dispatched a letter affirming Gaultier's official capacity. Utilising this verification from Versailles on 19 August 1710, Gaultier embarked on his espionage and intelligence gathering activities.

By September 1710, with the groundwork for negotiations seemingly viable, Gaultier sought guidance on his discussions with the Earl of Jersey

---

[130] *Mémoires du marquis de Torcy*, ed. A. Petitot and Monnerqué, t.II (t. LXVIII of the collection of Mémoires relatifs à l'histoire de France), Paris, 1828, p.16.
[131] *Ibid*, p.18.

concerning Shrewsbury. Following these instructions, Gaultier reported back to Torcy, lauding Jersey's disposition: "[...] If everyone were like him, the trials would soon be over. What he told you about the feelings of the Directors of his company [Great Britain] would give us all great pleasure."[132] By the close of September 1710, the English Tories were fervently pursuing peace, even at the cost of distancing themselves from their allies.

For a period, Abbé Gaultier was instructed to halt his clandestine communications with France to focus on his role as an official mediator. Torcy repurposed his involvement, assigning him as a negotiator in the efforts to release Marshal de Tallard, captured since the Battle of Blenheim in 1704.

Gaultier also played a significant role in managing the concerns of James Stuart, King James II's son, who was displaced by the 1688 revolution. Acting as the primary representative for Stuart's interests, Gaultier reached out to key figures across the political spectrum, from Tories like Shrewsbury to prominent Whigs, including the Duke of Marlborough. Torcy, kept abreast of developments, issued targeted directives aimed at securing a victory that would not only advance the Jacobite cause but also signal a triumph for Catholicism. This strategy envisioned drawing Britain away from its Protestant allies towards an alliance with Louis XIV's Catholic France. In 1713, Gaultier expressed frustration over France's decision to deploy other clergy for handling the Pretender's matters, even threatening to withdraw his services.

Beyond the political manoeuvres, the British press played a crucial role in shaping public sentiment towards peace, a fact astutely recognized by Robert Harley. He was perhaps the first British politician to truly harness the power of media, enlisting pamphleteers such as Simon Clément and Abel Boyer, alongside William King, John Arbuthnot, Daniel Defoe, and Jonathan Swift. Swift, in particular, emerged as a leading figure in Tory propaganda, exerting significant influence over prominent

---

[132] Archives des affaires étrangères, C.P. Angleterre. 230, 1° 309. Torcy to Gaultier, 18 September 1710.

publications like "The Examiner" and "Post Boy."[133] This orchestrated media effort not only cultivated public opinion favourable to the Tories' agenda but also provided Tory ministers and members of parliament with potent ammunition to challenge their adversaries and advocate for their policies within the Houses of Parliament. Swift's "Conduct of the Allies" exemplifies the strategic mobilisation of public opinion to endorse governmental policies, a tactic gaining traction internationally and enhancing the impact of opinion-forming movements.

Harley, recognising the opportunity to broker a peace deal advantageous to British trade, chose to dispatch Gaultier to France to negotiate terms. Prior to this mission, on 28 December 1710, Harley relayed two critical pieces of information. Firstly, Great Britain intended to send Mr. Hill to the United Provinces to collaborate with the States General's deputies in seeking peace, secretly planning to present proposals originating from France. Secondly, and more significantly, Harley outlined a foundational principle for future discussions: "We will not insist on the full restitution of the monarchy of Spain to the House of Austria or, if we do, it will be only weakly and pro forma and we will be content provided that France and Spain give us good securities for our trade for the present and as soon as we have what suits us and we are in agreement with the two Crowns, we will declare it to our allies without worrying about anything they may say or think."[134] Upon reaching a satisfactory arrangement with these two crowns, Great Britain was prepared to independently announce the agreement, irrespective of its allies' reactions. This stance opened the door for direct negotiations with France, sidelining other allies in pursuit of commercial benefits and tacitly accepting Philip V's reign in Spain.

In January 1711, Abbé Gaultier returned to France after requesting an annual subsidy from the Earl of Jersey, seeking five to three thousand pounds sterling for his involvement and services.

---

[133] J.A. Downey, *Robert Harley and the press. Propaganda and public opinion...*, pp. 131-148 and 162-183.
[134] Archives des affaires étrangères, Angleterre. 230, 1° 437 i/v. Gaultier to Torcy, 28 December 1710.

By the 15th of January, he was in Nieuport and, by the 21st, had a significant meeting with Minister Torcy. Gaultier boldly inquired: "Do you want peace? I have come to bring you the means to deal with it, and to conclude it independently of the Dutch, who are unworthy of the King's kindnesses and of the honour he has done them so many times to turn to them to pacify Europe."[135]

Following this, there appears to be a period where Gaultier is not assigned specific duties, but he remains actively engaged with Shrewsbury and Harley. It's on January 21st that Torcy's diary first records Gaultier's name, indicating that until then, Gaultier's activities were shrouded in secrecy. Given the Dutch's rigid stance at the time, Louis XIV opted against proposing peace through Holland, turning instead to England, where Gaultier was ready with a new mission. In February 1711, Gaultier communicated to Torcy: "[...] as I have indicated to you, you have the freedom to make them in terms as general and as dubious as you wish, and it will suffice for us if they have some appearance of truth to use them to please or deceive our peoples and to engage the States General, willingly or unwillingly, to come to an accommodation...."[136] Time passed, and Gaultier, concerned about maintaining his credibility with the English negotiators, once again forwarded the British peace offer to Versailles.

On March 8, 1711, England witnessed a startling incident: Antoine de Guiscard, Abbé de la Bourlie, known for his active involvement in the Cévennes uprising, was apprehended on charges of espionage. During his interrogation, he launched an assault on Minister Harley using a penknife, inflicting serious injuries. This event and ensuing investigation not only exposed de Guiscard as a double agent and spy, but unveiled furthermore an entire deeply enigmatic and clandestine world, to which we will later return. This development significantly impacted the ongoing negotiations, introducing Henry St. John, Viscount Bolingbroke, as a new plenipotentiary. Bolingbroke was notably less inclined towards peace than Harley, his counterpart.

---

[135] Torcy, *Mémoires*, p. 18.
[136] Archives des affaires étrangères, C.P. Angleterre. 232, 1° 59. Gaultier to Torcy, 20 February 1711.

Shrewsbury, initially resistant to a distinct and clandestine peace agreement and hesitant to engage in similar dialogues with France, shifted his stance by April 1711. His continued resistance to the independent peace process (linked to the ambition of alleviating British debt through the South Sea Company, which necessitated the Spanish trade monopoly in the Americas) found opposition in St. John's perspective, who advocated for England to pursue peace notwithstanding prior commitments with its allies. Torcy, reflecting on the developments of 1710, showed support for peace barring Holland's sustained excessive demands. To this end, enticing England with substantial compromises was essential. Jonathan Swift encapsulated the prevailing sentiment within the Tory faction: "We must have a peace, be it good or a bad one. [...] In my opinion, we have nothing to save us but a Peace, and I am sure we cannot have such a one as we hoped ...."[137]

On 18 April 1711, Gaultier returned to Paris with a British response for Torcy, who later slightly adjusted his demands, focusing on issues related to English commerce, defensive measures against France, and initiating discussions in Aix-la-Chapelle and Liège. Gaultier presented the British memorandum to Torcy, urging its acceptance. Torcy, in turn, handed him two documents: one officially signed by him and another without a signature, to be used in a critical situation.

By 8 May, armed with Torcy's letter, Gaultier was officially recognised as a plenipotentiary and formal diplomat. The dialogue between London and Versailles, facilitated by Gaultier, progressed slowly, hampered by Harley's gradual recuperation and his engagement in personal matters. On 23 May, Harley was named Baron of Harley and Earl of Oxford and Mortimer, and on 29 May, he was appointed Lord of the Treasury. With these new titles, he assigned Matthew Prior, an English poet and diplomat, to head to Paris with Gaultier. Their roles were certainly crucial, and Marshal de Tessé (1648-1725) wrote of them: "two small, subordinate geniuses who have not failed to act in the great machine of peace."[138]

---

[137] J.A. Downie, Jonathan Swift..., p.150.
[138] Saint-Simon, t. XXIII, additions and corrections, p.549, letters from the maréchal de Tessé to the princesse des Ursins.

Prior acted primarily as a go-between and source of information, his responses contingent on directives from higher-ups. The necessity arose for a courtly figure, well-versed in formal matters, to be dispatched to London. Hence, Nicolas Mesnager (1658-1714), a count, diplomat, and recognised ambassador, was selected, and set off for London on 3 August, 1711, with Abbé Gaultier in tow. However, an unfortunate event at British customs compromised the confidentiality of his discussions with the British, providing Johann von Gallas, the Imperial Ambassador in London, with evidence to validate his doubts. Negotiations persisted into September of the same year.

By year's end, amidst vigorous negotiations, Mesnager received a mandate from the English Upper House prohibiting peace negotiations with any prince harbouring a Stuart Pretender. The retort was that the current discussions were merely preliminary and not yet a formal treaty, promising that James Stuart would depart the country once an agreement was reached (this stance is corroborated in a letter from Mesnager to Torcy, dated September/October 1711).

On 8 October 1711, the renowned London Preliminaries were finally signed, endorsing the Protestant succession in the British Isles, the demolition of Dunkirk's fortifications, the prohibition of the French and Spanish crowns' union, and trade benefits. Two accords emerged: an official one disclosed to Holland, and a clandestine one. Following the agreement, Mesnager returned to Versailles, while Gaultier remained in London to subsequently brief French diplomats in Holland. In Holland, Gaultier reached out to Torcy, suggesting an increase in Matthew Prior's compensation to deepen his covert ties with France.

The Dutch, aware of or suspecting these negotiations, remained vigilant against possible duplicity or information trade for monetary gain. Willem Buys, a Pensionary from Amsterdam, made his way to London. Gaultier, after discussing Holland's conditions with Torcy in Versailles, made his way back to London on November 26, 1711. Louis XIV specifically requested Matthew Prior to visit Paris en route to Holland, a directive meant to be kept under wraps. From late 1711 into early 1712, Gaultier was extremely active in British political circles, facilitating dialogues among Torcy, St. John, Harley, and Strafford, and delving into press dynamics amid rumours of covert deals between London and Amsterdam and critiques directed at Queen Anne in the Gazette.

The Congress of Utrecht was officially inaugurated on 29 January 1712, with Gaultier as a key figure in steering discussions and liaisons among the delegates, especially emphasising the importance of influencing Matthew Prior, who held sway over England's decisions. The proceedings were strained after the death of the Duke of Burgundy on February 18, raising concerns about a potential unification of the French and Spanish crowns, thus endangering the peace talks. By 23 March, Gaultier was back in Paris, bringing news that Harley's cousin had joined the negotiation efforts, aiding the English representatives. A crucial moment came when Philip V of Spain, albeit reluctantly for Louis XIV, relinquished his claim to the French throne, a move that eased tensions significantly. Gaultier was then tasked with conducting rigorous discussions with the English about Dunkirk's status (designated for England until peace was established). The underlying motive for the Tories' push for peace was the Whigs' preference for continuing the war; a hastened agreement risked jeopardising the standing of London's ministry.

Abbé Gaultier faced considerable opposition, not just from French exiles in London opposed to peace, but also from threats of violence against him. In response, Louis XIV elevated his status by officially appointing him as the secretary of the embassy in Utrecht. This strategic move meant that while harming a secret agent might be overlooked, attacking a diplomatically recognised figure would provoke international outrage and potentially derail the peace process.

In late 1712, French officials received accusations against Gaultier, including the allegation that he facilitated the issuance of a passport to a member of the exiled Huguenot Vaillant family, known for their intrigues against the French court. The accusations extended to misuse of St. John's name for passport issuance, engaging in the illegal sale of passports, treason, misconduct, and alcoholism, with calls for his replacement by someone more competent. However, these charges were debunked, and Gaultier found allies in British diplomats like Harley and Matthew Prior, who vouched for his integrity and opposed any replacement: "[...] there is one clergyman in whom we take a great interest, and that is Associate Gaultier."[139]

The situation progressed when, on 12 June, 1712, Queen Anne declared to Parliament her commitment to a swift peace based on the current balance of power, hinting at an imminent agreement with France. Gaultier's access to information on the allies' war intentions underscored the shift towards peace.

The definitive step towards ending hostilities came when Matthew Prior and Gaultier visited Paris on 10 August, alongside the newly titled Viscount of Bolingbroke, St. John. This visit catalysed the conclusion of peace between France and England by 21 August, 1712.

The negotiations took a definitive turn with the arrival of the Duc d'Aumont and the Marquis de Monteleon in London. Gaultier was put in touch with both of them, but did not get on well with the new French ambassador. In fact, Torcy had explicitly tasked Gaultier with forging a close relationship with Monteleon, a strategy that proved effective as Monteleon showed considerable favour towards Gaultier, extending him a generous grant of four thousand ducats from his bishopric in Toledo. However, this collaboration cast Aumont somewhat into the shadows, particularly in financial terms, and fueled speculation about the personal ambitions driving both Monteleon, who aspired to be named the ambassador to France, and Gaultier, who harboured aspirations for the cardinalate. Aumont, sensing the culmination of Gaultier's diplomatic role post-Treaty of Utrecht, suggested to Torcy that Gaultier's mission conclude with the treaty's signing. Indeed, Gaultier remained in Paris longer than anticipated.

In 1713, the Treaty of Utrecht was signed between France, Great Britain and Spain.[140] Gaultier departed London after addressing a financial issue related to James Stuart's mother. The Duke of Aumont, perhaps motivated by envy, dismissed Gaultier's involvement as trivial.

---

[139] Archives des affaires étrangères, Private correspondence. England. 237, 1re 142, Prior à Torcy, 24 May/1er April 1712.
[140] The conflict lasted until 1714 (Treaty of Rastatt, 6 March 1714), after the French armies commanded by Marshal de Villars had defeated the Dutch army, in order to be able to deal from a position of strength.

Of course, Gaultier's efforts were driven by loyalty to the French crown and the defence of Catholicism. This motivation was shared among many double agents who transitioned into official roles, yet the allure of financial gain cannot be overlooked. Beyond the rewards previously discussed (such as the funds from Monteleon), Gaultier was also offered tangible benefits like the abbey of Olivet by Louis XIV in 1712—though he declined it for a less dilapidated alternative, the abbey of Fontaine— and aspirations towards a cardinalate and the bishopric of Tournai. It's believed that Gaultier amassed around 35,000 livres for his service. However, it's worth noting that Pope Clement XI took issue with Gaultier for engaging with the adversaries of the Catholic faith and King Stuart, who was a staunch Catholic. Gaultier responded:

> No ecclesiastic has worked better or more effectively than I have for the preservation of religion, the restoration of James III and the peace of Europe. France, Spain, England and Savoy announce that it is to me that they will owe the peace.[141]

Ultimately, much like other double agents who stepped into diplomatic roles, François Gaultier emerged as a crucial figure in the peace negotiation process. His extensive correspondence provides invaluable insights into the intricacies of the peace treaty formation and the espionage-laden political dynamics between France and Great Britain from 1710 to 1712. The introduction of the Duc d'Aumont in 1712 highlights that Gaultier, despite his contributions as a French crown agent and his lack of noble status or title, earned his accolades through his adept negotiating skills, necessitating his deference to those of higher social standing. This pattern of behaviour was typical among agents of the era.

IV. Nicolas Mesnager (1658-1714), the Trader Turned Negotiator.

The career of this character deserves a closer look, given the importance of his role in the negotiations that led to the signing of the

---

[141] Foreign Affairs Archives, Private correspondence. England. 242, fos. 56-58, Gaultier to Clément XI, 12 September 1712.

Treaty of Utrecht. A specialist in commercial matters, he worked alongside a large number of agents and spies, particularly when he was given the diplomatic and partly secret mission of detaching England from the coalition that had been formed against France. This service earned him a pension of 10,000 livres from Louis XIV.

While Mesnager is recognised for his commercial and negotiation acumen, less is known about his espionage activities. Known as the "Count of Saint-Jean," he was appointed in 1700 as a delegate to the Council of Commerce for Rouen. His diplomatic endeavours included missions to Spain for trade purposes in the Indies and to Holland to engage with Heinsius in 1707. In 1711, he was sent to London and was one of the plenipotentiaries who signed the Treaty of Utrecht in 1713. Upon his death, he generously bequeathed 20,000 livres to support impoverished girls in the Rouen hospices.

However, his secret life is a reality, because historians agree that it is perhaps not his real name that has passed into posterity. In fact, it was his status as a wealthy merchant that allowed him to undertake numerous covert journeys, providing him with intricate knowledge of the economic and financial landscapes of the nations he visited. Mesnager consistently emphasised his foremost commitment to serving both the king and the state.

Nicolas Mesnager's 1703 memoir reveals his conviction that economic interests and state interests are closely intertwined. By 1710, France's exports included wine, brandies, salt, cloth, and fabrics, while it imported gold, silver, wool, silk, spices, and drugs, indicating a robust engagement in international trade. As an economist, Mesnager was a formidable negotiator, particularly evident during the Treaty of Utrecht negotiations, challenging the maritime powers of the time.

During his 1707 mission in Holland, Mesnager quickly gained access to influential figures who were sceptical of Louis XIV's son ruling Spain. He suggested that establishing peace could be facilitated through a trade agreement. The Dutch minister Duywenvorde, reflecting on Mesnager's suggestions regarding trade agreements post-war:

> We're in for a tough campaign. The English want to fight. It is said that M. de Vendôme also wants to and has the power to do so. We will repair the

losses of our troops more easily than you will be able to restore yours. If there is an action, and if we have an advantage, it will have considerable consequences, but if nothing is done on either side, a decision will have to be taken once the campaign is over. We won't be at war forever.[142]

Mesnager's diplomatic efforts in Holland not only earned him Louis XIV's recognition but also his admiration:

His Majesty was perfectly satisfied with the solid and consistent reasoning that you put forward against the objections made to you [...]. Personally, I have not seen dispatches more sensible, clearer and better written than yours, and I am very sorry that the distance you find to peace does not allow you to make longer use of the talents you have to deal with an affair of this importance.[143]

Nicolas Mesnager, with keen insight, recognised France's diminished military strength and redirected his focus from imperial ambitions to trade negotiations. Understanding that France's position weakened its leverage, he proposed shifting the geopolitical dialogue towards economic discussions. Although he anticipated interest from the United Provinces, it was England that engaged him for talks.

In 1711, Mesnager's discussions with Matthew Prior and St. John in France, particularly about American trade, facilitated two crucial summits on the matter. Abbé Gaultier served as the intermediary, ferrying diplomatic texts, including those by Mesnager, between London and Paris.

These negotiations in London paved the way for the Treaty of Utrecht, with Mesnager playing a key role as one of the plenipotentiaries. His work was closely monitored by Abbé Gaultier. Noted by English diplomats as an "authorised merchant minister of the Most Christian King," Mesnager was honoured with the title of Count "de Saint-Jean" by the Spanish king, acknowledging his contributions with substantial rewards. Nicolas Mesnager died suddenly in Paris in 1714, and was buried at Saint-Roch.

Ultimately, this character had a relationship with the world of espionage that we still know too little about, but he is also of interest to us

---

[142] Archives des Affaires étrangères, C.P., Hollande 213, fol. 112v°, letter of 12 January 1708, in the "Analyse de la négociation de M. Mesnager en Hollande de janvier à février 1708."
[143] Ibid. Holland, fol. 60, Torcy to Mesnager, 2 February 1708.

because he allows us to paint a picture of France in the context of the wars that fall within the scope of our work:

> The advantages that the French monarchy could not grant in political matters had to be granted in the economic sphere. The war was moving into the realm of merchants: the invasion was no longer about soldiers, it was about goods. [...] In the minds of the negotiators, economic concessions were now a given: they were the price France had to pay for its defeats and for keeping Spain in Louis XIV's family. The "political" victory was offset by an economic setback.[144]

V. The Attack of the 8 March 1711 and the Discovery of a First-rate Spy, Antoine de Guiscard (1658-1711).

The Marquis de Guiscard, also known as Abbé de la Bourlie, stemmed from a family with modest noble roots. He was the younger sibling to the Count of Guiscard, who Louis XIV had named the inaugural French governor of Namur. Initially ordained as a priest, Guiscard swiftly developed a notorious reputation for his libertine lifestyle. Seeking fortune and adventure beyond the ecclesiastical realm, he ventured into a military career, where his conduct soon drew criticism, resulting in his discharge from the army. Undeterred and marked by both bravery and bitterness, he aligned himself with the Camisards' insurrection, subsequently courting foreign courts with offers of espionage services. While it remains unclear if espionage was always part of his repertoire, his fervent drive quickly made him a marked figure in intelligence circles. By 1705, Guiscard had landed in England, where he encountered the English diplomat Richard Hill (Richard Hill of Hawkstone, known as "the Great Hill," 1655-1727). Guiscard presented Hill with his plans, in which Hill expressed his interest. They discussed plans to foment uprisings among the Catholics in France's southern regions, specifically in Dauphiné and Languedoc, while also suggesting the recruitment of numerous French spies. His zeal and determination were evident, and it's rumoured that Guiscard always carried a small vial of poison, a dark testament to his readiness to face the direst consequences should he ever be apprehended.

---

[144] Bély, Lucien, *op. cit*, p. 592.

By 1706, Guiscard had ingratiated himself with Queen Anne's government, securing a pension of 600 guineas for his proposed role in inciting an uprising in Normandy. He was even appointed to lead the military effort, though these plans ultimately fell through. However, within months, his standing with English diplomats, including Minister Harley, began to wane. Despite Harley's earlier promises of substantial financial rewards, these were not forthcoming, leaving Guiscard's situation precarious and not unlike that of many other spies and agents of the time. Impatient and disillusioned, Guiscard turned against the English government, a decision that led to his detection and arrest.

During the trial, Minister Harley, despite being ill, made a point of appearing before Guiscard during Council interrogations. In a dramatic turn, Guiscard, possibly under the influence of alcohol, attempted to stab Harley with a knife he somehow possessed. Miraculously, Harley escaped unharmed, thanks to his ornate brocade waistcoat, sparking widespread speculation about how Guiscard had managed to bring a weapon into such a secure environment. While some suggested a lapse in security, others theorised that Guiscard might have been acting on behalf of another, as yet unknown, employer. Harley had many enemies within the government, and Guiscard's allegiance had clearly shifted. Whether he was already serving another nation's interests remains a mystery. In any case, Guiscard was attacked by members of the government, and it was James Butler, the 2nd Duke of Ormond (1665-1745), who severely wounded him, though not fatally. Suffering and imprisoned in London's Newgate Prison, Guiscard was kept alive for further questioning but succumbed to his injuries shortly thereafter.

The incident significantly bolstered Harley's standing, both among the general populace and within the government. His brave confrontation with danger was celebrated across the country, with the press extensively covering the festivities in his honour. Harley, whose popularity had waned, found his position within the government and public perception greatly strengthened by the ordeal.

In 1713, the Pretender, travelled to Lorraine,[145] where he received a warm welcome from Duke Leopold of Lorraine. The Duke offered him

---

[145] Irish refugees flocked to Duke Leopold of Lorraine between 1698 and 1729.

the protection of his guards and officers, an offer James declined in favour of maintaining a low profile, adhering to his usual practice of remaining incognito. Jean-Baptiste de Noailles, the Bishop of Chalons, who was present at the Duke's court, remarked on James's humility and the dignified yet approachable manner in which he conducted himself:

> For example, he makes the milords and I sit before him in equal seats, even in armchairs; at meals, he always stands at the corner of the table, serves everyone, and often affects not to ask for what he is served until after those who have the honour of eating with him have taken some. He knows how to humble himself and make himself more human, without losing any of his air of dignity and majesty, which he maintains with gracious manners that can only be described as familiar.[146]

However, the Pretender's personal demeanour did not leave a favourable impression on everyone. Described as reticent and lacking fluency in French, his manners were found wanting.[147] What's more, his time spent in military campaigns with Marshals de Condé and Catinat had earned him a reputation for being despondent and melancholic.[148]

In 1714, Queen Anne Stuart showed openness to the idea of her half-brother, the Pretender, reclaiming the throne. The Earl of Oxford even suggested that James renounce his Catholicism, or at least keep it hidden, to facilitate his ascension, a proposal James steadfastly declined.

The Pretender was well-informed about the ongoing negotiations and understood that England, having negotiated the Treaty of Utrecht with determination, had secured a favourable position in the new European balance of power. With Queen Anne's health failing, she preferred her half-brother over the more distantly related George I of Hanover, son of Princess Sophia of Hanover, for the succession to the crown. The year 1714 was marked by the intense rivalry between Robert Harley, Earl of Oxford (1661-1724), who leaned towards the Whig party, and Henry St. John, Earl of Bolingbroke (1678-1751), a Tory, amidst the backdrop of the Pretender's refusal to convert to Protestantism. This religious stance

---

[146] Saint-Simon, Mémoires, Paris, Gallimard, collection de la Pléiade, under the dir. of Y. Coirault,
[147] Du Bosq, op. cit. citing Chateaubriand's novel *The Four Stuarts*, p. 41
[148] *Ibid*, p. 46

led the Whigs to question the trade treaty with France, resulting in parliamentary accusations of treason against those who facilitated the peace, stirring significant public and press reaction. Matthew Prior (1664-1721), an English poet and diplomat who often operated in secrecy, was compelled by the inquiry into the peace process to disclose everything he knew. His revelations forced Bolingbroke and the Duke of Ormond to flee to France for refuge, while Robert Harley faced the scrutiny head-on, managing to defend his actions successfully and preserve his life.

Another foreigner arrived at the same time, who suffered the same fate as the Princesse des Ursins. I am referring to Lord Saint-Jean, better known as the Viscount of Bolingbroke, who was responsible for the Treaty of London which forced the allies to conclude the Peace of Utrecht, and who, at the end of the London negotiations, was sent here to spend eight or ten days by Queen Anne, where he was received with such distinction, as I have already mentioned. His fate in England had changed like that of the Princess des Ursins in Spain, with the difference that our court was very angry at the disgrace of this minister and at not daring to see him. The new king had changed the entire ministry and put the Whigs back in their place, from where he had driven the Tories. The former took advantage of this return to exercise their particular hatreds. They attacked Queen Anne's ministers and made it a crime for them to have made peace. Prior, who had been heavily involved under Queen Anne's ministers, sold their secret and what papers he had to their persecutors, who were also his own, in order to escape oppression through this infamy. Bolingbroke, the most noted of all for having had the main part in the peace, also found himself in the greatest danger, and at the same time the least established. He fought for a while, and when he saw that there was no way out, he made a very nervous speech in the middle of Parliament, and at the same time very free and very strong against the harangue of the King of England, and immediately went to France. He came to live in Paris, but he did not go to court, nor did he publicly see our ministers and officials.[149]

Ultimately, the biggest loser in these political manoeuvres was Holland, which ceded commercial supremacy to London, marking a shift in economic power from Amsterdam to London.

---

[149] Saint-Simon, *Mémoires*, tome 11, Paris, ed. Hachette, 1874, 490 pages.

VI. The Duc d'Aumont's Journey to England (1712).

In 1712, the diplomatic relationship with France warmed significantly. The French Foreign Minister dispatched the Duc d'Aumont (Louis-Marie d'Aumont de Rochebaron, Marquis de Chappes, de Villequier, and Duc d'Aumont, 1691-1723), to join forces with Abbé Gaultier in England. Despite Gaultier's suitability for the diplomatic mission, his status did not empower him to make pivotal decisions. The Duke, who had occupied several prestigious positions at the French court, made his arrival in England on 12 January, 1712, and was immediately the focus of public attention. After dining in Canterbury where he was greeted by English officers, he spent the night in Settinburn. He then made his way through Rochester and entered London by evening, attracting crowds eager to catch a glimpse of him. It was at Blackheath that the Duke met Abbé Gaultier, accompanied by a gentleman from Lord Dartmouth, then Secretary of State. They dined at Lord Bolingbroke's, and the next day met the Duke of Ormond, who had replaced the Duke of Marlborough as commander of the English armies, and then visited the Duke of Buckingham. The English plenipotentiaries remained reserved, however, as the official meeting with the Queen had not yet taken place. Everything was still just pomp and circumstance, a welcome and an appetiser. The Duc d'Aumont remarked on this attitude towards Buckingham: "[he] overwhelmed me with the false courtesies of an old courtier such as himself...,"[150] and countered with discretion: "As I have not yet taken on a character here, I thought I could not make too many advances, especially with the people who had the honour of making up the Queen's council."[151]

The Duc d'Aumont's audience with Queen Anne in London was a significant moment in his diplomatic mission. Prior to the audience, he shared a meal with Bolingbroke, the Queen's vice-chamberlain, who later facilitated his reception by the Queen. This encounter provided the Duke with an opportunity to reflect on the contrasting aesthetics and atmosphere of Buckingham Palace compared to Versailles, which he noted with a

---

[150] Archives des Affaires étrangères, C.P., Angleterre 243, fol. 50-55, the Duc d'Aumont to the King, 19 January 1713.
[151] *Ibid.*

subtle critique meant to flatter Louis XIV: "His Britannic Majesty lives in a palace which does not impose and which is respectable only by its presence."[152] Lord Darmouth was the first to greet him in the antechamber, introducing him to the Queen, who was sitting in an armchair (she was suffering from an attack of gout at the time). Queen Anne engaged in conversation with the Duke, inquiring about France and its King. The Queen's remarks about her subjects being a "strange people" struck a curious note, especially considering the Duke's own reservations about the English populace. This interaction could be interpreted as the Queen's astute awareness of the Duke's sentiments and possibly her attempt at wry humour. The Duke detailed these observations and the subtleties of their exchange in a letter to the French Minister of Foreign Affairs:

> This vile rabble, which has not left my door for five or six days, is a motive for the greatest events, and a dangerous instrument in the hands of those who know how to handle it. But the most certain means of rousing this nation, so haughty and so independent, and of making it serve its own ends, is money, of which I have experienced their greed ever since I set foot in England.[153]

However, the Duke went on to note, this time focusing on the climate in England:

> I confess, however, that I am not bored and that I love these first cries of the people as much as I love my music. All I would like is for the fog, the air and the coal smoke not to be so hard on my throat. You need a clear voice to start with in this country.[154]

But the Duc d'Aumont must have had a rather peculiar character, which is admitted by historians, since he even attacked the French agent Mesnager, despite the latter's instrumental role in facilitating Franco-British reconciliation. Mesnager's lower social standing became a point of contention for d'Aumont in a diplomatic environment where England valued negotiation skills over noble birth, in contrast to France's preference for entrusting diplomatic duties to those of high social rank, regardless of their diplomatic acumen. Queen Anne herself acknowledged

---

[152] *Ibid*, fol.52
[153] *Ibid*, fol. 53-54
[154] *Ibid*, fol.56, from Aumont to Torcy, 19 January 1713.

Mesnager's overly enthusiastic conduct, which, she implied, had overstepped the bounds of his social status, a viewpoint shared during an interaction recounted by Lord Dartmouth:

> He [the Duc d'Aumont] told me that the Queen had just told him that she had been less embarrassed with me than with Mesnager. He had given her a formal harangue and had remained in the middle of the road. The queen wanted to get him back on track but, instead of continuing, he started again and was unable to finish.[155]

The Duc d'Aumont's conduct towards Abbé Gaultier can therefore be comprehended more easily, within the context of adjusting to the diplomatic norms of the time. Recognising that agents deployed to the English court, despite their common birth, had become integrated within the circles of England's notable figures due to their roles as spies and double agents, d'Aumont saw the necessity to realign the dynamics. This shift from espionage to formal diplomatic relations signified a return to traditional practices where embassies and official dialogues took precedence over covert operations. Whether this transition was directly mandated by the king remains uncertain, yet it underscores the evolving nature of international diplomacy and the need to adapt to its changing demands.

Some time later, the Pretender was rumoured to be secretly part of the Duke's embassy and was actively sought. This suspicion put the Duke under considerable pressure, culminating in the arson of his lodging. Engaged in Jacobite intrigue, Minister Torcy cautioned him against these "outbursts," which could drag him into unfamiliar territory. Despite this, he was permitted to dispense financial incentives to operatives engaged by the French ministry. The Duke d'Aumont's personality was well recognised, and after the notorious fire incident, King Louis XIV feigned to attribute it to the chaotic state of the English capital. Perhaps the situation would have been different had peace been the overriding concern.

In any case, concern for the safety of the British ambassador in Paris prompted Torcy to augment the security around his residence. The

---

[155] *Ibid.* fol. 58.

apprehension of a diplomatic fallout that might jeopardise the peace negotiations was paramount.

In conclusion, regarding the Duke d'Aumont's mission in London, Lucien Bély, in his examination of ambassadors and espionage during the era of Louis XIV, offers a pragmatic perspective on the Franco-English rapprochement:

> [...] two nations ceased to be expressed as enemies, and this "reunion" took place in the midst of drama, because the event for a society was experienced with theatrical artifice. The danger of a break-up lent lustre to these first moments of official diplomacy.[156]

---

[156] Bély, Lucien, *Ambassadeurs...*, *op. cit.* p.370-371

CHAPTER 14

JACOBITES HIBRYD USE OF INFLUENCE AND INTELLIGENCE IN ENGLAND (1712-1713)

The propaganda we have discussed, intrinsically linked to power struggles, operates with the same discretion and manipulation inherent in espionage: the true intentions are veiled while information is strategically employed to serve specific goals. Furthermore, this method of propaganda is directly comparable to the activities of agents and spies, aiming to incite societal upheavals, even violent ones as seen in events like the Cévennes revolt. England, in particular, became a battleground for these covert operations: espionage was used to undermine political dynamics, recruit operatives to a cause, sway public opinion, sow division among opposition factions, infiltrate government bodies, and leverage external forces like the Jacobites in France. In the final analysis, we will draw a distinction between the notions of "party" and "cabal," the former involving people carrying out public operations, and the latter involving secretive, underground actions.

In 1712, John Keill (1671-1721) was appointed Royal Cryptographer, succeeding William Blencowe, who died the same year. Following in the footsteps of John Wallis and William Blencowe, he benefited from Louis XIV's lack of interest in cryptography and espionage. The latter was the business of great diplomats, who took a dim view of the rise to power of characters who had no titles of nobility. John Keill and the British government were aware of the situation, and were able to deal more easily with the Jacobites' attempts at destabilisation. Ill-served and ill-supported, their efforts were numerous but in vain, even if they still benefited from the help of a large part of the Scottish nobility in the Highlands, which remained poor.

I. Reversing a Political Situation.

In February 1712, Prince Eugène (1663-1736), a fervent advocate for continuing the war against France, visited London, aligning himself with the Whig party, which opposed the peace-seeking Tories. This visit was strategically timed, especially after the dismissal of the Duke of Marlborough, who had been instrumental in England's military efforts. Despite his war hero status, Prince Eugène received a lukewarm welcome from Queen Anne, prompting him to seek alliance with the Duke of Marlborough to advance their pro-war agenda. It's through the narratives of agents and spies that we learn about Prince Eugène's movements in England from January to March 1712. Jonathan Swift's efforts to sow doubt about Holland played into the complex political dynamics, with not all Tories fully persuaded towards peace. The Prince's presence in Holland didn't go unnoticed, with English spy Plunket alleging in correspondence that Eugène's London mission was to conspire with Marlborough and Jean-Gaspard de Bothmer (1656-1732), the Hanoverian envoy, to depose Queen Anne and install George of Hanover on the throne through turmoil and armed intervention. Financial incentives were purportedly offered to agents participating in this scheme, with reports from foreign diplomats of skirmishes occurring within London's core:

> According to our letters from Holland of 30 March, it was said in the streets of Ostend that a great riot had taken place in London on the 25th. Many people, armed with knives and bayonets, went through the streets shouting that Marlborough must be reinstated and the war continued. They killed every Tory they met. In the end, 150 of the most seditious had to be arrested and imprisoned. - It was thought that the affair might have been instigated by Prince Eugene, but others believe that he had no part in it as he had his leave audience with all the usual ceremonies.[157]

Ultimately, the disturbances were not linked to Prince Eugène, and the resultant turmoil did not escalate. The prevailing sentiment in England leaned strongly towards peace. The French Foreign Minister, Torcy, offered his perspective on these events, noting that Marlborough felt slighted by Prince Eugène's delayed visit. Additionally, the tepid

---

[157] *Correspondence of Baron Karg*, p. 559, Karg to Paolucci, 3 April 1712.

reception from Queen Anne and the Tories towards the Prince underscored the cool relations. Torcy acknowledged the conspiracy theories but provided clarifications on the connections with Bothmer, who was opposed to employing violence, and Marlborough, who was more inclined to finance influencers to stir unrest in London under the cover of darkness.

> Marlborough proposed to employ a band of people without any confession, to encourage them to run through the streets at night and, under the pretext of buffoonery, to insult passers-by; in short, to increase the licence little by little and to commit greater disorders from one day to the next. He claimed that once the people and inhabitants of London had become accustomed to the insults of these night runners, it would not be difficult to have such persons murdered as they saw fit to get rid of, and to blame the crime on this licentious gang.[158]

However, other correspondences suggest a more aggressive strategy proposed by Eugène, including instigating fires throughout the city. This would create chaos, during which Marlborough could seize the Tower of London and capture Queen Anne. This turmoil would potentially facilitate the toppling of Parliament, allowing for the exposure and punishment of those involved in the clandestine negotiations between France and England.

II. <u>Winning Over Agents to your Cause.</u>

It was Louis-Marie, Duc d'Aumont (1691-1723), who, from his station in London as an ambassador and diplomat, attempted to sway English politics towards France's interests. The Whigs, recognising the Duke's influence, directed their attacks against him. The Duke's disdain for the spies under his command, who were tasked with influencing public opinion, was evident. His accounts vividly illustrate the powerful roles of monetary incentive and media manipulation, as well as the significance of ideological persuasion. But we are also interested in ideas.

Indeed, the Duke had a penchant for oversimplifying the character of the English populace, branding them as mercenary due to England's

---

[158] Torcy, Jean-Baptiste Colbert de, *Mémoires du marquis de Torcy*, ed. A. Petitot and Monmerqué, Paris, 1828, p.126

commercial nature. He was unscrupulous in his efforts to manipulate the masses: "two of the most accredited ministers of religion have promised me the help of their word to contain the people, and to animate them when necessary or to combat the seditious speeches of their colleagues. There are lost children in the pulpit as there are in war. All we have to do is get them interested, starting with the vilest of the people. There is no one here exempt from the desire to have, and acquisitions are sure, provided that there are funds proportionate to the greed that reigns here."[159]

By frequenting circles of power and pulling various strings, Duc d'Aumont developed a keen insight into human nature, especially regarding spies and double agents, with whom he became familiar by observing their movements across different spheres. This was notably true for a spy known as Pleiss—possibly connected to the Danish von Plessen family, involved in commerce and politics—who was accused of being an informant for the House of Hanover. Duc d'Aumont detailed: "M. Pleiss, former Minister of State in Denmark and since then steward to the late Prince George, a very intriguing man, a declared enemy of Denmark, from which he was driven by the present King, and likewise an enemy of France and probably of the Queen of Great Britain, has left to come to London. He is going to Hanover, where he is to receive instructions from the Duke of Hanover concerning the cabals he is to create in England against France and the present government of Great Britain."[160]

The narrative around von Plessen underscores the House of Hanover's deployment of agents within London, aiming to cement their ascendancy following Queen Anne's reign. The Duc d'Aumont, promoting France's agenda in favour of the Pretender, a Catholic, naturally opposed von Plessen's manoeuvres. Nevertheless, von Plessen's operations were no secret, with vigilant eyes monitoring his every step.

Guiding minds:

Daniel Defoe, notable as a distinguished writer, also played a significant role in English political dynamics. Beyond his literary contributions, Defoe

---

[159] Archives des affaires étrangères, C.P. Angleterre 243, fol.184, the Duc d'Aumont to Torcy, 16 February 1713.
[160] Public Record Office (London), S.P., 100/2, fol.332, 20 August 1713, extract from a memorandum by the Duc d'Aumont.

adeptly navigated the political currents, engaging in espionage activities amidst the tumultuous interplay of political factions. He openly acknowledged his use of informants and his capacity to recruit individuals willing to betray their alliances, stating: "I have my spies and pensioners everywhere, and I confess that it's the easiest thing in the world here to recruit people to betray their friends. I have spies in the Commission, in Parliament and in the Assembly and, under the pretext of writing my story, I am told everything."[161]

Daniel Defoe waited until the death of Queen Anne to gather intelligence on the Jacobites for the House of Hanover. Lucien Bély asserts that he was a master spy, the head of a network "that served all the powers," and speaks of the "infiltration" of characters and minds:

From time to time I run the risk of fatal misunderstandings. I am, for this service, installed among rabid papists, Jacobites and reactionaries, a species which, I affirm, my soul abhors; I am obliged to hear treacherous impressions and outrageous remarks against the person and government of His Majesty and his most faithful servants and to smile at all this as if I approved of it; I am obliged to take all the scandalous and even scurrilous libels that come my way and keep them with me as if I had to gather material to put in articles; in fact, I sometimes go so far as to let things pass that are a little shocking, so as not to be suspected.[162]

In 1712, the Abbé Du Bos composed a political text, which, receiving approval from Torcy, was entrusted to Colonel Hooke for translation and dissemination within the Jacobite faction, likely as groundwork for the doomed Scottish venture. Amidst its battle against myriad influences, the English government reinvigorated the campaign of printed polemics, recognising it as a conflict beneficial to its interests with minimal repercussions. Queen Anne's cabinet thus reignited the libel conflict—a covert and camouflaged war of sway, engaging familiar figures. On the French front, numerous authors, employed by the state, awaited cues to counteract the critiques from English, Dutch, and Hanoverian adversaries.

---

[161] Mentioned by Lucien Bély in his work on spies and ambassadors at the time of Louis XIV: Deacon, Richard, *Histoire des services secrets britanniques*, Paris, 1976, p.70; the document comes from Portland Manuscripts, p.396.
[162] Mentioned by Lucien Bély, op. cit. *Ibid*, p.71; Public Record Office, S.P., 35/11/24, 26 April 1718.

Moreover, the manipulation extended to the physical aspect of the mediums used for these writings; the appearance and content of libels were altered, rendering them difficult to read or handle, as part of the broader strategy to guide public opinion:

> To counterfeit the German editions, you have to use bad paper that is very dirty, you have to use worn-out type, and what is printed in Greek has to be printed in bad type. You can tell the Paris editions by the Greek characters when they are too beautiful. The Ws must be of the same typeface; as this paper and typeface make an edition difficult to read, to relieve the eye it must be printed in a large typeface; at the very least, the case of the Lettres du Suisse edition must be used and the words and letters must not be squeezed.[163]

Of course, diplomats and ambassadors then took it upon themselves to discuss these writings and pamphlets with politicians, in order to influence decisions taken against a particular country, in this case Holland. Some ambassadors reacted to certain writings, because they knew full well that they had been transformed by well-known writers too: "...there is a printed document being circulated by the French under the title *Remontrances d'un Hollandais à M. le comte de S.P.*, which is interpreted as the Count of Sinzendorf, works to contradict and refute the false allegations of Abbé Du Bos, who is said to be its author, in order to disabuse this country of the weak who might be dazzled and fascinated by the fallacious sophistries of this abbé..."[164]

III. Return of the Pretender and the Treaty of Utrecht.

Despite this, Queen Anne was inclined towards peace, and the political dissidents in London were considering appealing to Dutch intervention once more. Prince Eugène, a staunch adversary of Louis XIV, was present in London, highlighting the tense atmosphere. The financial state of Holland was in shambles, lacking the necessary resources to continue its

---

[163] Lombard, A., *L'Abbé Du Bos, un initiateur de la pensée moderne*, Paris, 1913, p. 127.
[164] Archives des Affaires étrangères, C.P., Hollande 243, fol.270, letter dated 22 December 1712, accompanied by a letter from Audiffret dated 5 January 1712.

opposition effectively. To bypass prolonged discussions, France and England decided to proceed with a secret, bilateral treaty. Both London and Paris were aware that a failure in negotiations could potentially reignite the war, marking the Congress of Utrecht as a significant diplomatic debacle. Meanwhile, spies from both camps were vigorously attempting to sway the outcome, with sensitive information circulating stealthily among many ambassadors. This environment of mutual suspicion was palpable, and despite England's hesitation—stemming from its anticipation of guarantees from Holland—historians recognise that France and England harboured a diplomatic secret meant to be implemented should plans go awry:

> The Estates General have had our proposals printed; they are in all the gazettes. They hope that England will find them unreasonable and that Parliament will declare itself in their favour, but you know our secret, the Queen knows it too, and that we will not confine ourselves to these proposals alone, but we must not show our game to everyone, we will open up to the Queen's ministers of Great Britain when the time comes and when Her Majesty deems it appropriate.[165]

Queen Anne delivered her speech and thus came to a decision crucial for France, which was the surrender of the port and town of Dunkirk. In July 1712, the Duke of Ormond, Marlborough's successor as commander of the English forces, received orders to cease military operations in Dunkirk, as "the Queen no longer wishes to act against France, nor to pay those who do so."[166] Additionally, a contingency plan for a secret treaty in Dunkirk was in place, should Holland terminate the formal negotiations. This move publicly solidified the accord with France and dissolved the Grand Alliance. Correspondence from European intermediaries suggested Holland awaited Queen Anne's demise to reassume control.

Holland thus found itself "caught between two loyalties: the first to the English dynasty and the memory of King William, the second to the

---

[165] Archives des Affaires étrangères, C.P., Hollande 234, fol. 224-225, 8 May 1712, Torcy aux P.P.
[166] Archives des Affaires étrangères, M.D., Hollande 58-59, fol. 86-89, letter from St. John, 2 July 1712.

Grand Alliance against France."[167] What was certain in any case was that England's sense of autonomy was now firmly established, distancing itself from Dutch influence. The Dutch negotiators felt deceived, under the impression of being manipulated covertly. Meanwhile, some speculated that Queen Anne was laying the groundwork for the Pretender's restoration to the English throne.

The Allies therefore pressured the English and French plenipotentiaries, yet retained their intelligence operatives in London to monitor developments. Prince Eugène de Savoie considered withdrawing from the congress to present France with more moderate demands. London diplomats speculated that a potential return of the Pretender would face unanimous parliamentary opposition:

> It is said that a solemn suit will be brought in the next Parliament of England against the authors of certain satires made against the present establishment and in favour of the Pretender: and that this, like the affair of Sacheverell,[168] will be done with a view to discovering the sentiments of the nation in relation to the court of Saint-Germain.[169]

In August 1712, the arrival of an English envoy's wife on the continent sparked belief among French diplomats that the clandestine treaty at Dunkirk was indeed set to proceed. This speculation led to a renewed determination from Holland, which was vehemently opposed to a separate peace at Dunkirk, to engage more constructively in the negotiations. Meanwhile, Prince Eugène and the imperial faction remained intransigent.

These developments underscore the fragility of the peace process and illustrate how this covert war, fueled by spies and double agents, had the potential to sway the overall outcome. While it may be an overstatement

---

[167] Bély, Lucien, Espion et ambassadeurs, op. cit. p. 431

[168] Dr Henry Sacheverell was a Tory preacher, renowned for his harangues, one of which was delivered in St Paul's Cathedral, attacking the Whig government. London was shaken by the affair, which ended in a trial, and he was seen as the symbol of the battle between the Whigs and the Tories (in fact, Sacheverell had unleashed a furore because he questioned the whole of English politics since the Glorious Revolution of 1688). Edmund Burke (1729-1797) himself used it at the end of the 18ᵉ century, to oppose the Jacobite activities that resumed in 1791.

[169] Archivio Segreto Vaticano, Vatican City, Albani 90, fol. 438-9, Amsterdam, 4 December 1711.

to claim that these covert activities were the sole determinants, it's undeniable that unofficial dynamics could significantly influence the direction of formal negotiations.

Ultimately, the Treaty of Utrecht solidified the Protestant succession to the British throne, marking England's growing disinterest in continental politics and its separation from Dutch aspirations.

1. The Pretender's Fate Seemed Sealed:

The comprehensive discussions allowed France and England to confidentially align their interests, despite the existence of a secret treaty known to Holland, which might have lacked the influence to challenge it. Promises were exchanged to mitigate the impact of decisions that seemed too detached due to their official nature, especially concerning the Protestant succession and James III Stuart. The French diplomats were presented with a treaty draft, stipulating the irreversible departure of the Pretender:

> As the man who, during the life of King James, was called the Prince of Wales and, since his death, King of Great Britain, left France with the intention of never returning, Your Majesty promises to ensure that he never returns.[170]

To enforce this commitment, England reiterated its demand for the son of Louis XIV (Philip V of Spain) to formally renounce his claim to the French throne. This stipulation nearly derailed the treaty, provoking frustration and anger, which led the French to observe that in this confrontation, English "phlegm" was met with their "fury," signalling a profound discord.

Throughout the European diplomatic discussions, the multilingual proficiency of the plenipotentiaries was paramount, enabling them to converse with envoys from various nations effectively. This linguistic agility was exemplified by agent Matthew Prior, who, during a personal audience with Louis XIV, engaged in substantial diplomatic dialogue in French. French, in fact, emerged as the diplomatic lingua franca, even among English and Dutch negotiators at the Utrecht Congress,

---

[170] Archives of Foreign Affairs, C.P., Holland, fol. 63-71, P.P. to the King, 8 April 1712.

underscoring France's cultural and political ascendancy. This dominance was notably affirmed in interactions with monarchs considered Louis XIV's juniors, such as the King of Prussia: "Although I am willing to grant him the honours of a crowned head, there must be no parity between me and him; therefore the peace treaty must be signed simply in French [...]."[171]

The collective endorsement of Queen Anne's reign by the participating nations empowered England to independently determine its royal succession. By excluding the Pretender and sidelining Holland, England affirmed its central role in European diplomacy, leading to speculations that future European arbitrage might pivot from the British Isles. The London Upper House's insistence on France's immediate acknowledgment of Anne as Queen aimed to cement her unchallenged status. The French response, characterised by deliberate delays, was a strategic move well understood by the English:

> They (the English plenipotentiaries) were as dismayed by our reply as we were by their request. They naturally told us that we were right in principle, but that it was not their fault if the Upper House had taken the matter the wrong way, and that in a word it was their heads that were at stake, not to mention the danger to which the negotiations would be exposed if this House, over which the present ministry had no control on a matter of honour, were to become more heated.[172]

The arrangement was for France to issue a mere memorandum regarding trade, but wherein Queen Anne would be acknowledged as the sovereign of Great Britain. However, King Louis XIV's directives were explicit: despite the covert recognition of London's Protestant monarch since the early 1710s, the Utrecht negotiations were not deemed the appropriate venue for such a proclamation, and his envoys were instructed to either avoid responding or to do so only in noncommittal terms.

---

[171] Archives des Affaires étrangères, Hollande 249, fol. 1-9, French plenipotentiaries to the king, 1er March 1713.

[172] Szabo, Istvan, *The State Policy of Modern Europe from the Beginning of the Sixteenth Century to the Present Time*. Vol. I, Longman, Brown, Green, Longmans and Roberts, 1857, p. 166.

2. Informers, Agents and Spies, the Financial Cost:

In his book on spies and ambassadors in the time of Louis XIV, French historian Lucien Bély outlines the actual expenditures disbursed to informants working for the French monarch throughout the War of the Spanish Succession. These financial details are particularly revealing, not only because they involve entities seemingly peripheral to the struggle over the British Isles but also because they highlight the global dimension of the Stuart cause, set against the larger canvas of continental conflict:

- Austria: between 900 and 4000 pounds, with a peak in 1714 of 12,000 pounds, certainly paid to the Austrian plenipotentiaries;
- Holland: between 900 and 3500 pounds. This figure can certainly be explained by the decline in influence suffered by the Netherlands in 1714, to the benefit of England;
- Germany: £3,500 on average ;
- England: most of the figures are missing because, as we have explained, the agents erased all traces of corruption. But we can put a figure of £12,000 on the sums paid to the English plenipotentiaries in 1714.

CHAPTER 15

THE FAILURE OF THE JACOBITE'S CAUSE (1715-1745)

Following the death of Louis XIV in 1715, Europe entered a period of official peace. The United Provinces and England diverged both economically and politically, while France formally acknowledged the deposition of the Stuarts in favour of the ascension of the House of Hanover to the throne. This shift relegated Holland from its position as the preeminent maritime force, ceding the title to Great Britain. Despite France maintaining its continental dominance, its influence waned progressively. The primary focus for all was on economic stabilisation after almost four and a half decades of conflict. Although Europe seemed tranquil on the surface, the machinations of espionage and secret warfare persisted in the shadows, laying the groundwork for future conflicts that were inevitably on the horizon.

The period from 1689 to 1709, characterised by revolts and grand expeditions, set the stage for more significant rebellions and uprisings in Scotland, which, alongside Ireland, was a bastion for the Jacobite cause. This opposition, while seemingly superficial, masked the deeper ambitions of the Jacobite and Scottish nobility, who were disillusioned with their failed endeavours in the prior decade. France capitalised on this instability, leveraging it to challenge the newly established ruling house of Great Britain. The era spanning from 1715 to 1746, defined by events such as the Treaty of Utrecht, the demise of Louis XIV, and the calamitous Battle of Culloden, heralded the end of Jacobite aspirations.

In 1717, Jacques François Edouard Stuart, the "Old Pretender," accepted his permanent exile from France, settling in Rome. He would make one final bid for restoration in 1719. However, from 1740 onwards, the mantle was passed to his son, Charles Edward Louis John Stuart, famously known as "Bonnie Prince Charlie," who endeavoured to reclaim his grandfather's throne.

This afterword seeks to elucidate the ongoing intelligence war waged between France and Great Britain from 1715 to 1746. Our aim is to provide a comprehensive yet succinct explanation, ensuring the reader is fully guided through the narrative. To achieve this, we draw upon the expertise of Christopher Andrew, Former MI5 official historian, co-convenor of Cambridge , University Intelligence Seminar and a prolific author. His seminal work, "The Secret World: A History of Intelligence," published in 2019,[173] offers illuminating insights into the era under discussion, serving as a critical reference for our analysis.

Post-1715, the Jacobite movement persisted in leveraging Scotland's vulnerable state, albeit their efforts were fated to end in failure. Despite the allure of the Stuart claimants, epitomised by the romantic figures of the "Pretender" and his son "Bonnie Prince Charlie," their era had definitively concluded. The economic considerations at the time gave even the staunchest supporters pause for thought. Additionally, the Catholic faith of the Pretenders proved to be an insurmountable obstacle for the majority of Scots. In 1715, a mere year following the coronation of George I of Hanover at Westminster, the indecisive Earl of Mar, alongside a modest entourage of nobles and devoted followers, unfurled the royal standard at Braemar. However, the country's response was lukewarm at best. The skirmishes that ensued against the diminutive government forces, led by Argyll, failed to deliver a decisive outcome. Even the arrival of the "Chevalier de Saint-George" in Scotland did not ignite the anticipated fervour. The troops eventually disbanded, and a disheartened "Old Pretender" retreated to France.

Prince Charles Edward, at the age of 25 and immediately following a thwarted French invasion of England, landed in Scotland with merely seven companions, resolved to "conquer or die." His valor, zeal, and charismatic aura, reminiscent of Mary Stuart's, convinced successive Highland chieftains to join his cause. He swiftly overcame the government forces and established his headquarters in Edinburgh. For a brief period,

---

[173] Andrew, Christopher, *The Secret World : A History of Intelligence*, Yale University Press, 960 p. 2019

he reigned over his makeshift capital, basking in the adulation of his courtiers and organizing the amassed Highland warriors. However, lacking artillery and facing hostility from the Lowlands, especially Glasgow and the Southwest, his position was tenuous. He advanced into England, reaching Derby within five weeks, inciting panic in London and prompting King George to contemplate flight to Holland. Yet, Charles Edward's circumstances were fraught with challenges: the Highlanders' discipline waned as they ventured farther from their homeland; the anticipated English Jacobite support failed to materialise; the hoped-for French reinforcements did not arrive; and a veteran English army, redirected from continental engagements, was on the march. Amid growing concerns, the chieftains opted to retreat to Scotland against the Prince's wishes. The inevitable clash at Culloden on 16 April 1746 decisively ended Charles's ambitions.

Over the span of more than five months, Charles Edward Stuart lived through a sequence of extraordinary escapades. The Highland communities, ranging from the humblest tenant farmers to the most affluent clan leaders, clandestinely sheltered him, covertly transferring him from one refugee to another. Despite a bounty on his head, the fidelity of the Highlands was unwavering. Ultimately, he made his way back to the continent, where he died over four decades later. His later years were marked by a nomadic exile, soured by disillusionment and alcoholism, rendering him a figure more apt to be forgotten than the hero of his brief period of acclaim. The Jacobite aspiration, akin to another "ancient ballad," had reached its conclusion. Even the Episcopalians eventually pledged allegiance to the House of Hanover.

But it was also from 1721 that Edward Willes (1693-1773), who succeeded John Keill, became the official cryptographer. Taking advantage of a catastrophic situation for French intelligence, but also of his great expertise in cryptography, he supplanted Louis XV's secret services and ensured that the Jacobite cause was quickly eradicated. Relying, as Louis XIII of France had done in 17th-century Europe, on a solid and highly experienced network, he thwarted all attempts to land Jacobites in Scotland, and set up an entire network specifically designed to track down Charles-Edouard Stuart. Up until the 1750s, the Jacobite leaders, who had enjoyed favourable treatment as a result of royal pardons, were harshly repressed. Louis XV did not have many spies to contend with, as they were forced to avoid the English spy service, which was everywhere.

I. The Mar Rebellion (1715).

In 1715, the death of Louis XIV of France marked a turning point, suggesting a semblance of stability across Europe. This event came on the heels of the 1713 Treaty of Utrecht, a significant agreement that laid the foundations for a new entente among European nations. Notably, Great Britain, which had faced criticism for its prior policies, began to establish a more stable and accepted approach in international relations.

In Scotland, however, the Jacobites still wanted to believe in the restoration of their old rights, in particular those that had belonged to the aristocracy under James II Stuart. For the time being, France had to organise the succession to its King Louis XIV and was therefore only observing the revolt from afar.

This rebellion was spearheaded by John Erskine, the 6th Earl of Mar (1675-1732). Known colloquially as "Bobbing John" and brother to the esteemed judge James Erskine, Mar was a scion of the ancient Scottish nobility. Initially a supporter of the Union of Crowns in 1707, his political journey saw him navigating the complex terrain between the Tories and Whigs, culminating in his exile in Scotland. The rebellion also saw participation from English Jacobites, some of whom held seats in the British Parliament and others who were apprehended in Oxford in October. In England, the uprising was bolstered by notable figures such as James Radclyffe, the 3rd Earl of Derwentwater (1689-1716), William Widdrington, the 4th Baron Widdrington (1678-1743), Charles Radclyffe, the 5th Earl of Derwentwater (1693-1746), Edward Howard, the 9th Duke of Norfolk (1686-1777), and Sir John Hynde Cotton (1686-1752). These individuals launched their own campaigns in concert with the Earl of Mar in Scotland, under the leadership of William Gordon, the 6th Viscount Kenmure. (1672-1716).

On the 6th of September, 1715, the Earl of Mar made a bold proclamation, declaring James VIII the King of Scotland and Ireland, effectively igniting the Jacobite rebellion. In response to this act of defiance, the British Parliament enacted legislation that would transfer the land of landlords who supported the Jacobite cause to their tenant farmers, should these tenants choose to remain loyal to the government. This incentive was met with considerable support. Despite being a less than stellar military leader with a competent force at his disposal, the Earl of Mar managed to secure minor victories within central Scotland. However, his indecisiveness at critical moments during October allowed the Duke of Argyll, a staunch Hanoverian, to bolster his ranks. On the 22nd of October, James II elevated Mar to the role of commander-in-chief. The two opposing forces, led by Argyll and Mar respectively, clashed at Sheriffmuir on the 13th of November, 1715. Mar prematurely left the battlefield, under the impression of having clinched a decisive victory, thereby scattering his forces. Concurrently, from the 12th to the 14th of November, the English Jacobite contingent under William Gordon, having come close to triumph, ultimately capitulated at Preston.

On the 22nd of December, the Pretender made his arrival at Peterhead, Scotland, yet after a series of manoeuvres, he opted to re-embark from Montrose on the 4th of February, 1716. In the aftermath, while many conspirators faced execution, others found mercy under the Indemnity Act passed in July 1717. By 1721, the vacillations of the Earl of Mar regarding his stance on the Jacobite cause led to a loss of trust among his ranks. Ultimately, he accepted a pension from George I. Following his involvement in the Atterbury trial in 1722, he withdrew to Aachen, where he died in May 1732.

The year 1715 therefore saw the failure of the Earl of Mar's uprising with the Battle of Sheriffmuir on 13 November 1715. As the defeat was short and indecisive, the Jacobites still had the means to organise a new rebellion. Their efforts were bolstered by military aid from Charles XII of Sweden, who was engaged in conflict against the House of Hanover. In 1716, cryptographer John Willes cracked the code of communications between Georg Heinrich von Görtz, the Swedish Prime Minister, and Count Karl Gyllenborg, the Swedish ambassador in London. Gyllenborg's marriage to a wealthy Jacobite heiress provided him significant influence in these talks. The intercepted letters revealed discussions among Swedish diplomats in Paris and The Hague, financial backing from Jacobites for the war on Hanover, and Charles XII's military strategies. This intelligence exchange was aimed at securing Swedish support for another insurrection in Great Britain. As a result, George I ordered the arrest of Gyllenborg in January 1717, notwithstanding his diplomatic immunity. Released in August, Gyllenborg returned to Sweden to continue his intelligence activities with Görtz. This period was further complicated by the publication of secret correspondences of Charles I of England, involving the Stuarts and Jacobites in propaganda efforts (as noted by Christopher Andrew, these letters were officially disseminated by Parliament in a white paper, available in English, French, German, and Dutch editions).[174] In response, the House of Commons extended an official commendation to the King, celebrating divine and monarchical victory over the Jacobite and Swedish conspiracies.

The year 1718 brought a significant turn in the tide of European politics with the death of Charles XII of Sweden from a projectile wound to the head during the siege of Fredriksten, an event marking the cessation of Swedish support for the Jacobite cause.

This development, following the exposure of the secret correspondences between Georg Heinrich von Görtz, Prime Minister of Sweden, and Count Karl Gyllenborg, the Swedish ambassador to London, led the Swedish Foreign Ministry to implement a more secure system for encrypting diplomatic communications. John Willes also spent three years deciphering the correspondence of the Bishop of Rochester (Francis Atterbury), leader of the English Jacobites in Great Britain and abroad.

Parallel to the espionage dramas, England faced a significant economic upheaval involving the South Sea Company. Established in 1711 by Robert Harley in the aftermath of the Treaty of Utrecht, the company aimed to monopolise trade with the Americas. However, initial expeditions yielded disappointing results, and trade agreements with Spain began to deteriorate. By 1718, in a desperate move to stabilise its financial standing, the company undertook a substantial portion of the public debt.

---

[174] Chance, J.F. *"The "Swedish Plot" of 1716-17*. Letters exchanged between Count Gyllenborg, Barons Görtz, Sparre and others." English Historical Review, vol. 18 (1903), quoted by Christopher Andrew in *The Secret World.*

The subsequent speculative bubble in 1719, fueled by the company's overconfidence in American trade prospects and the facilitation of public debt acquisition, ultimately led to a catastrophic crash in share prices by September 1720. This financial disaster, known as the South Sea Bubble, not only bankrupted numerous investors but also unveiled extensive fraud among the company's directors, leading to incarcerations in the Tower of London, and several suicides.

II. The Jacobite Rising of 1719.

In 1719, the Jacobite cause found a promising yet ultimately ill-fated ally in Cardinal Alberoni, the Spanish King's minister renowned for his clandestine operations. Following covert discussions and secured promises of military support from Spain, an invasion force was mustered, aiming to unite with Scottish loyalists. However, adverse weather conditions led to the dispersal of the majority of the fleet intended to transport 5,000 soldiers to Scotland, resulting in a mere contingent of 300 Spanish troops making landfall at Loch Duich. Under the leadership of William Murray, Marquis of Tullibardine (1689-1746), and George Keith, 10th Earl Marischal (1693-1778), this force momentarily occupied a castle but was compelled to capitulate owing to insufficient support from the local clans. The remnants of this force faced bombardment by the Royal Navy on May 10, 1719, and retreated to Glen Shiel, only to be overcome by British forces on June 10, marking a swift and ignominious end to their campaign.

The fallout from the failed uprisings of 1715 and 1719 prompted the British Parliament to adopt a strategy extending beyond conventional military engagements, recognizing the potential for an endless cycle of conflict. Legislation such as the Disarming Act and the Clan Act was enacted in 1715 to mitigate future insurrections, alongside the establishment of strategic garrisons in key locations such as Fort William, Fort Augustus, and Fort George. The construction of the Wade Roads, orchestrated by General Wade (1673-1748),[175] facilitated rapid military

---

[175] In 1725, General Wade created militias called "Highlands Watches," hence the famous "Black Watch" regiment, made up of militias from the Monroe clan, to ensure

mobility across these points.

Adopting a "winning hearts and minds" approach aimed at quelling unrest through reconciliation and pacification, the British Parliament's subsequent endeavours included significant investments towards educational initiatives in the Highlands. Nearly £20,000 was allocated for the foundation of schools, predominantly managed by Presbyterians, thereby marginalising Episcopal and Catholic influences in the region.

In November 1721, amidst a decelerating financial climate in Britain, Francis Atterbury (1663-1732), a bishop in the Anglican Church known also for his clandestine activities, concurred to endorse an insurrection helmed by the Pretender, channelling his efforts through Jacobite intermediary George Kelly. This insurrection was meticulously timed to align with the English general election of 1722. Cautious to evade detection, especially in the aftermath of the exposed correspondences between Görtz and Gyllenborg, Atterbury chose to communicate solely through Kelly. This episode unveiled the inherent discord and internal strife prevalent among the Jacobite ranks, reminiscent of challenges faced by Nathaniel Hooke in his era, leading to the ultimate dissolution of their plans. We shed light on the Pretender's perennial misjudgments, notably his concurrent participation in a plot orchestrated by Christopher Layer, a rather unconventional lawyer from Norfolk.

In Rome, the Pretender encountered Christopher Layer, who presented a list of 114 influential individuals willing to support the Pretender's bid for the throne. Despite Layer's eccentricity, James took him seriously, even becoming the godfather to Layer's daughter. The scheme aimed at seizing the Tower of London, the Bank of England, and the Royal Mint, with plans to capture George I and compel his abdication in favour of a return to Hanover. Intriguingly, it was Philip of Orleans, desiring closer ties with England amidst the prevailing Anglophilia of the 1720s in France, who conceived the plan. Layer was apprehended, offered a defence, and ultimately faced execution at Tyburn in May 1723, disclosing no further conspirators. The investigation led by Sir Robert Walpole

---

peace in the Highlands. The regiment fought in 1745 at Fontenoy under the command of Colonel Monro.

implicated Francis Atterbury, betrayed by another Jacobite. Atterbury extricated himself from the plot in the spring of 1722 to avoid execution. Historical records, enriched by disclosures from the 1715 Earl of Mar's rebellion, now confirm Atterbury's direct involvement in the insurrection.

The Earl of Mar, after seeking refuge at the Court of Saint-Germain, assumed the role of Secretary of State. He later served the British crown as a double agent under the alias "Mr. Musgrave." In his efforts to extract information from Atterbury, Mar corresponded with him using the pseudonym "Mr. Islington," ensuring their communications were encrypted to facilitate Atterbury's capture. The Earl of Mar relayed these encrypted messages to Walpole for decryption through intermediary exchanges with Atterbury, mediated by Kelly.

On 24 August 1722, Atterbury found himself arrested and subsequently imprisoned in the Tower of London. In a revealing letter, he stated James Stuart "offered to make peace with George I, provided that George would 'deliver quietly to us the possession of our own Kingdoms,' but complained 'that divers of our Subjects continue daily to be questioned and imprisoned upon pretence of intelligence with us,' and that 'informers, Spy's and false witnesses are become so numerous....that no innocence is safe."[176]

However, in 1723, Walpole's investigation concluded with insufficient grounds to warrant further imprisonment for Atterbury. Opting therefore for a demonstrative measure, authorities decided on his lifelong exile, revocation of ecclesiastical rights, and designation as an enemy of the state. Atterbury, a diplomat of notable skill and eloquence, transformed his trial into a momentous debate in the House of Lords, rivalling the historical trial of Mary Stuart 137 years before. In May 1723, he boldly criticised Walpole. The trial was meticulously orchestrated, selecting witnesses to incriminate Atterbury, notably involving the Archbishop of Canterbury's interrogation of Mrs. Jane Barnes about Harlequin, a beautiful dog gifted by George Kelly, from the Earl of Mar to Atterbury's wife. Jonathan Swift, a friend of Atterbury and critical of the manipulated trial evidence, composed the satirical poem "Upon the Horrid Plot discovered by Harlequin, the Bishop of Rochester's French

---

[176] Christopher Andrew, *op.cit.*

dog." John Willes, called to testify, declined to respond to certain inquiries. Consequently, Atterbury was exiled to France, assuming the role of Secretary of State at the court of Saint-Germain. This move cast a pall over the Jacobites in southern England.

The tenure of the Earl of Waldegrave as the English ambassador to France, spanning from 1730 to 1741, is particularly notable for his diplomatic manoeuvrings amidst a backdrop of intrigue and espionage. The Earl, born to the 1st Baron Waldegrave and Henrietta Fitzjames—an illegitimate offspring of James II and Arabella Churchill—found himself in the midst of a lukewarm French intelligence landscape under the stewardship of Cardinal Fleury (1653-1743), the principal minister to Louis XV. The 1730s saw French diplomatic efforts underwhelmed by Fleury's disinterest in espionage, a situation further complicated in October 1736 when the oversight of foreign affairs shifted to Minister Germain-Louis Chauvelin (1685-1762). The relationship between Fleury and Chauvelin was strained; Fleury advocated for an alliance with Austria, a stance contrary to Chauvelin's adversarial position towards the same. In a twist of fate, Chauvelin "accidentally" conveyed a clandestine missive from the Pretender to Waldegrave, hinting at France's willingness to pivot towards Austria if it meant reinstating the Stuart dynasty in England. This gesture was ostensibly designed to undermine Cardinal Fleury by associating him with the Stuart Pretender's increasingly marginal role in European politics. Waldegrave's reaction to this delicate information was critical. By alerting Fleury to the clandestine correspondence, he not only navigated through the labyrinth of Franco-British diplomacy but also earned the gratitude of Queen Caroline, who was acting as regent during George II's absence in Hanover. Queen Caroline lauded Waldegrave for his astuteness in thwarting the covert plans.

We should also mention the eventful career of the Frenchman François de Bussy (1699-1780). Initially appointed as a secretary to the French Foreign Office in 1725, his diplomatic journey took him from Austria to Versailles and eventually to London as the French ambassador. His prior acquaintance with the Earl of Waldegrave in Vienna laid the groundwork for their future interactions in the realm of international relations. Bussy was adroitly manipulated into divulging crucial information to the English, a service for which he was reportedly compensated. By 1749, the nature of Bussy's activities had aroused suspicion, leading the Marquis d'Argenson (1696-1764), then Secretary of State for Foreign Affairs, to say of him: "He is a man of intrigue, a traitor, a bad man and greatly suspected of being won over by England? The English will be well warned of everything from now on."[177]

One man, however, could have turned the tide against Great Britain and in favour of the Jacobites: Jacques-Joachim Trotti de La Chétardie (1705-1759). Born into an old French family, his uncle was the confessor of Madame de Maintenon, wife of Louis XIV. He began his career in the army, becoming a colonel in 1734, and was soon sent abroad on diplomatic missions, assisted by his father-in-law, who was ambassador to Louis XV. He was very active and travelled all over Europe, taking part in the War of Polish Succession between 1733 and 1738. In 1734, however, he decided to pursue a career as a diplomat. Well-liked and well acquainted with Voltaire, he had a taste for intrigue and society life, and was a very refined and handsome man. Assigned to Russia, he was to work towards a rapprochement with France and a distension of that country's relations with England. To achieve his aims, he had to enter Russian politics, where two parties were in confrontation. The first, Russian nationalist, under the leadership of Princess Elisabeth Petrovna (1709-1762), and the second, pro-German, under the leadership of Anna Leopoldovna (1718-1746). He seduced Elisabeth and became her lover. He plotted with her, with the help of Versailles, to bring down the pro-German party. The coup worked and La Chétardie became a hero.

However, he was under constant surveillance, and his encrypted dispatches to France were intercepted, decrypted and read. Indeed, Peter the Great's secret services had also reached a certain level of excellence, as had those of Great Britain. In his letters, he insulted the Russian imperial family and was disgraced. He left the country in 1743 and returned to military life in France, where he was killed at Hanau in 1758 during the Seven Years' War, a conflict that perfectly symbolised France's international decline.

---

[177] D'Argenson, Mémoires, t. V, p. 434

III. The Jacobite Rising of 1745.

In 1737, amidst the ongoing conflict between Great Britain and Spain in the Caribbean, known as the War of Jenkins' Ear,[178] François de Bussy found himself in London under a veil of secrecy. Tasked with intelligence gathering regarding communications between Spain and the Jacobite sympathisers, Bussy's infamy for avarice preceded him. In a dramatic turn of events in February 1744, de Bussy betrayed the trust placed in him by revealing to the British authorities a comprehensive plan crafted by France. This plan aimed to facilitate the invasion of Britain to restore the 'Young Pretender,' Charles Edward Stuart, affectionately dubbed 'Bonnie Prince Charlie,' to the throne. This betrayal included divulging the identities of key English Jacobites entangled in the conspiracy, for which Bussy was handsomely rewarded with 2,000 pounds. The thwarting of the 1744 invasion attempt is attributed to adverse weather conditions near Dunkirk, which compromised the integrity of the landing fleet, alongside covert counteractions by the British. Despite Bussy's comprehensive betrayal, the astute manoeuvres of Henry Pelham's (1694-1754) government played a crucial role in neutralising the threat. Forewarned of the impending French operation, Pelham mobilised additional military support from Ireland and the Netherlands, facilitating the arrest of principal Jacobite conspirators before the operation could gain momentum. By the time Charles Edward Stuart, now going by 'Chevalier Douglas', reached Gravelines en route to Dunkirk, the British had effectively neutralised the threat.

In the summer of 1745, despite Versailles withdrawing its support for the Stuart Restoration efforts in England, Charles Stuart, fueled by unwavering determination and the loyalty of key Scottish clans, embarked for Scotland. Anchored by his confidence in the Highlanders' prowess, exemplified by their notable victory at Prestonpans on 21 September 1745, Charles envisioned a united front. By December, he had advanced to

---

[178] A war that mobilised enormous naval forces on the part of both countries. The result was disastrous for Great Britain. The name of the war refers to Captain Robert Jenkins, who in 1731 had his ear sliced off by the Spanish captain Julio Leon Fandin. Fandin is said to have told him: "Take it to your king, and tell him I'll do the same to him if I see him around here!"

Derby, flanked by devoted allies, including a covert operative of the English government masquerading as Oliver Williams, a fervent Jacobite whose real identity was Dudley Bradstreet. Williams' mission was to obstruct Charles's progress and distance him from London by any means necessary. Unbeknownst to Charles, as he reluctantly decided to retreat to Scotland, influenced by his council's apprehensions about the overwhelming odds posed by enemy forces, he was unwittingly ensnared by betrayal, and his troops would never reach London again. Moreover, it would seem that his privy council had advised him to make this choice, as the advance into English territory raised fears of a confrontation with three enemy armies, which was beyond their strength.[179]

This clash, the second significant battle on British soil since the uprising's inception, resulted in a devastating defeat for the Scots. Despite this setback, Charles evaded capture, thanks to the clandestine efforts of his network of spies and agents. Remaining concealed within Scotland, Charles eventually set sail again on 19 September 1746.

IV. The Battle of Culloden: The Jacobite Last Stand (1745).

The Battle of Culloden, fought on 16 April 1746, holds a particularly important place in the annals of Scottish and British history, and is of particular relevance to our book, as it is emblematic of more than just the Scottish army's defeat. This army, composed primarily of Highland clans in rebellion, alongside a smattering of Irish veterans, English supporters, and several hundred French troops, represented the collapse of an entire nation under subjugation. This battle, marking the last on British soil between two opposing national forces, saw the English troops bolstered not just by local Lowland Scottish loyalists but also by a significant contingent of Hanoverian soldiers, predominantly of Hessian origin. Historians have often interpreted this engagement as signalling the end of the feudal system that dominated the Scottish Highlands. In the end,

---

[179] Anecdotally, Christopher Andrew writes that Brastreet received only £120 from George II, but not the commission he was expecting and had apparently been promised. He later left the army and became an illusionist and conjurer.

however, the battle's outcome, marred by tactical missteps and the lack of substantive support from Louis XV of France, underscored the failure of the uprising. Louis XV's commitment to the cause was symbolised by sending Lord Jean-Baptiste de Boyer d'Eguilles (1708-1783) as a representative to stand with Charles Stuart.

Charles, commanding his forces, found himself at a numerical advantage with 9,000 men to his opponent's 5,000. Yet, this superiority did not translate into victory. Following a bold advance towards London, his forces retreated to Scotland, where they achieved minor successes but struggled significantly in capturing key locations due to logistical shortfalls. The campaign's overly cautious strategy, which should have decisively defeated the opposition and shifted the political landscape, instead resulted in strategic missteps leading to their undoing. The prolonged duration of the campaign, marked by relentless rain, drained Charles's forces before they even reached the battlefield. Clans, rallying behind their leaders to fight periodically before returning to their familial duties, found themselves weary. The exhaustive length of their campaign, coupled with the inability to relinquish their arms even momentarily, deeply demoralised the troops on the eve of battle.

However, the Highland warriors were renowned for their courage, operating in a terrain dotted with low marshy walls that favoured their signature battle tactic: the Highland charge. This manoeuvre involved waiting for the enemy to discharge their firearms before rushing in with the claymore, a formidable two-handed broadsword, screaming to disorient and drive the enemy back. Opposing them, the Duke of Cumberland strategically positioned his infantry in two lines, equipped with the newer bayonet rifles, preparing for the assault.

The battle commenced as Hanoverian artillery targeted the advancing Cameron clan, prompting an immediate, though uncoordinated, charge from the entire Scottish line. This fierce onslaught initially overwhelmed the enemy's front line but was halted mid-battlefield during intense hand-to-hand combat. This pause allowed the Hanoverian cavalry to encircle the Scots. In a battle that lasted less than an hour and concluded around midday, the Duke of Cumberland emerged victorious. The conflict resulted in approximately 1,250 Jacobite casualties, significantly outnumbering the 350 Hanoverian losses.

The aftermath of the Battle of Culloden was marked by a brutal crackdown that earned the Duke of Cumberland the infamous moniker "Butcher Cumberland." The wounded, prisoners, and even innocent bystanders who had merely sought to witness the conflict were mercilessly killed. Charles Edward Stuart swiftly fled the scene as the savage repression unfolded over the following months, with tens of thousands estimated to have perished. The captured leaders were executed by axe, a departure from the ghastly traditional punishment of being hanged, drawn, and quartered, but a grim fate nonetheless. But more than that, after more than fifty years of war between Scotland and England, the Duke of Cumberland finally had the chance to end the rebellion once and for all. So, he spared no expense.

The repercussions extended far beyond the battlefield, fundamentally altering Scottish culture. England's objective was to eradicate Scottish distinctiveness, seen as the root of rebellion. This led to a forced transformation of the Highland way of life. Clan chiefs were coerced into adopting speculative cash crop farming, such as sheep raising and enclosing moors, which resulted in the displacement of peasants from their ancestral lands. Many of these dispossessed Scots emigrated to the Apalachicola region in the United States. The swift defeat at Culloden, lasting less than half a day, not only subdued a nation but also irrevocably altered its identity and landscape. Charles Stuart was left with no choice but to escape into exile.

In the subsequent years, British intelligence closely monitored Charles, apprehending and executing several of his adherents. Despite this, Charles's network of agents remained potent, exuding confidence in their capacity to orchestrate a coup in London. In 1750, despite being a fugitive and sometimes disguising himself as a priest, Charles successfully infiltrated London by dispatching deceptive letters to an English ally within the city.

Arriving in Dover on 13 September 1750, Charles made his way to London by 16 September, taking refuge in the residence of Anne Drelincourt, Lady Primrose, situated on the Strand. There, he convened a meeting of approximately fifty Jacobites in a hall in Pall Mall. This gathering only served to reinforce his apprehensions: the political climate in London was starkly unfavourable for a coup d'état, with scant support from his followers. By 23 September, Charles permanently departed from Great Britain.

By the late 1750s, the English authorities had significantly improved their capacity to quell Jacobite dissent, bolstered by a sophisticated espionage network. A notable figure, known as "Pickle," infiltrated the Jacobite movement, a moniker inspired by Peregrine Pickle, a fictional character from Tobias Smollett's narrative. The true identity of "Pickle" remained a mystery until the mid-19th century, when historical inquiry into the Jacobite phenomenon intensified, spurred by figures such as Walter Scott. These investigations also unearthed legends of a hidden Jacobite treasure in the Highlands, a mystery purportedly solved only in the 2020s. Historian Andrew Lang, upon scrutinising certain archival materials, unveiled that this enigmatic spy was actually Alasdair Ruadh MacDonnell, chieftain of the MacDonell clan of Glengarry, living from 1725 to 1761.[180]

"Pickle" maintained covert correspondence with prominent figures within the British government, establishing covert channels with notable political figures including Prime Minister Henry Pelham, whom he affectionately termed his 'Great Friend,' and the Duke of Newcastle, to whom he referred as 'Mr Kenady'. Additionally, key individuals were cryptically identified by numerical codes, with the 'Old Pretender' labelled as 8, and Charles Stuart, the 'Young Pretender', as 80. Through Pickle's intelligence activities, the "Elibank Plot" of 1752, a conspiracy orchestrated by Alexander Murray of Elibank, was successfully neutralised. This scheme, reminiscent of Christopher Layer's plot of 1720, aimed at a bold seizure of St James's Palace and the Tower of London, the abduction of King George II and select members of the royal family to Hanover, and facilitating Charles Stuart's return from France to reclaim the British crown, set for November 10, 1752. However, upon Murray's arrival in England in October to consolidate the conspirators, he

---

[180] Lang, Andrew, *Pickle the Spy, or The Incognito of Prince Charles*, Longmans, Green and Co, London, New-York and Bombay, 1897, p. 320

discovered a prevailing sentiment of betrayal among them, shifting their focus to evasion rather than aggression. Amidst this tumult, the whispered name of Charles Stuart's mistress, Clementine Walkinshaw, permeated discussions, yet it was 'Pickle' whose clandestine efforts ultimately unravelled the plot. It was not until February 1751 that Murray was apprehended. Summoned by the House of Commons for stirring up Jacobite violence during an election, he was imprisoned at Newgate to stand trial. His trial was marked by a number of outbursts, such as his refusal to bow to the House, for which he was again charged with contempt. Yet, the tumultuous political landscape of England in June 1751, culminating in the dissolution of Parliament, inadvertently facilitated Murray's swift release. However, by November, the pendulum of political interest had swung back towards Murray, prompting plans for his re-arrest and return to Newgate prison. Forewarned by allies of his impending detainment, Murray orchestrated his escape, ultimately seeking refuge in France.

In 1753, the British government's relentless pursuit of Jacobite conspirators culminated in the arrest of one of the most active figures in the movement, Dr. Archibald Cameron (1707-1753). Cameron, who had been a staunch supporter and participant in Charles Stuart's endeavours since the 1745 uprising, was among a group of high-profile Jacobites, including Sir John Graeme, Henry Goring, Lady Primrose, Jeremy Dawkins, MacDonald of Lochgarry, and George Keith, Earl Marischal—who by then served as Frederick of Prussia's envoy to Paris. Cameron's trial became a spectacle of the government's determination to quash the Jacobite cause, and in a bid to deter future dissent, Cameron was executed on 7 June 1753, following traditional methods.

This event marked a turning point in the Jacobite struggle, as Charles Stuart found himself increasingly pursued by English intelligence, and those Jacobites who remained in England were forced into hiding, with many ultimately renouncing their allegiance to the Stuart cause.

By June 1753, the once fervent flame of Jacobite resistance in Britain and France had been effectively extinguished. It had been nearly eight decades of turbulent and often clandestine efforts to restore the Stuarts to the British throne, but this era was drawing to a close. The subsequent years saw the influence of Jacobitism wane, with its activities shifting from overt resistance to subtler attempts to exert influence within the government, though these efforts largely faded from the annals of British history.

The failure of the Jacobite cause was therefore the result of a great deal of procrastination on the part of France and Scotland, who were unable to find common ground, especially as the "pretender's" struggle turned into a losing battle, a kind of romanticism in which the result was less important than the battle itself. Charles-Edouard Stuart, son of Jacques-François Stuart, tried by all means to land in Scotland, and when he did, he did not win any major battles. Nevertheless, the Scottish revolts after 1715 were numerous and sometimes dangerous for the government of Great Britain. But Louis XV, following in the footsteps of Louis XIV, abandoned the battle of intelligence and espionage, which could have restored the situation. He preferred the actions of selected diplomats who knew how to make their mark in the countries to which they were sent, such as Jacques-Joachim Trotti de La Chétardie (1705-1759) in Russia. Louis XV preferred continental alliances to setback alliances, particularly with the Scots, without realising that a unified Great Britain would in turn become the arbiter of Europe after the Seven Years' War.

CONCLUSION

The Treaty of Utrecht led to the creation of the Triple Alliance in 1717, uniting France, Great Britain, the United Provinces, and the Holy Roman Empire to ensure the treaty's terms were upheld. This alliance aimed to further isolate James III Stuart, the Pretender, with the Emperor explicitly vowing never to welcome him into his territories. By the late 1710s, this coalition had effectively bolstered collective security in Europe, sidelining the Pretender from the international arena.

By 1715, marking the end of our focal period, the Pretender had departed from France, solidifying the Protestant succession. The Treaty of Utrecht thus reset the international stage, reaffirming the supremacy of lawful governance. Louis XIV's response to England in 1712 underscored this ethos: "Our reply was that Your Majesty did not wish to meddle in the future with anything to do with the succession to the crown of England, and that she referred to the decisions of Parliament, convinced that it should be left to each nation to settle these kinds of matters according to its own laws."[181] However, the King also emphasised the familial obligations of Queen Anne to prevent her brother from living in destitution.

On 27 August 1712, amid preparations by the Jacobites for new influence operations, the Pretender announced his impending exile, emphasising the absence of guaranteed comforts:

> It will not be possible for me to leave for a few days yet, I even have to send someone ahead, if only to take a house, and I cannot send him without first hearing from you to find out whether the King likes me as much to go to Châlon as to Reims, where it is said that there are bound to be some enemy

---

[181] Archives des Affaires étrangères, C.P. Hollande 232, fol. 109, the P.P. to the King, 30 January 1712.

parties, which would greatly restrict my walks, and where everything is excessively expensive.[182]

On 30 August 1712, Torcy emphasised the urgency of departure. On 14 September, the Duke of Lorraine had extended an offer of his Château de Bar, leading to the Pretender's eventual departure. This move signified his estrangement from England's evolving domestic agenda. Reflecting the era's sentiment, a French treatise titled "Memoir on the Genius of the English and the Current State of the English Court" was published on 29 October 1712. It marked the end of conflict and acknowledged Britain's attainment of political equilibrium, sidelining any prospect of a Stuart restoration amidst the Protestant ascendancy:

> The English maintain that the end of government is the preservation, good and happiness of the people. This is why they say that the monarchy of Great Britain is admirably well formed, being limited in such a way that the liberty of the people is secure without diminishing the power of the king; it is an instrument with three strings, which, being well in tune, produce an excellent harmony for the happiness of the kingdom: It is a mixed government of monarchy in the King, aristocracy in the Peers, and democracy in the Commons: the King appears as a great monarch, the Peers uphold their authority and the Commons their freedom, and they are all three to observe each other.[183]

Needless to say, towards the middle of the 18th century, a sort of Anglophilia took hold of France, valuing commerce over conflict and viewing England, in the midst of its Industrial Revolution, as a paradigm of a nation where domestic and foreign policies were in harmony. The Enlightenment period particularly saw this alignment as a prime example of reason applied to governance and political strategy.

The Treaty of Utrecht solidified the fracturing relationship between Holland and England. A rivalry persisted between these two maritime powerhouses: Holland aimed to hold England accountable for past actions, while England sought independence from such reminders. Queen Anne positioned Great Britain as the senior partner to the United Provinces, with

---

[182] *Ibid*, England 242, fol. 40, "James III" to Torcy, 27 August 1712.
[183] *Ibid*, M.D., England 138, fol. 16-38, "Mémoire sur le génie des Anglais, et sur l'état présent de la Cour d'Angleterre," 29 October 1712.

the Peace of Utrecht being more of an imposition than a proposal. The Queen's communications highlighted a European "balance" achieved through financial subsidies under the guise of securing the peoples' safety. She conveyed to the United Provinces: "Our conduct has always been based on the same principle. A sincere desire to preserve equilibrium in Europe, and to procure not only the security but also the increase of your State, has been the principal motive which has led us to support a war as long and as costly as the one from which we hope to emerge."[184]

Furthermore, trade agreements also regulated situations of war and peace. England and France found common ground here, because their mutual enemy was indeed Holland, and if everything was clear from this point of view, then there would no longer be any possibility of war between the two nations:

> When you want to get rid of old prejudices and look deeper into the matter, you will easily see that the interests of both crowns are met in this concert and in these mutual facilities. France will never ruin England through its trade and vice versa. She has nothing to fear: these are two great kingdoms, countries of great extent and great consumption. It will always be enough for each of the two nations to do its own trade without thinking about that of the others. They are not opposed to each other.[185]

The Treaty of Utrecht marked the end of a European war that had lasted 45 years. Lord Bolingbroke, in his correspondence with Harley, the Earl of Oxford, articulated the collective sentiment of the era: "The common happiness of the whole of Europe can only be expected from this happy intelligence which has prevented public demonstrations of perfect reconciliation."[186] And in another letter to Torcy he stated:

> At last, Sir, here we are on the eve of peace; let us not be shipwrecked in the harbour; but let us conclude as soon as possible a work on the success of which depends the happiness of so many peoples, of the present century and of those to come.[187]

---

[184] *Ibid*, C.P., England 243, fol. 45-46, letter from the Queen to the States General, 18 January 1713.
[185] *Ibid*, M.D., France 1425, fol. 101sq.
[186] *Ibid*, England 238, fol. 106, letter to Oxford, 8 June 1712.
[187] *Ibid*, England 240, fol. 201-203, Bolingbroke to Torcy, 2 December 1712.

This period of peace, brokered among France, Great Britain, and the United Provinces, endured a quarter of a century until it was ruptured by the War of the Austrian Succession in 1740. However, this ostensible tranquillity belied undercurrents of unrest, notably due to Jacobite scheming, which threatened the fragile accord even after the ink had dried on the treaty in 1713. Thus, the semblance of stability that Europe enjoyed post-Utrecht was tenuous at best.

By the year 1714, the era of soliciting external backing from Europe's influential figures had ceased. The Jacobites came to the realisation that each notable supporter they garnered also brought along political backing that could provoke disturbances across the political spectrum, affecting both Whigs and Tories.

At this time, although the aristocracy continued to dominate government roles, their authority increasingly hinged on the favour of political factions that commanded popular support and were susceptible to manipulation by foreign operatives. Consequently, the Stuart court found itself, albeit reluctantly, leaning on the Conservative party for support. This affiliation did not imply that all Tories were Jacobites or vice versa, but rather that Jacobitism represented the complex ambition of a potent minority that had the capacity to sway public sentiment, despite recurrent suppression by those in power.

For the Stuart claimant, any meaningful influence over English politics necessitated an alignment with the Conservative faction, a partnership fraught with challenges. The Conservatives championed the monarch's dominion and the Church of England's authority, while critiquing the perceived "corruption" and "despotism" of the governing ministers. The Stuart Court, while adherent to monarchical principles, showed a predilection for religious tolerance and displayed little enthusiasm for reform. The Catholic nobility, spanning Scottish, Irish, and English backgrounds, held positions in Saint-Germain-en-Laye and Rome, often regarding the prominent English clergy with scepticism. Their goal was to court the Whigs to mitigate their reliance on the Tory party alone.

The gradual convergence of Jacobitism with Toryism unfolded over time. A segment of the Tory party, marginalised by the Glorious Revolution of 1688, had sanctioned the Edicts of Toleration, embarked on various military campaigns, and ultimately witnessed the ascendancy of their rivals, the Whigs. Within the Conservative faction, a subgroup known as the "country" party, began veering towards Jacobitism in the 1690s, a movement that gained momentum during Queen Anne's reign. From 1710 to 1714, key Conservative figures such as Robert Harley, Earl of Oxford, and Henry St. John, Viscount Bolingbroke, sought to establish connections with the Stuart court, aiming to bolster their party's base.

When George I ousted the Tories from power after his accession to the throne in 1714, the party's leaders devised a plot, but it did not sit well with the expectations of the Court of St Germain, despite some of the anti-government riots that broke out in London.

The insurrection of 1715 demonstrated the organisational frailties of Jacobitism, particularly as the rebellion unfolded across Scotland and Northern England yet failed to secure victory. This failure, however, did not diminish the movement's allure or its status as a viable alternative to the prevailing Whig governance. For a brief period, Bolingbroke served as Secretary of State to the Pretender, only to depart from the court, disillusioned by the Jacobites' shortcomings in exile at Saint-Germain. Oxford, too, engaged in conspiratorial activities with them, alongside James Butler, Duke of Ormonde, a former Captain General of British forces who defected to the Jacobite cause. By 1721, the conspiracy had evolved into an intricate plot, which included plans for uprisings within London and an invasion by Spanish forces under Ormonde's leadership. Central to this conspiracy was Francis Atterbury, Bishop of Rochester, who, despite being a Conservative and a prominent Jacobite figure within England, was ultimately apprehended by the British authorities and sentenced to exile.

The period of political instability in Britain was marked by the inability of the government to ensure the security of both the populace and the elite, leading to a fragmented political landscape. During this tumultuous era, the Conservative Party found itself leaderless and engaged in uneasy alliances with their ideological adversaries, the Whigs. The Stuarts sought to rekindle their association with the Tories between 1731 and 1733, notably through figures like Henry Hyde and Lord Cornbury, who sought French support for a new rebellion. However, Tory distrust towards Saint-Germain and revelations of Bolingbroke's duplicity soured these efforts. From 1740 to 1744, Stuart sympathisers, including prominent Tories such as Sir John Hynde Cotton, Sir Watkin Williams Wynne, and James Barry, Earl of Barrymore, conspired to orchestrate a French-supported invasion. These plans were uncovered in January 1744, prompting several conspirators to join a coalition government known as the Broad Bottom administration, blending Whigs and Tories. Despite these preparations, Charles Edward Stuart's unexpected arrival in Scotland, leading a modest force, caught them off guard. His subsequent defeat at the Battle of Culloden in April 1746 marked a significant blow to the Jacobite cause. In 1750, on a clandestine trip to London, Charles assembled a group of Tory figures, led by Charles Noel Somerset, Duke of Beaufort, and John Fane, Earl of Westmorland. Despite the fact that a group of loyalists had created a popular opposition club in London (the Independent Electors of Westminster), they managed to persuade him to abandon a coup. After this date, the Conservatives distanced themselves from the Stuarts, so much so that in 1761, the renowned arch-conservative Sir John Phillips even fled from the Jacobite agents. The latter were no more than a minority of malcontents, who no longer had a voice in English political debate.

Contrary to what many historians assert, the Stuart court was not misled by its interactions with Tory circles. Indeed, as previously mentioned, Charles Stuart was initially hesitant to embrace this alliance. A few years prior, some individuals had taken the bold step of writing directly to the Pretender (George Granville, Lord Lansdowne; John Boyle, Earl of Orrery; and Alderman John Barber), although intermediaries remained the preferred mode of communication. The Stuart Papers reveal that Jacobite agents did indeed express their reservations and pledges of allegiance to notable figures at the court. Apart from the crisis in December 1745, the Stuarts never fully trusted the Tories regarding military support. Instead, it was the French, Spanish, and Swedes, supported by the Highland clans, who undertook military actions. The Tories' contribution was limited to organising riots or protests across the country (notably in the spring and summer of 1715, when party affiliates incited them in numerous English towns). These actions served either to distract the English army stationed on the coast or to undermine the Hanoverian government. Hence, Jacobite agents focused on swaying public sentiment.

Jacobite publicity and propaganda targeted primarily Tory audiences, employing pamphlets, billboards, caricatures, and newspapers as mediums. In May 1717, London publicist George Flint even forwarded to the Court of Saint-Germain a list that included the names of several influential Conservatives in London, York, and Newcastle, who were identified as potential recipients and readers of these materials. After his exile in 1728, Nathaniel Mist, the editor of the Tory-oriented Mist's Weekly Journal, became a steadfast correspondent for the Court of St Germain. He frequently commented on the parliamentary and London city affairs, notably during the excise crisis of 1733. In the years 1736-1737, Mist proposed financing a new publication, Common Sense, edited by his associate Charles Molloy. The Pretender himself had reached out to his supporters in England to contribute to this endeavour. Additionally, in 1750, a fervent anti-Hanoverian pamphleteer faced trial near London for seditious speech. His subsequent acquittal was met with great jubilation in Jacobite circles.

The conclusion of this discussion therefore extends beyond merely summarising the events described; it involves reevaluating them in light of the substantial contributions to the historiography of Jacobitism made possible by the Stuart Papers. This treasure trove of documents, coupled with diligent research in archives and studies on the intelligence war from 1688 to 1715, has facilitated the creation of a comprehensive portrayal of this period. It is evident, however, that additional investigations could further elucidate significant occurrences within the same timeframe, offering a deeper understanding of the complexities of this historical chapter.

Ultimately, the Stuart Papers shed light on the dynamics of an English political landscape in flux, shaped by European continental influences, persistent external meddling, and the sway of public opinion as stoked by a highly partisan press. While earlier narratives on Jacobitism tended to dwell on dynastic, religious, and constitutional themes—with considerable retrospection, especially concerning mid-18th-century events—current historical discourse, propelled by both seasoned historians and emerging scholars, has sought to refresh and reshape the research perspective. This shift highlights how Jacobite endeavours in Great Britain served as a significant source of national turmoil, occasionally plunging governments into crisis.

With the examination of the Stuart Papers, we can see illuminated the turbulent political landscape of England between 1688 and 1715, revealing a society fraught with complexity and contradictions. For nearly seventy years, Great Britain was ensnared in a web of domestic uncertainty, rife with factionalism, betrayals, and conspiracies that impeded national unification and state-building. It was not until the dawn of 1760 that a new vision of Britain emerged—one marked by confidence, imperial ambition, and the foundational values of Protestantism, liberty, and property rights. This research endeavour has sought to uncover the layers of a profoundly unstable and tumultuous period in British history. In doing so, we have also acknowledged the country's remarkable resilience in the face of both external and internal threats, a resilience bolstered by an array of enigmatic figures—spies, agents, and shadowy operatives—whose contributions to the crown and private interests intertwine with the broader narrative of geopolitics and international relations involving France and Holland.

In terms of espionage, France's decline began with the reign of Louis XV. However, Richelieu and Mazarin, the former during the reign of Louis XIII and the latter at the beginning of the reign of Louis XIV, were very fond of Rossignol, who was the man for the job. Louis XIII and Richelieu, then Louis XIV went to Juvisy sur Orge to visit him and prove once again that they had confidence in him.[188] Rossignol was recommended to Louis XIV, but the latter treated him less favourably than his predecessor.

On the English side, the famous Wallis began to outdo the French in the field of encryption and decryption, and William III took notice. Colbert, the minister of finance, called on Rossignol to examine the

---

[188] The only depiction of the meeting between Louis XIV and Antoine Rossinol is a painting by Pierre-Denis Martin, circa 1700. It appears in the book by the Former historian of MI5, Christopher Andrew : *The Secret World, A History of Intelligence*, published by Yale University Press and Penguins Books UK (2019).

kingdom's financial accounts, but when the minister died, Rossignol was definitively abandoned, along with the auditing of accounts. Wallis was Bishop of Bath and Wells, were sent by Walpole to England to do the same. So was the Duke of Marlborough. But the unification of Great Britain was nearing completion, making it a great power that now rivalled the greatest countries in Europe. The France of Louis XV, which was in crisis, could not resist and the Jacobite cause was therefore doomed. Peter the Great also made Russia a great country in terms of intelligence, which also outclassed France. If France had wanted to succeed with the Jacobites, it would have had to be in a position to still be the most dominant kingdom in Europe, which was no longer the case in the reign of Louis XV, but had been the case in the reign of Louis XIII and the early reign of Louis XIV. But it was Britain that, after years of internal and external political struggles, had managed to build its unity. Having in turn become the most powerful kingdom in Europe, it was now seen as its arbiter, and the kings of France subsequently paid the price, notably with the Seven Years' War, which symbolised the downfall for one and the glory for the other. The Jacobites' cause was therefore lost as soon as Louis XIV failed to continue the work of his father and his minister Richelieu in the field of espionage, and Louis XV merely witnessed their inexorable demise.

BIBLIOGRAPHY

The Foreign Affairs Archive, Paris:

- England : 42, fol. 56-58 (1712)/230, 1° 309 (1710)/230, 1° 437 i .v (1710)/232, 1° 59 (1711)/237, 1re 142 (1712)/238, fol. 106 (1712)/239, fol.61 (1712)/ 240, fol. 201-203 (1712)/ 240, fol. 279/242, fol. 96, 30 (1712)/243, fol. 45-46, (1713)/243, fol. 50-55 (1713)/243, fol.68 (1713)/ /243, fol.184 (1713).
- Holland : fol. 63-71 (1712)/58-59, fol. 86-89 (1712)/ 213, fol. 112v° (1708)/234, fol. 224-225 (1712)/ 232, fol. 109 (1712)/fol.190 (1712)/243, fol.270 (1712)/ 249, fol. 1-9 (1713).

Archivio Segreto Vaticano, Vatican City:

- Albani 90, fol. 438-9 (1711).

Archives de la Bastille:

- Bastille 10577, t. XI.

The National Archives, Kew :

- Letter from Princess Anne, november 18, 1688, SP 8/2/81, Part 2, Folios 152-153

Andrew, Christopher, *The Secret World : A History of Intelligence*, two editions at Yale University Press and Penguins Book UK, 960 pages, 2019.

Mémoires et journal inédit du marquis d'Argenson, (René-Louis de Voyer de Paulmy), ministre des Affaires étrangères sous Louis XV, publiés et annotés par M. le marquis d'Argenson, Paris, Jannet, 1857-1858, 5 vol.

Bély, Lucien :

- *Espions et ambassadeurs au temps de Louis XIV*, Ed. Fayard, 1990 ;
- *Les secrets de Louis XIV*, Le grand livre du mois, 2013.

Callow, John, *King in Exile, James II: Warrior, King and Saint*, 1689–1701, Sutton Publishing, Stroud, 2004, ISBN 0-7509-3082-9, 454 p., 2004

Caylus, Madame de, *Souvenirs de Madame de Caylus,* Ed. Mercure de France, 2003.

Chance, J.F. *"The "Swedish Plot" of 1716-17*. Letters exchanged between Count Gyllenborg, Barons Görtz, Sparre and others." English Historical Review, vol. 18, 1903.

Coombs, Douglas, *The Conduct of the Dutch. British Opinion and the Dutch Alliance during the war of the Spanish Succession*, The Hague-Ashimota, 1958.

Cottret, Bernard, *History of England, 16th-18th centuries*, PUF, "Nouvelle Clio," 1996

Cruickshanks, Eveline, *Ideology and Conspiracy: Aspects of Jacobitism 1689 - 1759*, John Donald Publusihers, Edinburgh, 1982.

Deacon, Richard, *Histoire des services secrets britanniques*, Buchet-Chastel, Paris, 1976.

Dedieu, Joseph, *Le Rôle politique des protestants français (1685-1715)*, Paris, 1920.

Downie, J.A, *Robert Harley and the press. Propaganda and Public Opinion in the Age of Swift and Defoe,* Cambridge University Press, 1979.

Du Boscq, G. and M. Bernos, *La Cour des Stuarts à Saint-Germain-en-Laye 1689-1718*, Paris 1912, VIII., Paris - Emile Paul -1912.

Duffo, François-Albert, *Lettres inédites de l'abbé E. Renaudot au ministre J.-B. Colbert* (Années 1692 à 1706) Lettres inédites de J.-B. Racine à l'abbé E. Renaudot (Années 1699 et 1700), 1931.

Dulon, Jacques, Jacques II Stuart, Sa Famille et les Jacobites à Saint-Germain-en-Laye, 1897, 158 pages.

Forbin Claude de, *Mémoires du Comte de Forbin (1656-1733),* Mercure de France, Paris, 1993.

Freschot, Casimir, *Histoire amoureuse et badine du congrès et de la ville d'Utrecht, en plusieurs lettres écrites par le domestique d'un des plénipotentiaires à un de ses amis*, Liège, Jacob Le Doux, S.D. (1714), in-12, front.

Girolamo, Cardano, *Proxeneta seu de Prudentia Civili Liber*, 2nd ed. Paris, 1652.

Gérin, Charles, *Le Pape Innocent XI et la révolution anglaise de 1688*, V. Palmé ed., 1876.

Hooke Nathaniel :

- *The Secret History of Colonel Hooke's negotiations in Scotland, in favour of the Pretender, in 1707 : including the original letters and papers which passed between the Scotch and Irish Lords and the Court of Versailles and St. Germains*. n. e., London, 1760, Memoir of the Scottish Lords, 1707, p. 83.
- *Mémoire des choses nécessaires pour mon voyage*, 31 January 1707, vol 2, p. 111

Gregg, James Edward, *James Francis Edward (1688-1766)*, Oxford University Press, 2004.

Horn, D.B., *The British Diplomatic Service*, Oxford, 1961.

Hugon, Alain, *Rivalités européennes et hégémonie mondiale, XVIe - XVIIIe siècle*, Ed. Armand Colin, 2002, 202 pages.

Lachs, P.S., *The Diplomatic Corps under Charles II and James II*, New Brunswick, 1966.

Lane, M., *The Diplomatic Service under William III*, Transactions of the Royal Historical Society, Cambridge University Press, 1927.

Lang, Andrew, *Pickle the Spy, or The Incognito of Prince Charles*, Longmans, Green and Co, London, New-York and Bombay, 1897.

Legrelle, Arsène, *La Mission de M. de Rébenac à Madrid et la mort de Marie-Louise, reine d'Espagne (1688-1689)*, 1894, 154 pages.

Lombard, A., *L'Abbé Du Bos, un initiateur de la pensée moderne*, Paris, 1913, p. 127.

Machiavelli, Niccolò, *The Prince*, London, Penguin ed., 1961 (translated by George Bull).

Macray W.D. :

- *Correspondence of Colonel... op. cit*, Memorandum given to M. de Torcy, 18 February 1703, vil 1, p.1
- *Summary Memorandum on Scottish Affairs*, 2 February 1704, vol 1, p. 48
- *Abridgment of Mr. Leviston's Memoirs*, 6 February 1704, vol 1, p. 78.
- *Mémoire donné à M. le Maréchal de Villeroy*, 10 mars, 1705, vol 1, p. 158.
- *The duchess of Gordon to me*, 5 August 1707, vol 2 p. 444

Ravaison, François, *Archives de la Bastille*, A. Durand et Pedone-Lauriel ed., Paris, 1866-1904

Saint-Simon, *Mémoires*, Paris, Gallimard, collection de la Pléiade, sous la direction de Y. Coirault.

Sainty, J.C., *Officials of the Secretaries of State (1660-1782)*, London, 1973

Sarmant, Thierry, Stoll Mathieu, *Régner et gouverner*, coll. Tempus, Ed. Perrin, 2019, 896 p.

Snyder, H.L., *The British Diplomatic Service during the Godolphin Minister*, in Studies in Diplomatic History, Hatton and Anderson eds, 1970.

Szabo, Istvan, *The State Policy of Modern Europe from the Beginning of the Sixteenth Century to the Present Time.* Vol. I, Longman, Brown, Green, Longmans and Roberts, 1857.

Thomson, M.A. *The Secretaries of State, 1681-1782*, Oxford, 1932.

Torcy, Jean-Baptiste Colbert de, *Mémoires du marquis de Torcy*, ed. A. Petitot and Monmerqué, Paris, 1828.

Valance, Edward, *The Glorious Revolution. 1688-Britain's Fight for Liberty*, London 2006.

Walpole, Horace, *Memoirs of the reign of Jing George the Second,* London, H. Colburn publishers, 1847.

Whitehead, Julian, *Espionage int the Divided Stuart Dynasty*, 1685-1715, 2020, 200 p.

Mémoires de M. le marquis de Feuquière, Lieutenant-général des armées du Roi, tome premier, A Amsterdam, 1761, 353 pages.

Correspondence between Baron Karg von Bebenburg, Chancellor of the Prince-Bishop of Liège, and Cardinal Paolucci, Secretary of State, 1700-1719: 1712-1719, Institut Historique Belge de Rome, 1968, 1364 pages.

Mémoires de Monsieur de Torcy : pour servir à l'histoire des Négociations, 1757, vol. 3, Ed. Kessinger Publishing, 2009, 276 pages.

Correspondence of Colonel N. Hooke, agent from the Court of France to the Scottish Jacobites, in the years 1703-1707 n.e, 1870, compiled by William Dunn Macray, two volumes.

Letters and correspondence, public and private, of the Right Honourable Henry St. John, Lord Visc. Bolingbroke, during the time he was secretary of state to Queen Anne, London, Printed for G.G. and J. Robinson, University of Michigan, 1798.

Mémoires du marquis de Torcy, ed. A. Petitot and Monnerqué, t.II (t. LXVIII of the collection of Mémoires relatifs à l'histoire de France), Paris, 1828.

Correspondence du Baron Karg de Bebenbourg, Chancelier du prince-évêque de Liège, Joseph-Clément de Bavière, archevêque électeur de Cologne, avec le cardinal Paolucci, secrétaire d'Etat, 1700-1719 : 1712-1719, Institut historique belge de Rome, 1968, 1364 pages.

INDEX

A

Aberdeen (Scotland) 173, 178, 179
Académie Française (Paris) xi
Acevedo y Rosales (Isidro Casado, Marquess of Monteleon, Milanese diplomat) 211, 212
Act (Licensing) 37, 71
Act (Test) 67
Agde (Cap of) 117, 120
Aglionby (William, English physician, historian and diplomat) 113
Aigues-Mortes (France).117
Aix-la-Chapelle (Treaty of, Germany).28, 58, 198, 208
Akerhielm (Samuel, 'the Elder', Swedish diplomat)132
Alba (Duke of, Spanish ambassador)190
Alberoni (Giulio, Italian Priest and statesman in Spain)241
Alès (France).112
Alès (Pierre d', also known as 'le Baron d'Alès').112
Alexander the Great.8
Alliance (Auld).52, 87
Amboise (Conjuration of).45
Amsterdam18, 95, 125, 149, 150, 209, 218, 230, 266
Andrew (Christopher, English professor and historian).xiii, 3, 236, 240 243, 247, 260, 263
Anet (Castle of, France).178
Angoulême (France)171
Anne (Queen of Great Britain and Ireland).xii, 16, 17, 20, 22, 28, 36, 38, 43, 57, 68, 69, 72, 74, 80, 85, 91, 92, 103, 105, 112, 120, 128, 133, 135, 138, 142, 143, 145, 149, 153, 155, 156, 160, 161, 163, 164, 168, 169, 170, 178, 179, 183, 185, 198, 201, 204, 210, 211, 216, 217, 218, 219, 220, 224, 225, 226, 227, 228, 229, 230, 232, 253, 254, 257, 263, 267
Ansbach (Caroline of Brandebourg d', Wife of King George II of England, also known as 'Queen Caroline').244
Antoine (Nickname, Banker and spy).195
Arbuthnot (John, Scottish physician, satirist and polymath, also known as 'Dr Arbuthnot').201, 202, 205
Archambaud (Jean-Albert d', also known as 'Abbé Bucquoy' or 'Manicamp', the Duke of Marlborough's spy)144, 145
Argenson (Mars-Pierre de Voyer de Paulmy, 1er marquis d', French Minister)127
Argyll (Scotland)93
Aristotle.8
Arlington (Henry Bennet, 1st Earl of Arlington, member of the 'Cabal')58, 59, 61, 65, 77
Arlington (Isabella Bennet FitzRoy, Duchess of Grafton and 2nd Countess of, daughter of Henry Bennet).65
Armstrong (Thomas, English Army officer and politician, also known as 'Henry Lawrence').86

Arnaud (Camisard prophet and spy)116
Arouet (François-Marie, known as 'Voltaire', French writer and philosoph).245
Ashley (Anthony Cooper, 1st Earl of Shaftesbury, member of the 'Cabal')58, 77
Assassination Plot (the).129, 130
Asturias (Balthasar Charles, Prince of, son of King Philip IV of Spain).50
Atholl (John Murray, 2nd Duke of Atholl).93, 160, 161, 164, 173
Atholl Brigade (The)93
Atterbury (Francis, Bishop of Rochester and Jacobite)145, 240, 243, 257
Aubigny-sur-Nère (France)66
Aughrim (battle of)70
Augicourt (Truffier, Lord of, French Spy)21
Augustus (Fort, Scotland)241
Aumont (Louis-Marie-Victor de Rochebaron, marquis de Chappes et de Villequier, 2e duc d', Pair of France).22, 25, 133, 211, 212, 219, 220, 221, 222, 225, 226
Austria (Mary-Anne of, Habsbourg Princess).50
Austrian Succession (War of the).256
Avaux (Jean-Antoine de Mesmes of, French diplomat).33, 76
Avignon (France)117
Azzurini (Antonio, Cadinal, Count, diplomat and double agent)195, 196

B

Balaruc (France)120
Balustrode (Anne, 2nd wife of John Parker)129
Bamfield (Joseph, Colonel in the British Army)86
Bank of England (The)71, 242
Bank of Scotland (The Royal).71
Baptist (Jean, Count of Arco, German officer, diplomat and double agent).195
Bar (Castle of, France)254
Barber (John, jacobite Lord Mayor of London)258
Barbezieux (Louis François Marie Le Tellier, marquis de, Secretary of State)20, 127
Barcelona.188
Barclay (George, Sir, British army officer and Jacobite conspirator)89, 102, 127, 128
Barclay (William, Scottish diplomat).102
Barnevelt (Nickname, English catholic double agent)197
Barrier (Treaty of the)135, 200, 201
Barrillon (Jean-Paul, marquis de Branges, seigneur d'Amoncourt, de Mancy, de Châtillon-sur-Marne, French Ambassador to King Charles II of England).106
Barry (James, 4th Earl of Barrymore, Scottish Jacobite)258
Bartet (Isaac, First Secretary of Mazarin)11
Bastille (Castle of the, Parisian prison)13, 38, 39, 86, 124, 126, 127, 144, 145, 197, 263
Bavaria (Maximilian I, Duke of Wittelsbach of)44
Bavaria (Maximilian II Emanuel Ludwig Maria Joseph Kajetan Anton Nikolaus Franz Ignaz Felix, Elector of).28, 47, 49, 184, 185, 189, 190, 191
Bavière (Elisabeth-Charlotte de, comtesse de Simmern, aslo known as 'Princesse Palatine')44
Bayle (Pierre, French philosopher and author)107

Beaufort (François de Bourbon-Vendôme, 2e duc de, grandson of the King Henri IV of France).64, 158, 258
Beauvaisis (French Royal regiment of).158
Beauvilliers (Paul de, duc de Saint-Aignan, French politician).176, 187
Bebenburg (Johann Friedrich Karg von, German Chancellor)133, 224
Belcastel (Sieur de, protestant nobleman from the Cévennes)114, 118, 119
Bellay (France)114
Bellings (Richard, Sir, Irish courtier, Knight secretary to Catherine of Braganza and spy).61
Bély (Lucien, French historian)7, 20, 22, 33, 123, 199, 215, 222, 227, 230, 233, 263
Bergheick (Spanish diplomat)189, 190, 191
Berlin108, 132
Bern (Switzerland).112
Bernard (Nickname of a Protestant pastor and spy).109
Bernaville (Charles le Fournier de, Governor of the Bastille in Paris).144
Berne (Gazette of).36
Bernos (M. French historian)17, 100, 264
Berrick, or Berwick (Jacques Ier Fitz-James, duc de, Jacques II Stuart's son, nephew of John Churchill).22, 89, 119, 120, 128, 129, 130, 147, 148, 174, 177, 179, 187, 193
Berwick (Treaty of).50
Bielke (Nils, Count, Swedish officer and politician).132
Bill of Rights69, 75, 153
Billant (Moïse, French Huguenot peasant).113

Birkenhead (William, Spy)102
Bishops' War.49
Black Cabinet, Black Chamber (known as 'Cabinet Noir' or 'Darkroom'.xi, xii, 5, 14, 15, 16, 35, 39, 40, 53
Blencowe (William, grandson of John Wallis).16, 72, 155, 184, 223
Blencowe (William, British cryptographer, grandson of William Wallis)16, 72, 155, 184, 223
Blenheim (battle of)148, 164, 169, 184, 193, 205
Bluche (François, French historian).123
Bodleian Library (Oxford)181
Bolingbroke (Henry St. John, 1st Viscount of).17, 18, 20, 27, 38, 101, 145, 150, 151, 196, 200, 201, 202, 207, 208, 209, 210, 211, 214, 217, 218, 219, 229, 255, 257, 258, 267
Bonrepaus (François d'Usson, Marquis de, French officer and diplomat)87
Bordeaux113
Boscq de Beaumont (G., du, French historian)17, 75, 76, 89, 100, 264
Bothmer (Jean-Gaspard de, Baron, German diplomat in London).224, 225
Boucoiran (France).115
Boufflers (Louis-François, duc de, French Marshal).148, 186
Bouillon (Emmanuel-Théodose de la Tour d'Auvergne, Cardinal of).36
Boulogne (France)25, 129
Bourbon (French Dynasty)56, 190
Bourbon-Malause (Henri-Armand, marquis de Miremont, French Huguenot officer)112
Bourges (France).168

Bourke, or Bourk (Theobald, Tobias, called 'Toby', Jacobite agent and spy)22

Boyer (Abel, French pamphleteer in London).205

Boyle (John, 5th Earl of Cork and Orrery, Scottish Jacobite).258

Boyne (battle of the).23, 70, 76, 81, 90, 106, 108, 112, 128, 154

Bradstreet (Dudley, Irish adventurer and secret government agent, also known as 'Oliver Williams').247

Braemar (Scotland).236

Braganza (Catherine, Queen consort of England, Scotland and Ireland, Charles II's wife)57, 64

Brandenburg (State of, Germany).2, 75, 108, 109, 116, 132, 150

Breadalbane (branch of the Clan Campbell)93

Breda (Treaty of).58

Brest (France)63, 126, 175

Briançon (France).187

Brixham (England).68, 75, 81

Broglie (Victor-Maurice, comte de, French marshal)112, 113

Brougham (Henry, Whig lawyer and businessman)98

Brousson (Claude, lawyer and Protestant pastor).108

Bruce (Robert the, King of Scotland).42

Brunswick (Duke of)18

Brussels79, 112, 184

Brydges (James, 1st Duke of Chandos, paymaster general of the English forces).150

Buckingham (George Villiers, 2nd Duke of, member of the 'Cabal').58, 59, 64, 77, 219

Burnet (Gilbert, Bishop of Salisbury, Scottish philosopher and historian)55, 72

Bussy (François de, French nobleman, diplomat and double agent)244, 245, 246

Butler (James, 2nd Duke of Ormond, Irish statesman and soldier, Jacobite).195, 216, 218, 219, 229, 257

Butler, Henrietta (Lady Henrietta FitzJames, Viscountess Galmoye)244

Buys (Willem, Dutch diplomat).150, 185, 209

C

Cabal ministry (known as 'CABAL', group of high counciliors of King Charles II of England : Clifford, Arlington, Buckingham, Ashley, Lauderdale).58

Caillaud (Etienne, merchant and spy).15, 107, 110, 111, 129, 130, 131

Calais (France)17, 18, 60, 91, 100, 129, 196

Callières (François de, Sieur de Rochelay et de Grigny)11, 130, 172, 175

Callow (John, English historian)103, 264

Camaret (battle of)125, 126

Camargue (The, French region).118

Cambridge (England)3, 67, 154, 236, 264, 265

Cameron (Highland Scottish Clan).89, 93, 248

Cameron (Richard, Scottish leader of the militant Presbyterians)55

Cameron of Lochiel (Archibald, Scottish physician and Jacobite agent).251

Cameronians (Scottish political faction).55

Camisards (The, Rebel French Protestants)111, 112, 114, 115, 116, 117, 118, 120, 137, 215
Campbell (Archibald, 9th Earl of Argyll).79, 154, 161
Campbell (Highland Scottish Clan).88, 90, 93
Campbell (John, 1st Earl of Breadalbane and Holland, also known as 'Slippery John')160
Campbell of Glenlyon (Robert, 5th Laird of Glenlyon)90
Cannon (Alexander, Major-General of Jacobite forces)89
Canterbury (Archbishop of).67, 74, 243
Canterbury (England)219
Capell (Arthur, 1st Earl of Essex).78
Cardano (Girolamo).9, 265
Cárdenas (Alonso de, Knight of Santiago, Spanish ambassador).50
Carlton House (London).97
Carron (James, Scottish agent).165
Carruthers (Bruce, American sociologist and historian)72
Castanet (Henri, Camisard chief).117
Catalonia (The, Spanish region).120, 175, 188
Catholics (political faction).1, 19, 33, 43, 45, 55, 56, 57, 59, 60, 61, 62, 64, 65, 66, 67, 68, 69, 70, 73, 74, 75, 76, 77, 78, 79, 80, 81, 85, 86, 99, 100, 101, 102, 105, 106, 107, 108, 109, 110, 113, 114, 119, 120, 125, 141, 158, 159, 160, 161, 180, 197, 204, 205, 212, 215, 217, 226, 236, 242, 256
Catinat de La Fauconnerie (Nicolas de, seigneur de Saint-Gratien, French officer)107, 217
Cavalier (Jean, Chief and Camisard prophet)112, 113, 117, 118, 120
Caylus (Marthe-Marguerite Le Valois de Villette de Mursey, marquise de, author and memorialist)146, 264
Cecil (William, 2nd Earl of Salisbury, Viscount Cranborne).45
Celle (Germany).18
Cévennes, Cévennes War (The, France).107, 108, 109, 111, 113, 114, 116, 137, 207, 223
Châlons-en-Champagne (France)128, 146, 217
Chamillart (Michel, Frenc Secretary of State)17, 18, 20, 32, 34, 114, 147, 171, 176, 177, 178, 179, 183
Channel (English).35, 45, 46, 47, 48, 49, 102, 178
Charleroi (Belgium).184
Charles I (King of England, Scotland and Ireland).xi, xii, 2, 20, 42, 43, 44, 45, 46, 47, 48, 49, 50, 51, 53, 56, 57, 60, 70, 99, 100, 240
Charles II (King of England, Scotland an Ireland)xii, 13, 20, 27, 43, 44, 54, 55, 56, 57, 58, 59, 60, 61, 62, 64, 65, 66, 67, 73, 74, 75, 76, 77, 78, 79, 81, 99, 105, 130, 265
Charles XII of Sweden (King of Sweden).131, 239, 240
Chauvelin (Germain-Louis, Marquis de Grosbois, French politician).244
Chevreuse (Honoré-Charles d'Albert de Luynes, 3e duc de, French Marshal)21, 48, 148, 173, 175, 176, 177
Chisholm (Highland Scottish Clan).89
Chudleigh (Thomas, British ambassador)86
Churchill (Arabella, mistress of King James II Stuart)128, 129, 147, 244
Churchill (Sir Winston Leonard Spencer).126, 184
Civil War (The, England).xi, 9, 16, 43, 50, 53, 67, 75

Clan Act (The).241
Clanranald (Clan McDonald of, branch of McDonald Clan).89
Clément (Simon, French pamphleteer in London)205
Clement X (Pope).78, 212
Clément XI (Pope)212
Clifford (Thomas, 1st Baron Clifford of Chudleigh, member of the 'Cabal')58, 59, 61, 76, 77
Clignières (Nickname of a Dutch diplomat)115
Coke (John, Sir, English Secretary of State)45
Commons (House of).23, 57, 77, 149, 150, 240, 251
Commonwealth (The)54, 75
Compagnies Franches (French light troops)109
Condé (Louis II de Bourbon, French Marshal, known as 'le Grand Condé')15, 31, 78, 201, 217
Constantin (Nickname of a French spy and prisoner)126
Coombs (Douglas, English historian)38
Copenhagen136
Corbie (France).47
Corsica.119
Cottret (Bernard, French historian).51, 264
Council (King's)5, 21, 31, 174
Counter-Reformation (The)45
Courtin (Honoré)13, 28
Covenanters (Scottish religious and political movement).54, 55
Cowper (William, 1st Baron Cowper, High Chancellor).21
Crécy (Louis de Verjus, Count of).11, 130
Croissy (Charles Colbert, Marquis de, Secretary of State).xii, 20, 27, 28, 58, 61, 65
Croker (John Wilson, Irish author and politician).98

Cromwell (Oliver, Lord-protector)23, 43, 53, 54, 56, 70, 75, 86, 154
Crone (Matthew, Jacobite spy).17, 101
Crozon peninsula (France)126
Cruickshanks (Eveline, English historian).51, 125, 264
Culloden (battle of). 235, 237, 247, 249, 258
Cumberland (Prince Rupert of the Rhine, Duke of, brother of Charles I Louis)48
Cumberland (William Augustus, Prince and Duke of, son of King George II of Great Britain).248, 249
Cutz (Nickname of a British spy).114

D

Danckelmann (Eberhard von, German diplomat)116
Danger (Eustache, valet to Nicolas Fouquet, former finance minister of Louis XIV, hypothetical spy and 'Man in the Iron Mask').59
Dapifer (Alain, Seneschal of Dol-de-Bretagne)42
Darassus (French Protestant diplomat)116
Darien Company (The, Scotland)71
Dauphiné (the, historic region of France).107, 110, 115, 116, 117, 215
Davenant (Charles, English economist and pamphleteer).36, 136, 137, 138, 139, 143
David Ist (King of Scotland).42, 43
Dawkins (Jeremy, Jacobite agent)251
Dedieu (Joseph, French priest, author and historian).111, 264
Defoe (Daniel, English writer, merchant and spy)170, 200, 201, 202, 205, 226, 227, 264
Denain (battle of)34, 198

Denmark (Prince George of, Duke of Cumberland, Husband of Queen Anne of Great Britain).69, 74, 103
Denmark18, 69, 73, 103, 226
Descartes (René).16
Desmarets (Nicolas, French Controller General of Finance).183, 188
Disarming Act (The)242
Dol-de-Bretagne (France)42, 87
Douai (France)34
Douglas (James, 2nd Duke of Queensberry and 1st Duke of Dover, Scottish politician).161
Dover (Treaty of)42, 56, 61, 62, 63, 64, 76
Dover18, 42, 56, 61, 62, 63, 64, 76, 249
Downey (J.A., English historian).49
Drake (Francis, Sir).48
Drelincourt (Anne, Viscountess Primrose, aslo known as 'Lady Primrose')249, 251
Dresden180
Drummond (Anne, Countess of Erroll, mother of Charles Hay, 13th of Erroll).160, 167
Drummond (Highland Scottish Clan).89
Drummond (James, 3rd Earl of Perth, brother of John Drummond, 1st Earl of Melfort)141, 158, 159
Drummond (James, 4th Earl of Perth, Scottish peer and politician, son of James Drummond (3rd Earl of Perth).161, 164, 165
Drummond (John, 1st Earl of Melfort)38, 89, 101, 102, 141, 158, 172
Drummond (John, Scottish banker, merchant and politician)149, 150, 151
Drummond (Mary, Countess Marischal, daughter of James Drummond, wife of William Keith (9th Earl Marischal, 4th Earl of Perth).159
Du Wal (Mathias, Irish sailor and double agent)136
Dublin112, 153
Dubos (Jean-Baptiste, known as 'Abbé Du Bos', French author, diplomat and propagandist)143
Duffo (François-Albert, French historian)124, 264
Duich (Loch, Scotland)241
Dulon (Jacques, French historian)264
Dunbar (battle of).54
Dunkeld (battle of).90
Dunkirk (France)57, 60, 64, 172, 175, 177, 178, 179, 190, 209, 210, 229, 230, 246
Dunn Macray (William, English librarian, cleric and historian).181
Dunottar Castle (Scotland)159
Dunoyer (Madame, Nickname of a journalist and spy).145
Dussen (Bruno, Van der, Dutch Diplomat)185
Dutch Republic.23, 24, 35, 37, 38, 42, 57, 58, 66, 67, 71, 80, 87, 91, 105, 106, 108, 130, 135, 149, 150, 151, 155, 157, 180, 184, 185, 188, 196, 202, 203, 207, 209, 213, 227, 228, 230, 231, 240, 264
Dutch War.28, 74, 77, 109, 113, 115, 118, 120, 126, 142, 190, 191, 192, 211, 231

E

Eguilles (Jean-Baptiste Boyer, seigneur d', French politician).248
Elibank Plot (The).250
Elizabeth Ist (Queen of England and Ireland).48
England1, 2, 3, 5, 8, 9, 10, 12, 13, 16, 18, 19, 20, 22, 23, 24, 25, 27, 28, 36, 37, 38, 41, 42, 43, 44, 45, 46, 48, 49, 50, 51, 52, 53, 54, 56, 57,

58, 59, 60, 61, 62, 64, 65, 66, 67, 68, 69, 70, 71, 72, 73, 74, 75, 76, 78, 79, 80, 81, 83, 85, 86, 87, 88, 89, 91, 92, 95, 97, 98, 99, 100, 101, 105, 106, 107, 108, 109, 110, 111, 112, 114, 115, 116, 119, 120, 121, 123, 124, 127, 129, 130, 131, 132, 133, 135, 136, 137, 138, 139, 141, 142, 143, 145, 146, 148, 149, 150, 151, 154, 155, 156, 157, 161, 162, 164, 167, 168, 170, 171, 178, 179, 185, 186, 187, 188, 189, 191, 195, 196, 197, 199, 200, 201, 203, 204, 207, 208, 210, 211, 212, 213, 214, 215, 217, 218, 219, 220, 221, 223, 224, 225, 226, 229, 230, 231, 232, 233, 235, 236, 237, 238, 240, 242, 244, 245, 246, 249, 250, 251, 253, 254, 255, 256, 257, 259, 260, 261, 263, 264

English Civil War (The).9, 16, 43

English Revolution (The)55, 56, 66, 85, 123, 138

Episcopal War (The, Scotland).50

Epstein (Stephan R., British economic historian)72

Erasmus.8

Erskine (David, 9th Earl of Buchan, Jacobite)173

Erskine (James, Lord Grange, brother of John, 6th Earl of Mar).238

Erskine (John, 6th Earl of Mar, also known 'Bobbing John').129, 238, 239, 243

Estrées (Victor Marie, comte et duc d', French Marshal).189

Exclusion Bill (The)77

F

Fane (John, 7th Earl of Westmorland, Scottish Jacobite)258

Farquharson (Highland Scottish Clan).89

Fénelon (François de Salignac de la Mothe-Fénelon, Archbishop of Cambrai, French writer and teacher).21, 148, 194

Fenwick (John, Sir, 3rd Baronet, English Army officer politician, Jacobite conspirator).127, 129

Ferguson (Sarah Margaret, Duchess of York)66

Feuqiières (Antoine de Pas de, Marquis de, General of the French army)93

Finch (Daniel, 2nd Earl of Nottingham, 7th Earl of Winchilsea, Secretary of State).101, 112, 113

Firth of Forth (The, Edimbourg estuary)91, 175, 178

Fitz Alan (Robert, 7th Great Stewart)43

Fitz Alan (Walter, Anglo-Norman baron, Ist Stewart of Scotland)42, 43

Flanders.33, 45, 48, 49, 50, 155, 171, 190

Fleming (John, 6th Earl of Wigton, Jacobite)173

Flemming (Charles, Jacobite spy)160, 178

Fleury (André Hercule de, French Cardinal and Principal Minister to Louis XV of France)244

Flint (George, London publicist)259

Florisson (Nickname, Belgian merchant and spy)190

Flotard (David, Camisard chief)117

Fontainebleau (France)177

Forbin (Claude de, Comte de Forbin-Gardanne, French naval officer)91, 92, 177, 178, 178, 179, 264

Fort William (Scotland).90, 241

Fox (Charles James, British Whig politician).98

France (Louis de, also known as 'le Grand Dauphin').74
France.xiii, 1, 2, 3, 5, 7, 10, 12, 15, 18, 19, 20, 22, 23, 24, 25, 27, 28, 31, 33, 36, 37, 38, 39, 40, 41, 42, 43, 44, 45, 46, 47, 48, 49, 50, 51, 53, 56, 57, 58, 59, 60, 61, 62, 63, 64, 65, 66, 68, 69, 70, 72, 73, 74, 75, 76, 77, 78, 80, 81, 83, 84, 85, 86, 87, 88, 89, 90, 91, 92, 93, 98, 99, 100, 106, 107, 108, 109, 110, 111, 112, 116, 119, 120, 123, 124, 127, 128, 129, 130, 131, 132, 135, 136, 137, 138, 139, 142, 143, 144, 145, 146, 147, 148, 149, 151, 154, 155, 156, 158, 159, 160, 161, 162, 163, 164, 165, 167, 168, 169, 170, 172, 173, 177, 178, 179, 183, 185, 186, 188, 190, 191, 193, 195, 196, 197, 198, 200, 201, 202, 203, 204, 205, 206, 208, 209, 211, 212, 213, 214, 215, 218, 219, 220, 223, 224, 225, 226, 229, 230, 231, 232, 235, 236, 237, 238, 242, 244, 245, 246, 248, 250, 251, 252, 253, 254, 255, 256, 260, 261, 264, 267
Franche-Comté (French region).15, 31
Fraser (Alexander, 11th Lord Saltoun, Jacobite)173
Fraser (Lowlands Scottish Clan)89
Fraser (Simon, 11th Lord Lovat, Marquess of Beaufort, Jacobite)158, 160, 161, 163, 171
Fraser of Castle Leathers (James, Major, Scottish soldier and double agent)161
Frederik (Charles, Duke of Schleswig-Holstein-Gottorp, prince of Sweden).184
Fredriksten (Siege of).240
Freschot (Casimir, French historian)xiii, 29, 264
Fronde of the Princes (The, French civil War).8, 31, 78

Frontignan (France)120
Fuller (William, English spy)17, 101
Fürstenberg (Wilhelm Egon von)28

G

Gallas (Johann, Count of, Emperor's ambassador in London)203, 209
Galmoye (Regiment of).154
Galoy (British royal regiment of).115
Gaultier, or Gautier de Saint-Blancard, or Saint-Bernard (François, Protestant writer and divine, Huguenot spy).107, 108, 109, 151
Gauthier, Gaultier (François-Louis, Abbot, « also known as « l'Abbé Gaultier', French spy).17, 22, 28, 191, 194, 203, 204, 205, 206, 207, 208, 209, 210, 211, 212, 214, 219, 221
Gazette (London)38
General Letter Office (The)86
Geneva107, 114, 115, 119, 184
Genoa.187
George (Fort, Scotland)241
George I of Hanover (King of Great Britain and Ireland)20, 21, 43, 85, 92, 97, 98, 131, 135, 162, 198, 217, 224, 236, 239, 240, 242, 243, 244, 247, 250, 257
George II (George Augustus, Prince of Wales, King of Great Britain and Ireland).92, 244, 247, 250
George III (King of Great Britain and Ireland).97
George IV (King of Great Britain and Ireland)97, 98
Gérin (Charles, French historian).67
Gertuydenberg (Netherlands)191
Gévaudan (The, French historical region)109, 117
Ghent (Belgium).189
Glasgow (Scotland)153, 237

Glencoe (Clan Maclain of, or Clan Iain Abrach, branch of McDonald Clan)89
Glencoe (Scotland).70, 76, 89, 90
Godolphin (Sidney, 1st Earl of Godolphin, Minister of the Crown)20, 266
Gordon (George, 1st Duke of, also known as 'Marquess of Huntly', Scottish peer)159, 164
Gordon (Henrietta, Lady, 2nd Duke of Gordon, 5th Marquess of Huntly, wife of George Gordon, 1st Duke)167, 170, 176, 266
Gordon (Highland Scottish Clan)88, 89, 159
Gordon (William, 6th Viscount of Kenmure and Lord Lochinvar)169, 238
Goring (Henry, Jacobite agent)251
Görtz (Georg Heinrich von, Baron von Schlitz, Swedish First Prime Minister of Sweden and diplomat)239, 240, 242, 264
Goslinga (Sicco van, Dutch officer and diplomat)197
Goyon de Matignon (Charles Auguste, Comte de Gacé, French Marshal).177, 178, 179
Graem, Graham (John, Earl of Alford, Jacobite politician and Secretary of State of James Francis Edward Stuart)251
Graham (John de Claverhouse, 1st Viscount Dundee, Jacobite army officer, also known as 'Bluidy Claver' or Bonnie Dundee')89, 154, 160
Grand Alliance (war of, also known as the 'League of Augsburg War', 'War of the English Succession", or the 'Nine Years War')1, 15, 18, 76, 80, 81, 85, 106, 107, 108, 123, 129, 130, 229, 230

Grandval (Sieur de, French double agent).127
Grant (Highland Scottish Clan)89
Grant of Grant (Ludovick, 1st of Grant and 8th of Freuchie, also known as the 'Highland King', Jacobite)173
Granville (George, 1st Baron Lansdowne, British poet, writer and politician, Jacobite).258
Gravel (Robert de, French Ambassador)28
Gravelines (France)246
Gravisset (Paul, Huguenot Pastor and spy).107
Great Britain (Isle of)xiii, 3, 20, 43, 51, 52, 54, 73, 87, 91, 92, 103, 155, 189, 203, 205, 206, 211, 212, 226, 229, 231, 232, 235, 236, 238, 240, 242, 245, 246, 250, 251, 252, 253, 254, 256, 257, 260, 261, 266
Gregg (James Edward, English historian)194, 265
Gregg (Pauline, French historian)47
Grémonville (Jacques Bretel de, known as the 'Chevalier de').28
Grenoble (France).114
Gualterio (Philippe-Antoine, Cardinal to the French court)166, 195
Guénégaud (street of, Paris).143
Guilleragues (Gabriel Joseph de Lavergne, Comte de)11
Guiscard (Antoine, Marquis of, knonw as 'Abbé de la Bourlie').xii, xiii, 117, 118, 119, 207, 208, 215, 216
Guise (Marie de, also known as Marie de Lorraine, Queen of Scotland) 43
Guyenne (The, French historical region)112
Guyon (Michel, Sieur de Rouvray, French naval officer).119

Gyldenstolpe (Nils, Swedish Count and diplomat, dubbed 'the Fox')132
Gyllenborg (Carl, Count, Swedish statesman and author)239, 240, 242, 264

H

Habsbourg (Ferdinand II of).47
Habsburg (House of).8, 36, 44, 46, 48, 49, 130
Hall (James, Scottish clergyman and spy)159, 160
Hamburg (Germany).49, 136
Hamilton (Anne, 3rd Duchess of Hamilton, mother of James Hamilton, 4th Duke of Hamilton)167
Hamilton (Gustavus, 1st Viscount Boyne, Jacobite).173
Hamilton (James, Earl of Arran, 4th Duke of)23, 160, 162, 164, 167, 168, 169, 171, 172, 173, 179
Hanover (House of).72, 84, 226, 227, 236, 237, 239
Hanover (Sophia, Princess of the Palatinate, Electress of Hanover, mother of King George Ist of England).43, 92, 153, 217
Hanover (State of, Germany)2, 18, 29, 43, 72, 73, 84, 85, 91, 92, 135, 142, 144, 151, 153, 156, 157, 162, 170, 171, 196, 198, 217, 224, 226, 227, 235, 236, 237, 239, 240, 242, 244, 247, 248, 249, 250, 259
Harcourt (Henri, 1er duc d', French Marshal).22
Harcourt (Simon, 1st Baron of, High Chancellor).21
Harlay (Nicolas-Auguste de, Comte de Cély et de Bonneuil).130
Harley (Robert, 1st Earl of Oxford and Earl Mortimer, Minister of the Crown)xii, 20, 38, 98, 125, 145, 149, 150, 151,195, 196, 201, 202, 204, 205, 206, 207, 208, 209, 210, 216, 217, 218, 240, 255, 257, 264
Hastings (battle of).43
Hatzel (Jean Gaspard, Royal syndic of Strasbourg)132
Hay (Charles, 13th of Erroll).159
Haystoun (John Hay of, Sir, English diplomat).133
Hedges (Charles, Sir, English lawyer and politician).111
Heinsius (Anthonie, Grand Pensionary of Holland)27, 115, 151, 183, 185, 190, 195, 196, 197, 213
Helvétius (Jean-Claude-Adrien, French physician and agent)125
Hennequin (Pierre, Seigneur de Boinville).11
Henri IV (King of France)51
Henrietta Maria of France (Queen consort of England, Scotland and Ireland).xi, 9, 43, 57, 58, 61, 73, 99
Henrietta of England (Princess of England and Duchess of Orléans)27, 57, 58, 59, 60, 61, 64
Herbert (Philip, 4th Earl of Pembroke and 1st Earl of Montgomery).45, 65, 111, 138
Hesse-Cassel (William V, Landgrave of)48
High Council (The)79
Highlanders.88, 90, 165, 167, 168, 237, 246
Highlands Watches (Regiment of the)241
Highlands87, 88, 90, 93, 157, 163, 164, 169, 173, 174, 236, 237, 241, 242, 247, 248, 249, 250, 258
Hill (Camisard prophet and spy).116
Hill of Hawkstone (Richard, English diplomat, also known as 'the Great Hill'). 215

Hippisley (John Coxe, 1st Baronet)98
Holt (John, Sir, High Chancellor Commission).21
Holy Roman Empire (The)253
Holyrood (Palace of, Edimbourg)168
Hooke (James Nathaniel, 2nd Baron Hooke, son of Nathaniel Hooke the Jacobite).181
Hooke (Nathaniel (English historian, nephew of Nathaniel Hooke the Jacobite)181
Hooke (Nathaniel, Baron, Jacobite).22, 103, 153, 154, 155, 156, 157, 158, 159, 160, 162, 163, 164, 165, 166, 167, 168, 169, 170, 171, 172, 173, 174, 175, 176, 177, 179, 180, 181, 185, 186, 189, 190, 227, 242, 265, 267
Hopkins (Paul, Scottish historian).102
Howard (Edward, 9th Duke of Norfolk)238
Howard (Elizabeth, Lady, Duchess of Gordon, wife of George Gordon, 1st Duke of Gordon)159, 167, 170, 176, 266
Howard (Thomas, 14th Earl of Arundel)46, 47
Howards (Charles, 3rd Earl of Carlisle, Lord High Treasurer).21
Huc (François, French Huguenot, refugee and spy).109
Hugon (Alain, French historian)145, 265
Huguenots.51, 68, 80, 84, 107, 111, 123
Hutchins (George, Sir, High Chancellor Commission)21
Huxelles (Nicolas Chalon du Blé, Marquis de Cormatin et d', French Marshal).22
Hyde (Anne, first wife of James, Duke of York, mother of Queen Mary II of England and Queen Anne of Great Britain).74
Hyde (Edward, 1st Earl of Clarendon).57
Hyde (Henry, 4th Earl of Clarendon and 2nd Earl of Rochester)112, 219
Hyde Park (London)23
Hynde Cotton (John, Sir, 3rd Baronet)238, 258

I

If (Castle of, France).38
Indulgence (Declaration of)67, 74
Innes (Lewis, Principal of the Scots College at Paris).159
Innes (Thomas, Scottish historian, brother of Lewis Innes).158
Innocent XI (Pope)67, 100, 265
Inveraray (Scotland).90
Ireland20, 51, 54, 62, 70, 76, 81, 89, 90, 105, 106, 108, 112, 123, 128, 153, 154, 167, 175, 180, 185, 235, 238, 246
Isles of Scilly (England, naval disaster of 1707).113
Istvan (Szabo, Hungarian historian).232, 266
Italy.45, 188, 196

J

Jacobites, Jacobitism (Political party)1, 2, 3, 5, 41, 43, 51, 52, 66, 69, 70, 72, 73, 76, 81, 85, 89, 90, 91, 92, 93, 97, 98, 100, 101, 102, 105, 106, 123, 124, 125, 126, 127, 128, 141, 145, 154, 155, 156, 157, 159, 160, 162, 163, 164, 168, 169, 170, 172, 174, 176, 179, 183, 185, 186, 188, 189, 198, 201, 205, 221, 223, 227, 230,235, 236, 237, 238, 239, 240, 241, 242, 243, 244, 245, 246, 247, 249, 250, 251, 252, 253,

256, 257, 258, 259, 260, 261, 264, 267
Jeffreys (George, 1ST Baron Jeffreys, High Chancellor).21
Jenkins (Leoline, Sir, British lawyer).86
Jenkins (Robert, Welsh master mariner).246
Jenkins Ear (War of the)246
Jermyn (Henry, 1st Earl of St Albans).58, 60
Joani (Nicolas, Camisard chief)117
Johnstone (William, 1st Marquess of Annandale, Scottish Jacobite)160
Jonathan's Coffee-House (meeting place in London, also for share-trading).71
Jurieu (Pierre, Calvinist pastor, author and pamphleteer).107, 108, 109, 110, 111, 112
Juvisy (Castle of, France). xi, 260

K

Keck (Anthony, Sir, High Chancellor Commission)21
Keill (John).16, 223, 237
Keith (George, 10th Earl of Marischal, son of William Keith).241, 251
Keith (William, 9th Earl of Marischal, Scottish Jacobite)159, 173
Kelly (George, Jacobite agent)242, 243
Kensington (England)17, 101, 102
Kent (The, England).17, 81
Keppoch (Clan McDonald of, or Clan Ranald of Lochaber, branch of McDonald Clan).89
Ker of Kersland (John, born John Crawford, Scottish spy)160
Kérouaille, Kéroualle (Henrietta Mauricette de Plencoët de)65

Kérouaille, Kéroualle (Louise de Plencoët de, Duchess of Portsmouth, Countess of Fareham, Baroness of Petersfield).xii, 13, 62, 63, 64, 65, 66
Kew (Russia).45
Killiecrankie (battle of)89, 160
King's Cabinet (France)xi, 12, 87
King's Council (France).5, 21, 31, 174
Kinnaird (Patrick, 3rd Lord, Jacobite).173
Kinsale (Ireland).70, 76
Kirkcudbright (Scotland)175
Klaits (Joseph, English historian).36

L

La Baume (Nicolas Augustus de, marquis et maréchal de Montrevel)113, 114, 116, 117
La Chapelle (Jean de, French spy and pamphleteer)36
La Farelle (Nickname of a French agent)115
La Hague (France)38, 86, 109, 115, 137, 151, 181, 190, 196, 197, 240, 264
La Hougue (Battle of, France).35, 70, 76, 90, 110, 124
La Mottraye (Aubry de, French explorer and diplomat).148
La Reynie (Gabriel Nicolas de, Lieutenant General of the Paris police)123
La Rochelle (France).107
La Vallière (Françoise-Louise de la Baume Le Blanc, Duchesse of, official mistress of Louis XIV)64
Lamoignon de Basville (Nicolas, marquis de La Mothe, comte de Launay-Courson, French Intendant).109
Lang (Andrew, British historian).250, 265

Langlade du Chayla (François, Abbot and archpriest of the Cévennes).111
Languedoc (The, France).109, 113, 114, 115, 117, 118, 119, 215
Laporte (Pierre, also known as 'Rolland', Camisard prophet and chief).117, 118
Lauderdale (John Maitland, 1st Duke of Lauderdale, member of the 'Cabal').58, 77
Lauzun (Antonin Nompar de Caumont, 1st duc de)100
Layer (Christopher, Jacobite lawyer)242, 250
Le Blanc (Claude, French Intendant).33, 34
Le Vigan (France).109
Lefevre (Monsieur, Antwerp Postmaster and double agent)166
Legge (William, 1st Earl of Dartmouth, English Secretary of State).219, 220
Legrelle (Arsène, French historian).147, 265
Lennox (Charles,1st Duke of Richmond, Lennox and Aubigny, son of Louise de Kérouaille).65, 66
Leopold 1st (Holy Roman Emperor, King of Hungary, Croatia and Bohemia).67, 86
Leopoldovna (Anna, born Elisabeth Katharina Christine von Mecklenburg-Schwerin, also known as 'Anna Carlovna', Regent of Russia)245
Lérida (battle of).120
Leviston (Thomas, Scottish spy)157, 158, 266
Licensing Act (The)37, 71
Liege (Belgium).29, 133, 208, 264, 267
Lille (France).34
Limerick (Treaty of).70, 81, 102

Linch (Marc, Irish sailor and double agent).136
Lionne (Hugues de, marquis de Fresnes, seigneur de Berny, French minister and diplomat).28, 58
Livingston (William, Viscount Kilsyth)158, 160
Llyod's of London (English bank).71
Lockhart of Lee (George, also known as 'Lockhart of Carnwath, Jacobite politician).159
London (Tower of).23, 38, 145, 154, 162, 225, 241, 242, 243, 250
London (Treaty of).62, 218
London.17, 20, 23, 28, 34, 36, 37, 38, 48, 50, 54, 58, 61, 62, 67, 69, 71, 74, 75, 86, 87, 89, 90, 100, 101, 102, 103, 106, 109, 120, 124, 125, 127, 128, 132, 133, 136, 137, 139, 145, 148, 149, 150, 151, 154, 161, 162, 174, 176, 194, 195, 203, 208, 209, 210, 211, 213, 214, 216, 218, 219, 222, 224, 225, 226, 228, 229, 230, 232, 237, 239, 240, 241, 242, 243, 244, 246, 247, 248, 249, 250, 257, 258, 259, 265, 266, 267
Lord (House of)23, 37, 57, 62, 243
Lorraine (France)45, 46, 92, 216
Lorraine (Henri di, 4e duc d'Elbeuf, Comte de Lillebonne, de Rieux et baron d'Ancenis, peer of France)66
Lorraine (Leopold 1st, Duke of Lorraine and Bar)216
Louis XI (King of France) 7
Louis XIII (King of France) xi, xii, 2, 8, 42, 44, 45, 47, 48, 237, 260, 261
Louis XIV (King of France). xii, 1, 2, 3, 7, 8, 9, 10, 12, 13, 14, 15, 16, 17, 18, 19, 20, 21, 24, 26, 27, 28, 29, 30, 31, 32, 33, 35, 36, 37, 38, 39, 40, 42, 43, 44, 51, 52, 53, 56, 57, 58, 59, 61, 62, 64, 65, 66, 68, 69, 70, 72, 73, 74, 75, 76, 77, 80,

81, 83, 84, 85, 87, 88, 90, 92, 93, 100, 101, 105, 106, 107, 108, 109, 110, 111, 112, 113, 114, 118, 121, 123, 124, 126, 127, 128, 129, 130, 131, 132, 135, 138, 142, 145, 146, 147, 148, 155, 161, 162, 163, 166, 170, 171, 173, 176, 178, 180, 183, 184, 185, 186, 187, 188, 189, 190, 191, 192, 195, 199, 202, 205, 207, 209, 210, 212, 213, 214, 215, 220, 221, 222, 223, 227, 228, 231, 232, 233, 236, 238, 245, 252, 253, 260, 261, 263
Louis XV (King of France).3, 40, 181, 237, 238, 244, 245, 248, 252, 260, 261, 263
Louvois (François Michel Le Tellier, comte de Tonnerre, marquis de)15, 20, 21, 31, 60, 76
Louvre (Castle of the, Paris). 57, 99
Lowlands (The, Scotland). 93, 163, 237
Lubières (Sieur de, governor of Orange) 114
Lully (Jean-Baptiste) 27
Luxembourg (François-Henri de Montmorency-Bouteville, duc de Piney and) 32, 184
Luynes (Hôtel de, Paris) 175
Lyon (France)38, 117
Lyon (John, 4th Earl of Strathmore and Kinghorne, Jacobite).173

M

MacCarthy Reagh (Eleanor Susan, wife of Nathaniel Hooke the Jacobite).181
MacDonell (Donald, 2nd of Sandaig and 1st of Lochgarry, Jacobite agent)251
Machiavelli (Niccolò di Bernardo dei)9, 265
MacKenzie (Highland Scottish Clan)88

MacKenzie of Fraserdale (Alexander, Scottish politician).161
Mackey (John, Spy)102
MacLaine (Sir, Scottish merchant).156
MacLean (John, Sir, 4th Baronet of Duart and Morvern).163
Macpherson (James, Scottish author and historian).98, 181
Madrid (Spain)22, 147, 189, 190, 265
Maginn (Patrick, also known as 'Father Patrick' or 'Priest Patrick', political agent and spy).61
Maintenon (François d'Aubigné, Madame de)24, 141, 146, 153, 163, 176, 188, 189, 190, 191, 245
Malplaquet (battle of)101, 180, 183, 186
Malplech or Malplet (César, Camisard prophet and chief, brother of Elie Marion)117
Malvezzi (Virgilio, Italian writer and politician).50
Mancini (Hortense, Duchess of Mazarin).65
Mar Rebellion (The).92, 162, 180, 238, 239
Marchiennes (France)34
Marion (Elie, Camisard prophet and chief, brother of César Malplech).117
Marlborough (John Churchill, 1st Duke of, Minister of the Crown).20, 23, 98, 103, 125, 126, 144, 145, 147, 148, 150, 151, 153, 155, 164, 170, 183, 184, 185, 186, 193, 194, 195, 196, 197, 198, 199, 201, 202 204, 205, 219, 224, 225, 229, 261
Marlborough (Sarah Churchill, born Jenyns, Princess of Mindelheim, Countess of Nellenburg, Duchess of)69, 103

Marly (Castle of, France).28, 142, 184
Marsaille (battle of the)32
Marsault (Nickname of a French agent and spy)111
Martin (Pierre-Denis, French painter, also known as 'Martin le Jeune')xi, 260
Martinozzi (Laure, Duchess of Modena and Reggio, mother of Mary of Modena).100
Mary II (Queen of England, Scotland and Ireland)17, 20, 43, 68, 69, 70, 74, 75, 77, 80, 81, 85, 99, 100, 101, 105, 106, 135, 160, 168, 181, 158
Masham (Abigail Hill, Baroness, cousin of Sarah, Duchess of Marlborough and favourite of Queen Anne).151, 204
Massué, or Massue (Henri, Marquis de Massue et Ruvigny, Lord of Galway, French Huguenot officer).58, 112
Maule (James, 4th Earl of Panmure, Scottish Jacobite).169, 173
Maurel (Abdias, also known as 'Catinat', Captain of the Camisard cavalry)112, 119
Maynard (John, Sir, High Chancellor Commission).21
Mazarin (Jules, french First Minister).12, 20, 65, 86, 99, 100, 260
Mazel (Abraham, French Protestant prophet and fighter)111, 119
McBean (Highland Scottish Clan)89
McDonal of Glencoe (Alasdair Ruadh Maclain, Chief of the Glencoe McDonald of Keppoch).90
McDonald (Highland Scottish Clan).89, 90
McDonnel (Clan McDonell of Glengarry, also known as 'Clan Ranald of Knoydart and Glengarry, Highland Scottish Clan)89
McDonnel of Keppoch (Highland Scottish Clan)163
McGillivray (Highland Scottish Clan).89
McGregor (Highland Scottish Clan)93, 163
Mckay (Highland Scottish Clan)88, 89
McKenzie (Kenneth, 3th Count of Seaforth)93
McKinnon (Highland Scottish Clan).89
McKintosh (Highland Scottish Clan)89
McLachlan (Highland Scottish Clan)89
McLean (Highland Scottish Clan)89, 93
McLeod (Highland Scottish Clan).163
McPherson (Highland Scottish Clan)89
Meirol (Sieur de, Protestant nobleman)118
Melfort (Lady).17, 101
Menorca (Spanish Balearic island).188, 191
Menzies (Highland Scottish Clan).89
Mesnager (Nicolas, French diplomat, also known as the 'Count of Saint-Jean').22, 125, 193, 209, 212, 213, 214, 220, 221
Methuen (John, English diplomat)23
Mèze (France)120
Middleton (Charles, 2nd Earl of Middleton, Jacobite 1st Earl of Monmouth).86, 102, 141, 142, 145, 146, 158, 161, 163, 164, 179
Millenges (Marie, first wife of John Parker).129
Mirmand (French royal regiment of)115

Mirmand (Pascal, lawyer and Protestant pastor)109, 115, 116
Mist (Nathaniel, British printer and journalist).259
Modena (Marie Béatrice Eléonore Anne Marguerite Isabelle d'Este, princess of, Queen Consort).24, 68, 69, 74, 75, 78, 80, 99, 100, 101, 126, 141, 153, 161, 163, 189
Moerdijk (Netherlands).191
Mohun of Okehampton (Charles, 4th Baron)23
Molesworth (Robert, 1st Viscount)23
Molière (Jean-Baptiste Poquelin).27
Molloy (Charles, Irish lawyer and writer)259
Monaco (Prince of).118
Monasterol (Nickname of the envoy of Maximilien-Emmanuel, Elector of Bavaria)184, 189
Monck (George, 1st Duke of Albermarle).54
Monmouth (James Scott, 1st Duke of Buccleuh, 1st Duke of, son of King Charles II of England)67, 74, 78, 80, 128, 154
Monro (George, British Army officer).242
Mons (Belgium)189
Montagu (Charles, 1st Earl of Halifax and Manchester, Lord High Treasurer)21
Montagu (Edward Wortley, grandson of the 1st Earl of Sandwich, Ambassador)148
Montagu (Edward, 1st Earl of Sandwich)149
Montagu (Lady Mary Wortley, wife of Edward Wortley Montagu)148
Montélimar (France)114
Montespan (Françoise-Athénaïs de Rochechouart de Mortemart, known as 'Madame de', official mistress of Louis XIV).64

Montesquiou (Pierre of, comte d'Artagnan, French Marshal)34
Montgomerie (Alexander, 9th Earl of Eglinton, Jacobite)173
Montpellier (France)108, 119
Montrose (James Graham, 1st Marquess of, Scottish general)54
Montrose (Scotland).93, 175, 239
Moray of Abercairny (William, Lord, Jacobite).173
Mordaunt (Charles, 3rd Earl of Peterborough).23
Moulin de l'Agau (massacre of the)113
Mount Saint-Michel (France)38
Munro (Highland Scottish Clan)88
Murray (David, 5th Viscount of Stormont, Scottish Jacobite peer).160
Murray (Jacques, Scottish agent).173
Murray (William, Marquis of Tullibardine).241
Murray of Elibank (Alexander, known as 'Count Murray', British Army officer and Jacobite).250

N

Nairn (David, Jacobite Under-Secretary of State in Rome)97
Namur (Belgium).110, 184, 215
Nantes (Edict of).68, 75, 80, 107, 108
Nantes (France).52, 70
Naples (Italy)191
Napoleonic Wars (The)98
Neerwinden (battle of)32
Netherlands (United Provinces).xiii, 1, 18, 24, 41, 44, 46, 51, 58, 67, 73, 74, 75, 86, 116, 139, 143, 151, 184, 189, 190, 197, 233, 246
Neufville de Villeroy (François, Marquis and 2e duc de, French Marshal).164, 266
Newcastle (England)92

Newgate (prison of, London)xii, xiii, 102, 216, 251, *Naseby (battle of)54
Nice (France).118
Nicholson (Thomas, Bishop of Edimbourg).159
Nicolle (Huguenot spy).112
Nieuport (Belgium)184, 207
Nîmes (France)109, 114, 117, 119
Noailles (Adrien Maurice, comte d'Ayen and 3e duc de, French Marshal)120
Noailles (Jean-Baptiste-Louis-Gaston de, Bishop of Châlons-sur-Marne).217
Noiraye (Daniel Voysin de la, French Chancellor)20
Norris (John, Sir, Admiral of the Fleet).120
North (Douglas, English historian).72
North Sea (The).178
Nottingham (England)69, 101, 112, 113, 148

O

Obrecht (Ulrich, French spy and pamphleteer).36
Olivier (Nickname of a French Protestant pastor and spy).115
Onslow (Nickname of the great-nephew of the Jacobite John Parker)128
Orange (France)114
Orléans (Philippe, duc d', brother of the King Louis XIV)44, 57, 185
Orval (Jean Robert Lefebvre of, French politician)34
Osborne (Thomas, 1st Duke of Leeds)79
Ostend (Belgium).224
Oxenstierna (Axel Gustafsson, Count, Swedish chancellor).132

Oxford (England).xii, 16, 20, 38, 77, 98, 137, 150, 181, 194, 195, 196, 208, 217, 238, 255, 257, 266

P

Pajot (Louis-Léon, Comte d'Ons-en-Bray).15
Palatinate (Charles I Louis, Elector of the).44, 46, 47, 48, 49
Palatinate (Frederick V of the, father of Charles I Louis).44
Palatinate (The).45, 46, 47, 48, 49, 50
Paolucci (Fabrizio, Italian cardinal and diplomat)133, 224, 267
Papist Plot (The).79
Paris.xi, 15, 17, 27, 29, 37, 46, 47, 49, 57, 66, 110, 143, 144, 163, 166, 175, 178, 180, 191, 195, 203, 208, 209, 210, 211, 214, 217, 218, 221, 228, 229, 240, 251, 263
Parker (John, English army officer and Jacobite conspirator, also known as 'Colonel Parker').123, 127, 128, 129
Parker-Bowles (Camilla, Queen consort of the United Kingdom and the other Commonwealth and realms)66
Parliament of Great Britain (The).73, 91
Pelham (Henry, British statesman and Prime Minister).246, 250
Pequet (Monsieur, Nickname of a French spy)166
Percy (Algernon, 10th Earl of Northumberland).45, 50
Perrault (Charles, French writter).xi
Perrinet (Alexandre, marquis d').113, 116, 119
Peterhead (Scotland)239
Peterson (William, Scottish diplomat)156

Petkum (Hermann von, Danish Diplomat and Ambassador).184, 185, 190, 191
Petrovna (Elizabeth, Empress of Russia)245
Peytaud (Jean, French Protestant officer and agent).115
Philip V (King of Spain)183, 184, 189, 191, 192, 202, 206, 210, 231
Picardy (French region).21, 25, 46
Pignerol (Fortress, France)38, 60
Pitlochry (Scotland)89
Plessen (Carl Adolph von, Danish Minister of state and double agent)226
Poitou (The, historical French region).109
Polignac (Melchior de, French diplomat and poet).191, 192, 194
Polish Succession (War of the).245
Pomponne (Simon Arnauld, lord and marquis de, French Ambassador).28
Pontchartrain (Jérôme Phélypeaux, comte de, Secretary of State)20, 102, 144, 145, 174, 177, 189
Pontchartrain (Louis Phélypeaux, comte de Maurepas et de, Secretary of State)20, 123
Pont-Saint-Esprit (France).114, 115
Pope (The).12, 67, 78, 87, 100, 177, 193, 212
Portes (Sieur de, Protestant nobleman).118
Portland (England)102, 227
Portland (William Bentinck, 1st Earl of, English Ambassador to France)110, 126, 130
Portugal.28, 57, 58, 118, 175
Poussin (Jean-Baptiste de, French diplomat and spy)36, 136, 137, 138
Prendergast (Thomas, Irish spy)102
Presbyterians(religious and political party).77, 79, 170, 242
Preston (battle of).54, 239
Prestonpans (battle of).246
Prior (Matthew, English poet and diplomat).23, 25, 28, 208, 209, 210, 211, 214, 218, 231
Protestants (political faction)1, 23, 33, 45, 48, 52, 56, 57, 58, 67, 68, 71, 74, 75, 77, 78, 79, 80, 84, 85, 91, 92, 95, 101, 102, 105, 106, 107, 108, 109, 110, 111, 112, 113, 114, 115, 116, 117, 118, 119, 120, 130, 131, 135, 137, 142, 145, 151, 153, 160, 188, 193, 196, 198, 205, 209, 217, 231, 232, 253, 254, 260, 264
Provence (French region)118
Prussia75, 132, 232, 252
Pyrenees (Treaty of the).57

R

Radclyffe (Charles, 5th Earl of Derwenwater).238
Radclyffe (James, 3rd Earl of Derwentwater)238
Ramillies (battle of)170
Ramsay (Elizabeth Auchinleck, daughter of Gilbert Ramsay of Balmain, mother of John Drummond the merchant).149
Ramsay of Balmain (Gilbert, Sir, 1st Baronet of Bamff)149
Rastatt (Treaty of).211
Ravaison Mollien (François, French archivist and author)144, 266
Ravan (Edme, marquis de Miennes de Vielbourg).158
Rawlinson (William, Sir).21
Reformation (The)68
Regency Act (The)135
Regensburg (Treaty of)84
Renaudot (Eusèbe II, French priest and author, spy for England).124, 141, 264

Renneville (René Auguste Constantin de, French spy)39
Restoration (The)43, 55, 57, 72
Revolution (French).177
Revolution (Glorious, or 'Bloodless')xii, 1, 8, 23, 43, 51, 53, 55, 56, 66, 67, 68, 70, 71, 73, 83, 85, 87, 98, 123, 124, 125, 130, 131, 135, 138, 205, 230, 256, 265, 266
Revolution (Industrial)254
Rhône (The, French river)114
Rich (Robert, 2nd Earl of Warwick).47, 50
Richelieu (Armand Jean du Plessis, Duke and Cardinal, French Prime minister)xi, xii, xiii, 2, 8, 16, 44, 47, 48, 49, 50, 260, 261
Richmond, Richmond Park (England)89, 129
Rijksarchief (Algemeene, Dutch historian).197
Robertson (Highland Scottish Clan, also known as 'Clan Donnachaidh' or 'Duncan').89
Rocayrol (Tobie, French Protestant agent).117
Rochefort (France)175
Rochegude (Marquis of)115
Roe (Thomas, Sir, English diplomat).49
Roger (Nickname of a French agent).142
Rohan (Henri de, duc de)48
Rohan (Marie de, duchesse de Chevreuse)48
Rome (Italy).22, 37, 97, 98, 133, 180, 235, 242, 256, 267
Romney Marsh (England)102
Roquelaure (Antoine-Gaston, marquis de)120
Rose (Toussaint, marquis de Coye).12, 13
Ross (Highland Scottish Clan)88

Rossignol (Antoine, French codebreaker).xi, 2, 14, 16, 50, 53, 260, 261
Rossignol (Charles-Bonaventure, son of Antoine)16
Rottenbourg (Nicolas Frédéric, Comte de).22
Rotterdam (Netherlands)15, 107, 110, 111, 142, 166
Rouen (France)212
Rouillé (Nickname, agent and spy).190
Roussillon (The, French historical region)120
Rouvière (Nickname of a Camisard agent)117
Roxburghe Club (Scotland).181
Royal Navy (The).71, 242
Royal Swedish (French regiment)164
Ruadh Mac Donnell of Glengarry (Alastair, 13th Chief, Clan MacDonell of Glengarry, also known as 'Pickle')250, 251, 265
Ruisen (Van der, Sieur, Dutch diplomat).115
Russel (Francis, 4th Earl of Bedford).50
Russell (Edward, , 1st Earl of Oxford, English Admiral).98
Russell (William, Lord).78
Russia.3, 245, 252, 261
Rye House Plot.86
Ryswick (Treaty of)81, 111, 123, 130, 131, 133, 135, 142

S

Sacerdoti (the Duke of Savoy agent, also known as the 'Jew Sacerdoti')187
Sacheverell (Henry, English high church Anglican clergyman, also known as 'the bloody flag officer')230
Sacheverell riots (The).230

Sagnol de la Croix (Protestant pastor and agent)117
Saint-Germain-des-Prés (Abbey of, Paris)29
Saint-Germain-en-Laye (Castle and city, France)17, 24, 29, 51, 52, 69, 75, 81, 83, 85, 90, 92, 99, 101, 102, 105, 106, 111, 125, 127, 141, 142, 143, 145, 146, 149, 150, 153, 155, 158, 161, 162, 163, 165, 169, 171, 173, 176, 185, 186, 187, 188, 189, 194, 195, 203, 230, 243, 244, 256, 257, 258, 259, 264
Saint-Hilaire (Nickname, French spy).194
Saint-Hippolyte (France).115
Saint-Martin (Nickname of a Huguenot pastor and spy)107
Saintonge (The, French historical region).109
Saint-Petersburg.29
Saint-Romain (Abbé de, French diplomat).28
Saint-Simon (Louis de Rouvroy, duc de)11, 12, 93, 142, 144, 187, 194, 208, 217, 218, 266
Saints-Maurice and Lazarus (Orders of).136
Sarmant (Thierry, French historian).11, 266
Sarsfield (James, 2nd Earl of Lucan)70
Saumur (France).161
Saurin (Jacques, also known as 'Saurin-Jonquet', French protestant pastor)114, 115
Savoy (The)32, 107, 212
Savoy (Victor-Amadeus II, King of Sardinia, Sicily, Duke of).116, 117, 120, 187
Savoy-Carignano (Prince Eugene Francis of, also known as 'Prince Eugene', field marshal in the Army of the Holy Roman Empire and Austrian Habsburg dynasty).34, 150, 183, 185, 188, 195, 196, 224, 225, 228, 230
Saxony(German region).18
Schomberg (Frederik Herman de, 1st Duke of).57, 75, 109, 110
Scotland.41, 42, 43, 51, 52, 54, 55, 62, 71, 72, 73, 79, 86, 87, 88, 89 90, 91, 92, 103, 105, 111, 139, 143, 154, 155, 157, 158, 159, 160, 161, 162, 163, 164, 165, 166, 167, 169, 170, 171, 172, 173, 174, 175, 177, 178, 179, 185, 187, 188, 189, 190, 193, 235, 236, 238, 239, 241, 246, 247, 248, 249, 257, 258, 265
Scott (Anne, 1st Duchess of Buccleuh, Wife of the Duke of Monmouth)67
Scott (Walter, Scottish author and poet).98, 250
Scottish Guard (The, France)87
Scrope (John, High Chancellor Commission)21
Secret Intelligence Fund86
Séguier (Pierre, also known as 'Esprit Séguier', Camisard chief).111
Seignelay (Jean-Baptiste Colbert, marquis de, Secretary of State)20
Seissan (Monsieur de, French officer).120
Sète (France)120
Seton (James, 4th Earl of Dunfermline, Scottish Jacobite)160
Settlement (Act of)73, 135
Seven Years War.3, 245, 252
Sévigné (Marie de Rabutin-Chantal, marquise de).xii
Sheriffmuir (battle of)93, 180, 239
Shovell (Cloudesley, Sir, Admiral of the Fleet)113, 117
Sidney (Robert, 1st Earl of Leicester).45, 46, 47, 49, 50
Simpson (Jones)Scottish spy)123, 124, 126, 127

Sinclair (Alexander, 9th Earl of Caithness, Jacobite).173
Sinzendorf (Philipp Ludwig Wenzel, Count of, Austrian diplomat and statesman)228
Skelton (Bevil, British foreign envoy and diplomat).86, 144, 186
Slains Castle (Scotland).159
Sobieska (Marie-Clementine, Polish Princess, wife of James Francis Edward Stuart).97
Somers (John, 1st Baron Somers, High Chancellor)21
Somerset (Charles Noel, 4th Duke of Beaufort, Scottish Jacobite)258
South Sea Bubble241
South Sea Company (The)208, 240
Spain.10, 21, 28, 45, 46, 47, 48, 49, 50, 57, 74, 78, 86, 120, 175, 183, 184, 185, 190, 191, 202, 206, 210, 211, 212, 213, 215, 218, 231, 240, 241, 246
Spanish Succession (War of).xiii, 33, 35, 38, 111, 120, 125, 135, 137, 138, 142, 155, 233, 264
Sparre (Erik, comte de Sundby, colonel in the French army)131, 240, 264
Sparre (French royal regiment of)154, 164, 165, 170
Spencer (Diana, Princess of Wales)66
Spencer (Robert, 2nd Earl of Sunderland)80, 86, 98
Stair (James Dalrymphe, 1st Viscount of)23, 90
Stair (John Dalrymphe, 2nd Earl of)90, 180
Steinkerque (battle of)110
Stewart of Appin (Highland Scottish Clan).89, 163
Strasbourg (France)28, 36, 133, 158
Stratford (William, English priest).150

Strickland (Thomas John Francis, also known as 'Abbé Strickland').146
Strickland (Winifred, Lady, mother of Thomas Strickland)146
Stuart (Charles, 6th Earl Moray of Darnaway, Jacobite)173
Stuart (Elizabeth, Electress of the Palatinate, Queen of Bohemia, also known as 'the Winter Queen', mother of Charles I Louis)44
Stuart (Henry Benedict, also known as the 'Cardinal of York', son of James Francis Edward Stuart).97
Stuart (James Charles VI, King of Scotland, James I, King of Scotland, England and Ireland).43, 72, 73
Stuart (James II, King of England and Ireland, James VII, King of Scotland)1, 2, 3, 10, 12, 15, 18, 19, 20, 24, 27, 33, 36, 43, 44, 51, 52, 53, 55, 56, 59, 60, 61, 66, 67, 68, 69, 70, 72, 73, 74, 75, 76, 77, 79, 80, 81, 83, 84, 85, 86, 87, 88, 89, 90, 91, 95, 98, 100, 102, 105, 106, 108, 109, 112, 113, 123, 124, 125, 126, 127, 129, 130, 135, 136, 137, 138, 141, 142, 147, 153, 154, 158, 161, 203, 205, 212, 231, 238, 239, 244, 253, 254, 264, 265
Stuart (James V, King of Scotland).43
Stuart (James, Francis, Edward, son of James II, also known as 'Old Pretender', or 'Pretender', or 'King over the Water', or 'Chevalier de Saint-George').3, 17, 24, 43, 73, 80, 83, 84, 85, 87, 90, 91, 92, 93, 97, 98, 100, 101, 108, 129, 131, 133, 134, 142, 145, 146, 147, 149, 153, 155, 156, 161, 163, 170, 171, 174, 176, 178, 179, 80, 185, 186, 187, 188, 189, 193, 194, 195, 205, 209, 216, 217, 221,

226, 228, 230, 231, 232, 235, 236, 239, 242, 244, 246, 250, 252, 253, 254, 257, 258, 259, 265
Stuart (Louisa Maria Teresa, Royal Princess, daughter of King James II Stuart).100
Stuart (Mary, Princess Royal and Princess of Orange, wife of William II of Orange)73
Stuart (Walter, 6th Great Seneschal of Scotland).43
Stuart Papers.98, 99, 258, 259, 260
Sutherland (Highland Scottish Clan)86
Sweden.18, 49, 92, 131, 132, 239, 240
Swift (Jonathan, Anglo-Irish writer, essayist, satirist and Anglican cleric)199, 200, 201, 202, 205, 208, 224, 243
Switzerland.22, 36, 107, 109, 114, 116, 145, 185

T

Talbot (Charles, 1st Duke of Shrewsbury)98, 204
Tallard (Camille d'Hostun de la Baume, duc d'Hostun, Comte de, French Marshal).36, 124, 125, 148, 149, 203, 205
Tay (River).175
Teissèdre (Louis, French protestant spy, also known as 'La Roque', 'Théophile Vignaud', 'Antoine Fontanes', 'Sallien').115
Tessé (René III de Froulay, comte de, French Marshal)208
Thames (River)81
Thirty Year's war45, 49, 50
Tilladet (Jean-Marie de La Marque de, French Priest and author).158
Torbay Bay (England)68, 75, 130
Torcy (Jean-Baptiste Colbert, marquis de)14, 17, 18, 20, 24, 27, 28, 32, 111, 133, 137, 138, 143, 144, 146, 148, 155, 156, 165, 166, 169, 170, 173, 177, 183, 184, 185, 186, 187, 188, 189, 190, 191, 192, 194, 195, 196, 198, 203, 204, 205, 206, 207, 208, 209, 211, 214, 220, 224, 225, 226, 227, 229, 254, 255, 266, 267
Tory (English Government)xii, 1, 17, 23, 36, 77, 92, 97, 98, 125, 135, 137, 138, 143, 147, 150, 151, 156, 194, 196, 199, 200, 201, 202, 203, 204, 205, 206, 208, 210, 217, 218, 224, 225, 230, 238, 256, 257, 258, 259
Toulon (France)120, 196
Tourville (Anne-Hilarion de Costentin, comte de, French Admiral).35, 110
Townshend (Charles, 2nd Viscount of, Minister of the Crown).20
Tracy (Robert, Sir, High Chancellor Commission)21
Treby (George, Sir, High Chancellor Commission)21
Trémoille (Marie-Anne de la, Princesse des Ursins).21, 208, 218
Trevor (John, Sir, High Chancellor Commission).21
Trevor (Thomas, 1st Baron Trevor, High Chancellor Commission).21
Trinity College (Dublin)153
Triple Alliance28, 253
Trotti de La Chétardie (Jacques-Joachim, French officer and diplomat).245
Trumbull (William, Sir).27
Turenne (Henri de la Tour d'Auvergne, vicomte de).31, 75, 78, 99
Turin (Italy).117, 187
Tyrconnel (Ireland)89

U

Ugbrooke Park (England).61
Union (Act of).52, 73, 91, 135, 187
Utrecht (Congress of, Treaty of, Peace of, Negotiations of, Holland).xiii, 18, 29, 37, 92, 115, 120, 135, 180, 193, 195, 197, 198, 199, 202, 203, 210, 211, 213, 214, 217, 228, 229, 231, 232, 235, 238, 240, 253, 254, 255, 256, 264

V

Valance (Edward, English historian).87, 266
Valence (France).114
Valin (Gérard, French historian)71
Van der Burg (Jean-Alexandre, French officer, criminal and double agent)127
Vanderbent (Agatha, wife of John Drummond the merchant).150
Vatican (The).28, 33, 67, 230, 263
Vauban (Sébastien Le Presle, marquis de)31, 126
Velada (Antonio Sancho Dávila y Toledo Colonna, marquis of, Spanish officer and diplomat).50
Vendôme (Philippe de, Duc of, great-grandson of King HenrI IV of France)65, 66, 190
Vernon (James, English Secretary of State)23
Versailles (France)27, 34, 40, 76, 80, 88, 102, 111, 125, 138, 141, 146, 174, 176, 179, 189, 192, 195, 204, 207, 208, 209, 219, 244, 245, 246, 265
Vialas (Noah, British Huguenot pastor).119
Vienna (Austria).29, 46, 47, 49, 188, 198, 199, 244
Vieuville (Charles Ier de la)48
Vilette (Nickname of a French spy).115
Villars (Claude Louis Hector, duc de, French Marshal).22, 32, 35, 101, 117, 118, 119, 189, 211
Villefranche (France)117, 118, 119
Villeneuve (Sieur de, Switzerland)114
Villiers (William, 2nd Duke of Jersey, English peer)204, 205, 207
Vivarais (The, French historical region)112, 114, 115, 116

W

Wade (George, Irish FieldMarshal).241
Waldegrave (James, 1st Earl of, English politician and ambassador)244
Waldensians, or Vaudois (adherents of a reformed church tradition).107, 116
Wales (William Arthur Philip Louis, Prince of).66
Walkinshaw (Clementina Maria Sophia, mistress of Charles Edward Stuart).251
Wallis (John).xii, 16, 51, 53, 70, 72, 102, 155, 223, 260, 261
Walpole (Horatio, 1st Baron Walpole, English diplomat, brother of Robert Walpole,)23, 100, 101, 266
Walpole (Robert, 1st Earl of Oxford, Sir, Prime Minister of Great Britain).242, 243, 261
Walter (Lucy, also known as Lucy Barlow, mother of the Duke of Monmouth).67
Ward (Edward, 8th Baron Dudley, High Chancellor Commission).21
Waters (James Placid, Abbott)98
Watson (Robert, Scottish politician)98
Weingast (Barry, American political scientist and economist)72

Wentworth (Thomas, 1st Earl of Strafford, 3rd Baron Raby)47, 133, 151, 196
Wenworth (Peter).37
Westminster73, 78, 236, 258
Whigs (The, English political party)1, 17, 36, 51, 74, 75, 77, 85, 86, 88, 90, 92, 98, 100, 105, 110, 125, 126, 129, 136, 137, 138, 145, 147, 156, 169, 194, 196, 198, 199, 200, 201, 205, 210, 217, 218, 224, 225, 230, 238, 256, 257, 258
White (Ignatius, Irish Ambassador to the United Provinces)86
Whitehall (Palace of, London)64, 65, 69, 100, 113
Whitehead (Julian, British historian).85
Widdrington (William, 4th Baron Widdrington)238
Wilkes (John, British politician and journalist, Lord-Maire of London)98
Willes (Edward, English Anglican bishop and cryptanalyst).237, 239, 240, 244
William (Fort, Scotland)90, 241
William II (Count of Nassau, Prince of Orange)44
William III (William Henry of Orange, Stadtholder of Holland, Zeeland, Utrecht, Guelders, and Overijssel, King of England, Scotland and Ireland)xii, 1, 10, 16, 18, 20, 23, 32, 36, 37, 43, 44, 51, 53, 55, 56, 58, 66, 69, 70, 71, 74, 75, 76, 77, 79, 80, 81, 83, 84, 85, 87, 89, 90, 95, 100, 101, 105, 106, 108, 109, 110, 112, 123, 125, 126, 127, 129, 130, 131, 132, 135, 136, 137, 138, 142, 149, 153, 154, 160, 260, 265
William 1st (King of England, known as 'the Conqueror' or 'the Bastard')43
Williamson (Joseph, English agent and politician, also known as 'Captain Williamson')89
Williams-Wynn (Watkins, 3rd Baronet, Scottish Jacobite).258
Worcester (battle of).54
Wrede (Fabian, Count, Swedish diplomat)132
Wright (Nathan, Sir, High Chancellor).21

Y

York (Duke of)59, 61, 67, 73, 74, 77, 78, 99, 100, 105, 259
Ypres (Belgium)190

Z

Zurich.109